# A Life of Risks Taken

ℰ⊘ℛ

# Seymour Ubell

©2014
Nightengale Press
A Nightengale Media LLC Company

# A LIFE OF RISKS TAKEN

For information about Nightengale Press please
visit our website at www.nightengalepublishing.com.
Email: publisher@nightengalepress.com

Library of Congress Cataloging-in-Publication Data

Ubell, Seymour,
A LIFE OF RISKS TAKEN/ Seymour Ubell
ISBN 13: 978-1-935993-70-4
Memoir

Copyright Registered: 2013
First Published by Nightengale Press in the USA

July 2014

10 9 8 7 6 5 4 3 2 1

Printed in the USA and the UK

Marsha and me on our honeymoon, March, 1982.

Dear David & Jennifer —

I am not just a pretty face

Enjoy!

Love —

Seymour

To my Mother and Father

# Chapter 1

ഏരു

## Turning Point
### 1948

Poppa crashed to the pavement in midtown Manhattan. A massive coronary took his life the next day. My father was forty-four years old, leaving Momma a widow at forty-three. The date was June 24, 1948. I was sixteen years old, just two months from my seventeenth birthday.

Sitting at our kitchen table, looking at my Poppa's empty chair, my head cradled into my two fists, anger spat from my lips, "Now?—Now! When I need you the most, you go and die on me! You son-of-a-bitch!" I sobbed.

The anger and resentment came from out of nowhere and rushed through me. I felt a crushing pain in my chest that paralyzed me where I sat. The feelings, mixed with my tears, choked me. Denial raced over me in hundreds of sobs of no.

I didn't hate my father. I could never hate him. I loved him. Yet he abandoned me and left me with a mountainous responsibility—it was his obligation, his liability. He was the husband. He was the father. I was the son. I was supposed to go to university and prepare for my life. My older brother went to college. Now he was married and as good as gone. My inheritance was Poppa's family, the one I was now solely responsible to take care of.

Today, more than a half century later I still feel the unfairness of that situation. No one ever said that life was fair. What gave me the right of entitlement? I was a kid. What did I know about life or what was in store for me? I had not a clue of what I was going to do that very day.

How was I going to succeed in this world without an education? I knew I was not the scholar that my brother Earl was, but I was intelligent. I had good judgment—I thought, and was smart enough to know the importance of a college degree when looking for a job. Now that dream was smashed. I did not deserve this disaster. My inner voice screamed. The future became a brick wall that I smashed into.

Poppa was a loving father, but dying young is not a loving deed.

"Oh, yes, oh, yes," I heard my father's voice whisper, "Now, you, my son, must be a man and think of your family. They are yours now." His imagined voice faded away.

For a while, I remained ambivalent—almost numb in the face of the future. But days and weeks passed. Something strange emerged. The pain subsided. I felt suddenly matured, a microscopic view of myself, that now I was a man. Was that the reason my father had died? Did he do this just for me, nudging me to the edge of the next plateau of my life? I wondered.

## A Life of Risks Taken

As I got older, I began to understand that my father's heritage forever served to make me a better person. His insights developed in me a more politically aware individual. I inherited his work ethic, his honest approach to business dealings—and so much more. He and my mother imbued in my three brothers and me a unique understanding of other people's feeling and points of view. Our birthrights were the ability to learn, to gather and retain what we were taught. That was our legacy.

What greater gifts could parents leave for their children? Only the gift of life was more valuable. As you read in the chapters that follow I will tell you the depth of the teachings my father's unsigned and unwritten will left to me—and to my brothers.

&#8360;&#8658;&#8467;

Our neighborhood in East Flatbush, Brooklyn was my entire world, composed of mostly first-generation Jewish immigrants living in crowded apartments in small sixteen-family buildings or in the string of four-and six-family houses.

Our kitchen window looked out on Millie's Candy Store, the traffic and information center of our community. The newspaper stand at the entrance to the shop had dozens of papers for sale: *The New York Times, The New York Herald Tribune, The Daily Mirror, The Daily News, The World Telegram, The Wall Street Journal, The Post, The Journal American, The Jewish Daily Forward, The Freiheit, Il Progresso, La Prensa,* and so much more. At the time, we were a city and a country of newspaper readers. Some of my friends only read the sports pages or the comic strips. But they read. We all did. My family purchased our newspapers and magazines there, but the older guys would stand around and read for nothing. Against the wall, a few men were always pitching pennies—closest to the sidewalk line wins!

We did not have a telephone. A phone was a luxury. Friends and relatives could only reach us by mail or at the pay phone in Millie's store. We depended upon the teenagers who wasted time at Millie's to fetch us if we had a call, for which they got a nickel tip. Cigarettes cost twenty-five cents.

Four groups of people, living or working in this area were held in the highest esteem. The utmost respect went to our parents. The kids I knew—including me and my brothers—never dared to say a disrespectful or challenging word to their mothers or fathers. In our apartment that was the rule. It was a line never to be crossed.

Our teachers followed next with an almost equal level of respect. Public School 135 was the brain trust of the community. Our class room was our chapel and our teachers were feared and respected.

I recall being ill, home in bed for about two weeks. I cannot remember if I had the mumps or measles. All I could do was read, listen to the radio, or sleep. The greatest compliment came when my homeroom teacher came to visit me. When Mom heard that Mrs. Walsh was to make a treasured visit, she started to clean the already clean apartment. It was as if President Roosevelt, Mayor LaGuardia or Eleanor Roosevelt was going to be the guest of honor.

# A Life of Risks Taken

A teacher's "kind" visit was like getting the Congressional Medal of Honor. A "bad" visit—for deportment issues—was Alcatraz.

Mom served Mrs. Walsh tea and *mandel* bread in the living room on the coffee table. This was truly high tea served with honor and respect. Our family never ate in any other place except the kitchen. Mrs. Walsh assured Mom that I would easily catch up with the lessons I missed because of my absence. She did not want me to do any work at home. Reading, of course, was fine. The most important goal was to get well.

"And all the boys and girls in the class miss his smiling face." Mrs. Walsh took a bit of mandel bread. "This cake is good. What do you call it?"

Momma grinned from ear to ear.

"Vee call dis cake mandel bret," Momma answered in her best English.

This was followed by a ten-minute explanation of how to bake it.

The final two groups for whom the level of respect was extremely high were our doctor and, last but not least, the police. We never saw the police as our enemy. They were the helpful team ready to assist when needed.

When a group of kids was standing around outside the candy store on our street, talking, laughing, perhaps being a little noisy, and having fun, a patrol car would pull up. Officer Orlando, a cop from the Seventy-first Precinct, would get out of his car and instruct us, "Ten o'clock, kids. Time to go home and to bed."

The officer might also say, "Hey, Bernie, you little

wise guy, put that cigarette out or I make this report out to your father."

All of us did exactly what the policeman ordered us to do, not out of fear—well, maybe a little—but because we listened and did what adults told us to do. We were taught to have manners.

ꙮ

My friends and I spent a lot of time at Millie's as kids. We bought a stick of gum with a baseball card wrapped inside—the cost, one cent. Chocolate-covered candy was two cents. If you picked one with pink on the inside, it was free. A five-cent ice-cream cone was a special treat. A real pack of Lucky Strike cigarettes cost twenty-five cents, or, for a single penny, one Chesterfield cigarette that we implied was for our father.

At twelve or thirteen years old, Skinny Bernie, Robby, Fat Bernie, and me, the four of us disappeared with a pocketed penny smoke. One by one each of us took our first drags, until it was down to a quarter of an inch.

Returning home, I brushed my teeth and rinsed my mouth, not wanting Mom to detect the smell of smoke. But there was no hiding it from the her super sensitive nostrils. She was like a detective. As I left the bathroom, Mom called out in a strong voice,

"Come over to me—right this minute!" she commanded.

"I have homework," I said, almost mumbling.

"I SMELL SMOKE IN THIS HOUSE," she said in a firm voice.

"I didn't—"

12

"If I have to come to you, then you will be sorry."

"Okay, Okay." I surrendered.

Mom, smelling my clothes, said "You've been smoking!"

Whack!

Me, holding my arms over my head to protect myself, "It was just one drag."

"Don't you raise your hands to me!"

"It was just one drag."

Whack!

"I'll give you just one drag. You are lying. And I will drag you to your father and see what he has to say when he gets home."

"Momma, no, please, don't! I promise, never again."

"Well, we'll see. I'm going to save this little piece of information."

I was grateful, not wanting Poppa involved in this stuff. That would be very dangerous.

There was no discussion about the consequences of smoking, no appeal to intellect of understanding between parent and child. Those conversations never existed. The only danger I understood about smoking was that I would get the crap kicked out of me if caught. There was just a smack and a command. "You will not smoke or I will beat your brains in."

ॐ

Situated next to the candy store was Mr. Katz's shoulder-pad factory, where eight workers made pads for the garment center. I worked at Katz's shop for a couple of weeks as a teenager, earning sixty-five cents an hour.

# A Life of Risks Taken

On the corner of East Forty-Eighth Street and Church Avenue, Halpern's Appetizing store dominated the cross section. Here we bought bagels, lox, herring, cream cheese, halvah, and other special treats. Poppa loved that stuff, so we happily received all those Sunday breakfast goodies.

But, Mr. Halpern was not the nicest person. When we walked into the shop on the way home from school to buy a sour pickle, he watched us like a hawk, though we never once thought to steal anything. Mr. Halpern had a son and a daughter who went to school with us and were always eating. Both were dreadfully overweight and we often teased them about being fat.

In our home, eating was a special ritual, particularly on Friday nights. The preparation for the Friday-night dinner would take Mom a whole day. A typical meal included soup with *luchen* (noodles) or matzo balls, roasted chicken with a Ritz cracker stuffing, a green vegetable, roasted potatoes, Jell-O with sliced bananas for dessert, and a large challah bread. There were no candles, no prayers; we were all just happy being together, safe.

The sound of the bugle—"Dinner is ready"— summoned everyone from various corners of the apartment. It was like the call of Tarzan in the movies, when all the monkeys would rush to his side for instructions.

Four boys and Dad in ten minutes would eat what took four-to-six hours of preparation. Conversations were simultaneous. Over the din, Mom ordered me, "Eat your vegetables. Drink your milk."

We watched as Poppa took a quick shot glass of whiskey. It went down quickly as he crunched his eyes from the bitter taste. "Ahhh."

14

# A Life of Risks Taken

Mom never sat down to eat. She ate standing and serving, while her four sons devoured their dinner.

Suddenly, Poppa would have something to say, and we all would get immediately sha, shtil, silent and still. He instructed use in a clear, high-pitched Yiddish.

One Friday, not long after I was caught smoking, was a special lecture: "The war in Europe is not going to end there. Soon a war will start in Asia. And the world will be in a terrible condition. In our country, President Roosevelt is trying to keep us out of this awful situation. But I know, and he knows, that very soon we will be sending our young men to Europe and join the battle against the Nazi einschlus. And what I fear the most is that one of my sons will be part of that. This is a dreadful time in our country and in the world. Read the newspapers and books. Learn and be smart," he commanded, "all of you. Study hard, be smart! Become educated, because when you are educated and intelligent, the army will find a better place for you than as a foot soldier."

We listened intently. No one ate, or touched a spoon, or made a noise. I loved these moments. He looked around the table. His eyes met mine and his face changed. His glare frightened me.

"If I ever again hear that you are smoking, you will be a sorry boy. And that goes for the rest of you as well," he commanded.

I guess Mom didn't keep any secrets from Poppa. I was lucky that time. I figured she had interceded on my behalf and told Dad she had given me a couple good of smacks. He must have been satisfied—but still, he had to say something.

Each of us left the table with a speedy "Thanks, Mom." And that was it. No one took a dish or a single fork or spoon from the table. None of us ever helped with the cleaning up. Momma did everything. She and Poppa were left alone at the table. Mom ate the rest of her dinner, and Poppa had a cup of tea with a small square of sugar between his teeth. A piece of honey cake or strudel lay on a plate beside his cup.

Afterward in the living room, sitting very relaxed in his blue-velour chair, Poppa would light up a Camel cigarette, take a deep drag, and exhale, releasing of all the stress he had accumulated during the day. Now he was in his home and he could rest.

&#8359;&#8250;&#8238;

Another neighborhood staple, Harry's Luncheonette was a home away from home. Harry's wife, Frieda, prepared delicious bacon, lettuce, and tomato sandwiches or tuna salad on a toasted bagel, with a chocolate malted, both for thirty-five cents. There were no electric toasters. The bagel was sliced in half and put into the oven.

Frieda was a great cook and a terrific person, kind and trusting. She had two daughters away at college. Marilyn was a junior at Bryn Mawr College, and Selma, a freshman at Smith College. As I got older, I began to respect those parents whose efforts to earn a living for their families facilitated the single-minded goal of giving their children a better life through higher learning. Frieda and Harry were doing just that for their daughters, though Frieda did most of the work.

# A Life of Risks Taken

Frieda always gave us a break when we didn't have enough money. We paid thirty-three cents or thirty cents for a grilled cheese sandwich and a coke. Once she took only twenty-five cents from me when that was all I had.

Harry, on the other hand, was a do-nothing person. He sat in the back of the store with a baseball cap on top of his bushy head and read the sports pages of the Daily Mirror. Whenever it got busy, my friend Bob Mazur would put on an apron and help out. For that he, too, was paid sixty-five cents an hour.

Close to the corner of East Forty-Ninth Street and Church Avenue was a food store where most people in the neighborhood shopped. Three local businessmen ran it. Morris was the skinny five-foot-tall grocer. Lenny—with the moustache—was the fruit man, and Hymie was the finger-on-the-scale butcher.

That was my world. I never ventured beyond those three blocks or across the trolley tracks to the other side of Church Avenue. There was another life on that other side of the street—the land of Gentiles, people we never knew, never spoke to, and rarely talked about.

The Holy Cross Church, where the Catholic kids attended school, stood next to a cemetery of the same name. Their parents shopped at different stores. They dressed differently than we did. Gentiles didn't go to the same movie theater we patronized. We went to the Rugby Theater on Utica Avenue. They went to the Granada on Church Avenue or the RKO Kenmore on Flatbush Avenue.

Church Avenue separated our worlds. I grew up thinking non-Jews were different. I never thought about how they lived, what they did, who they voted for. As a young adult, I discovered that they had the same struggles and similar hopes as we did. The other side of Church Avenue was mostly Italian and Irish. The kids had names like Anthony, Frank, Mary, and Christina, names that were so strange sounding to our ears. Our friends had names like Hymie, Moishe, Mindy, and Sarah.

On Jewish holidays, our school had only about twenty non-Jewish students attending classes out of a population of close to five thousand boys and girls. Even my one Italian friend, Naldo, stayed home from school on Yom Kippur.

℘〇ℭ

The Rugby Theater was my paradise every Saturday. Just past ten in the morning my brother Alvin and I happily departed for the movie with Momma's bag of sandwiches, fruit, and candy. We would have food for at least three days, just in case we got lost coming home. We watched a double feature, plus one or two cartoons, and a weekly chapter of Dick Tracy or The Shadow, followed by the closing with the World News of the Day—all of it twice. Admission was eleven cents.

There were some movies we were able to recite to Momma from memory—verbatim. She smiled with pleasure.

We were supposed to come home after a few hours, but we often got caught up in the films. One time we stayed too long.

Around four o'clock in the afternoon, Momma's heart began palpitating; the emergency S.O.S. We had not returned from the movies. It was already close to four in the afternoon, we had been at the Rugby Theater almost six hours.

# A Life of Risks Taken

*Where are they? Have they been kidnapped? Are they lost? Was there a accident?*

Poppa, who had a suspicion we'd just lost track of time, came on a mission of mercy. He walked up and down the aisles calling our names in a loud whisper.

"Al-vin! Sey-mour!" he called, trying to muffle the sound of his voice.

We were far away by then—our eyes frozen on the screen, our ears in total concentration. Dick Tracy was about to be shot, the Shadow was going to be thrown off the Empire State Building. No one knew what would happen until next Saturday.

In a flash, I saw Poppa through the corner of my eye. He saw us. I elbowed Alvin. He did not move. I elbowed again, much stronger.

"Whaaaat?" he moaned.

"Poppa is looking for us," I said.

We both jumped from our seats, the half-empty bag of popcorn falling to the floor.

"If I didn't come and get you, I am sure you would have slept here," Poppa whispered in a firm voice of reprimand.

೪൦ഌ

It was a hot July day, two weeks after Poppa's death. The sound of the whistling tea kettle tempted me into the kitchen. The smell of freshly baked mandel bread swept through our apartment.

The July heat rushed through our tiny four-room flat. Finally, with the kitchen windows open, the white print curtains began to dance to the tune of a welcome gust of air, cooling the kitchen. Outside, the summer sun beat down on the black-tarred street. There was the rare sound of a car driving by. Kids were playing stickball or marbles, perhaps jump rope or stoopball. Down the block, a neighbor turned on the fire hydrant, and kids ran in and out of the spray. A symphony of neighborhood sounds mixed with the tune of Jewish music, the local news, and a Yiddish soap opera from Mom's chosen radio station WEVD, which played all day long.

Mom's head tilted slightly to the left, resting on her clenched fist.

I kissed her cheek and said, "Momma, a cup of tea for me as well. Any mandel bread left?"

She rose to the counter where the cakes were on a plate, covered with waxed paper.

"I'll have a piece and sit with you," I said.

Mandel bread was Momma's version of chocolate-chip cookies. The hand-rolled dough rose to a round, crusty mound in the oven, the raisins and nuts baked in.

A zift—a deep sigh—slipped from Momma's lips, with it a look of disbelief. She shook her head from side to side. From the corner of her eye, a tiny tear slipped slowly down her cheek.

Abandonment is a horrific experience. Our family irrevocably altered. We were lonely, depleted and confused. I had never known the feeling of fear. Now—not yet seventeen—I felt the pressure of responsibility. I was in a panic. Who other than my father would be able to take care of us?

Like a magician's coin trick—see it now, swoosh, it disappears into thin air—there was no warning, nor the slightest signal. Poppa was here one day, the next day gone. Death increases the feeling of powerlessness.

He vanished. As had his humorous storytelling, advice-giving, and his kissy-huggy, quick-to-anger, swift-to-forgive personality.

ഇൗര

The funeral took place on June 26th, 1948, as Jewish custom calls for a speedy burial. People came by the hundreds to the I. J. Morris Funeral Home on Church Avenue and Kings Highway. My father lay in an open coffin. A talus draped around his shoulders, a yarmulke on his head, he lay there quiet and still, his face, powdered white, already ghostly.

I looked at my father—religious cap and a prayer shawl? Poppa was not devout. He didn't dwell in religion. He found religion  hypocritical, make-believe. Poppa was a political realist. He believed in a better world for the working classes. He valued education and good health care for everyone, long before it was a modern-day political issue. He believed in justice for the human race, regardless of color or creed. He openly loathed the economic discrimination that flourished in his wonderful America. He was wise before his time. And he died before his time. He never saw his sons succeed in life or meet their wives or hold his grandchildren.

I stared into the coffin—Poppa's unblinking face was sterile and still. He was only forty-four years old, yet he looked tired, old. I had never noticed that before.

He was always kidding around and so I questioned it the moment. Could this be real?

I whispered as I gazed down at him, "Poppa, you're

fooling around, right? If this is one of your jokes, it's not funny. Please get up. Let's go home."

My older brother Earl slid his hand under my arm and led me away from the coffin. With all my strength, I squelched my sobs, crushing the truth of his death between my teeth. I would not accept the truth.

We—Momma, Earl, Alvin, Bobby, and I, together with my Aunt Rose, Uncle Louis, cousins Ruth, Sarah, and Irene—sat in the front as the eulogy began.

A gray bearded man in a black suit, a white shirt, and a black tie, stood on a platform behind the lectern. He, too, had a talus around his shoulders and a yarmulke on his head.

The man in black called Dad by his Jewish name, Chatzkal. Who was this guy talking about Poppa? He did not know my father. He was neither friend nor *mishpucha*, family. I never saw him in our home. He was not telling those gathered about the kind things my dad did, about the stories Poppa used to tell us, or the funny jokes he came home with from work at "The Place." Not a word was said about our going with Poppa to soccer games, wrestling matches, picnics in Prospect Park or the Russian baths. The man never mentioned Poppa's politics though it was a critical part of his life. Why was nothing being said?

This man did not know that Poppa napped on the blue-velour chair in our living room. When he slept, my brothers and I tiptoed quietly around him so as not to disturb him. There had to be quiet in the house when he rested. He breathed heavily, like a gentle drum rhythm—a deep inhale followed by a musical, thumping snore, like a refrain from the Russian song "Meadowlands," one of Poppa's favorites.

This man on the podium did not know our history. He did not know the story about the fire in our apartment building when the fire chief ordered all the tenants to evacuate their apartments. Daddy was asleep in his chair. Not one of us dared to wake him. Poppa might go down in flames, but we would not wake him!

Suddenly getting up the courage, my brothers Alvin and Bob and I quietly walked into the living room, approached Poppa's chair and with a slight tremble, whispered, "Daddy . . . Daddy."

He did not move. His breathing was playing our song.

Finally, Bobby, the youngest, touched him on his leg, swift as a frog's tongue.

Poppa raised his head quickly, "Whaaa—what's happening here?" His voice was deep and demanding.

We all stepped back and stifled the glee of our bravery. In his singsong voice, Bobby whispered, "Poppa, the building is on fire and they want us to come downstairs."

The bearded man wore rimless spectacles that balanced off the tip of his nose. His lips were moving, but I heard nothing.

How could he know our laughter as Poppa, making ghoulish sounds, guided us down the stairs in the darkened hall, while in front of the building three fire engines and an army of firemen all waited for the Ubells? Our neighbors applauded as we exited the building. Poppa lifted Bobby into his arms, kissed his baby boy and set him down, as Alvin and I huddled around him in safety. Standing in his undershirt, suspenders holding up his trousers, he lit up a Camel cigarette and exhaled the streaming smoke from his lips and nose.

The stranger on the podium said nothing about my father teaching me how to sell a suit of clothes or pull up a lay of cloth on the cutting table. He had not uttered a single honest word about my father. All he spoke of was God—a God that gives, a God that takes, a God that does so many things, a God we should trust—a God my father never believed in.

If Poppa could hear this man, he would have told the impostor to get down from the podium and let one of his sons speak on his behalf. Or Poppa might say jokingly, "I am getting up out of this coffin, and I'll take a taxi to the cemetery."

Oh, the anguish and my shame! How I regret not telling the true story of my father! To this day, more than sixty years of my life have sped by, and still, I feel the remorse over that choice. But how could I have said what I wanted to say? I was just shy of seventeen years old. There was no one to guide me. I was lost.

⚘

Sitting *Shiva*. White sheets covered the mirrors and pictures that hung from walls. We were told to sit on small wooden stools with our shoes off. I would do neither. People brought food, candies and all kinds of cakes. Our uncles, aunts, cousins, and friends mourned and wept, and tried to console us. It was exhausting. It was also unreal. A death in the family was something that happens to other people—not to us.

# A Life of Risks Taken

With all our relatives and friends coming to visit, this was the first time I had ever seen my mother sit silently. She watched us all as if frozen to her tiny wooden stool. She did not serve anyone. She did not welcome anyone. Her calm frightened me enough to make me fear that she, too, was going to die.

My Uncle Jack, Momma's brother, came from out of nowhere. We had not seen him for several years. They hardly spoke to each other. When he entered, Jack was the only one Momma got up to greet. The silence between them was obvious as they gently kissed each other's cheeks. He embraced her, and Momma wept on her brother's shoulder. Jack wiped a tear from his face, gently guided his sister back to her seat and sat down beside her. All that separated them in the past, was now gone.

Uncle Jack slept on the couch. For five days he prepared our meals, washed dishes, made the beds, swept up, made coffee, and took over the household. His actions were my first understanding of the importance and the power that connects blood relatives. Family is there when you need them.

After *Shiva* ended, Uncle Jack kissed Momma goodbye and disappeared. It was three years later when we saw Uncle Jack again, with his beautiful and charming wife, Natalie, and his lovely daughter, my cousin, Iris.

ଛଔ

Back in my mother's kitchen in early July, it was four o'clock in the afternoon. Momma finished serving the tea, while I munched on the mandel bread. Suddenly, she feigned a spit to her finger.

"Peh, peh! You should live until a hundred and twenty-one," she said in her Yiddish accent, a voice so familiar to my ears, that even today I can still hear her special intonation.

"Momma, the blessing is 'you should live until a hundred and twenty years, not twenty-one."

"I don't want you to die suddenly," she whispered.

I smiled. Once again she lifted her finger and began the ritual, a simple, tiny gesture, one that is centuries old, to ward off all evil spirits.

Tightly curled up in a knot, deep in the back of my mind, laid the throbbing sense of obligation. I must find a job. I would be seventeen years old the next month. The future weighed heavily on my shoulders. I was responsible now—reluctantly—but still responsible.

# Chapter 2

ᘒᘓ

### Early Childhood Memories

"Poppa, tell me how I was born. Pleeeeeeease!" I called out at seven or eight years old.

My dad would repeat that same story over and over. He probably told that story at least a hundred times to my brothers, Alvin and Bob, and me.

Poppa didn't just tell a story. He acted out each and every part. We laughed so much it hurt. Our childhood laughter was, as I found out later in life, one of the few joys in our home. Unknown to me and my brothers at the time, life between my parents lacked affection.

Speaking only in Yiddish with a deep stage voice, Poppa began, "It was a steamy summer day in August of 1931. You, my dear Shimon, were born during a terrible depression."

He hummed dark-sounding music.

"What's a depression, Poppa?" Alvin spoke up.

Poppa looked puzzled for a moment. He gathered his thoughts.

# A Life of Risks Taken

"A depression is . . . a depression is . . . no one has a job. Everyone is very frightened. There is no money, no food, no anything."

Alvin and I looked at each other. Although we heard the words, we could not grasp the essence of the word. All we understood was that it was bad.

"We were lucky, because I had a good job and a good trade. Momma and I and Earl felt safe, and we were going to have a beautiful and healthy baby. And we knew that every child brings their own luck into the family. We knew you would bring us good things."

I bounced up and down in our bed. "I'm the lucky baby!" I cried out.

Poppa pretended trumpets.

"One day Momma said to me, 'Hurry, Charlie, I think the baby is coming. We must rush to the hospital.'"

Poppa mocked a look of shock. Then he turned to me, suddenly serious. "Momma was very brave as we both walked carefully to the hospital more than twenty blocks away. We stopped a few times so your Momma could rest. A very heavy baby was not easy."

I smiled.

"Trucks were whizzing by on Kings Highway. Cars were honking, trolleys clanging. It all made me nervous. People were staring at us. But we walked carefully and slowly.

"When we reached this big hospital and walked in, a nurse quickly came to us and gave Momma a wheelchair. In a few minutes, she was taken away, and I went into the waiting room. I paced up and down that room. All the expectant fathers sat together and smoked cigarettes."

"Did you smoke?" I asked.

Poppa nodded.

I was lying on my stomach on my bed, my head propped up on my elbows. Bob was almost asleep, but Alvin was at my side in the same position. We watched our father.

"Momma was hoping for a girl," he teased.

I grimaced. I didn't want to be a girl.

"Finally after hours of waiting, the doctor came into the fathers' waiting room and announced, 'It's a boy!'"

Poppa had jumped with joy.

He whispered, "I always wanted a boy, but I was trying to please Momma by agreeing with her."

Alvin turned to me, "I'm so glad you were a boy."

"Me, too!" I screeched with joy.

Again trumpet music. Ta Dahhh!

I was the second son born to Hilda and Charlie Ubell. I weighed a whopping nine pounds, six ounces. Poppa told me I was a strong, husky boy with blond curly hair.

"Everyone in the family and all the neighbors wanted to look into the carriage and see our beautiful new son," he told us. "We were thinking of selling tickets for people to look at you."

I giggled.

"The hundreds—no—thousands, of people who looked at you all wanted to know your name."

I laughed, knowing Poppa was making it up.

My father continued, "We agreed on your name. It would be Shimon, or Samson, a Jewish hero from a biblical story."

"Can you tell us that story?" I pleaded.

On a different occasion, Dad had told me that when the time came to fill out the birth certificate, Momma had said my name was Shimon, and the nurse had looked at her.

"That's a religious name. What this boy needs is an American name."

The nurse thought for a moment. "Seymour," she said.

Momma thought about it, said the name over and over, and then agreed.

This night, Poppa hummed, *"Rock-a-Bye Baby"*—that was the signal to go to sleep.

"Another time. It is late now." His voice turned stern. "We have to shut the light. You have to go to sleep."

"Please, tell me about Samson," I begged as Alvin climbed into bed.

I had heard it many times, but I loved that special time my father spent with my brothers and me. I loved his smell, his voice. More than once, he fell asleep before we did, while telling us the story. While he slept, I cuddled up under his arm, put my nose against his body and inhaled deeply.

After Poppa left, I lay there in the dark, feeling content and safe. Alvin was curled up on the edge of the bed, looking as if he might fall off any minute. Bobby already dreamed in a deep sleep.

# Chapter 3

ഩൠ

### A New Life in America

Coming to America in 1925 as a young man of twenty-one was very complicated for my father. It took courage and resolve to make such a choice. Leaving home, parents, friends, and loved ones is not easy. But America meant opportunity, and my father wanted a new life.

Aunt Rose, his older sister, had arrived in the states four years earlier in 1921. She met her husband, Uncle Louis, in a hat workshop in Manhattan. She was a trimming girl and he was the foreman. They both came from Sulwalki, Poland. They dated for about six months and were married at a rabbi's apartment on Hester Street in lower Manhattan.

Poppa hoped for similar fortune as he crossed the Atlantic Ocean in a ship overflowing with other hopeful immigrants. The conditions were difficult and took their toll on the passengers.

Hundreds of brave and determined people crowded his section aboard the ship. Only four toilets were available to these passengers. Accommodations were not clean and people became ill. Three children and an older man died. All were buried at sea.

On the third night out at sea, Poppa heard rumors that several waiters in the first-class upper-deck section had taken ill. Dad went to his suitcase and put on a clean shirt that he had been saving for his arrival in New York.

He offered the guard—who separated the first class from the steerage passengers—a few rubles in order to get into that section. The guard was stern. He refused to accept the money and turned my father back. Pop went to the other side of the boat and saw a young man who looked very ill. The man was one of the waiters. After Poppa talked with him, the waiter went to his boss and said he had someone who wanted to help serving or in the kitchen. Since so much of the staff was sick, Dad was hired on the spot.

It was his first American job. He moved his two suitcases into the wait-staff quarters. For the next two-and-a-half weeks, he shared a room with four other waiters, ate better food and worked as a busboy. At the end of the voyage, he was paid forty-eight dollars for his efforts. Shared tips amounted to an additional nine dollars. To his surprise, he was also given a check for fifty-five dollars for a partial refund of his fare. He was rich, healthy and very happy.

Arriving at Ellis Island in New York Harbor with thousands of other immigrants, Poppa presented his documents to the officer in charge. A doctor and a nurse examined this twenty-one-year-old man and concluded that he was strong and in good health.

# A Life of Risks Taken

He remembered seeing several people who were not allowed to enter, those who were sick. Some were put into isolation and others were just sent back. He was heartbroken to see those people, after a tortured journey, detained or deported.

Dad stood before an officer at the documentation desk. He knew almost no English.

"You are Haskell Abraham Yubouroffsky. Is that correct?"

My father nodded.

"You were born in Sulwalki, Poland?"

Poppa nodded.

"Your birth date is March 15th, 1904?"

Again Poppa nodded.

"I'm going to do you a big favor that will save you money and make you an American right away," the officer exclaimed.

Poppa smiled.

"I'm going to give you an American name."

The officer wrote on Poppa's entry certificate Charles Abraham Ubell and the same on the small identity card. *Stamp! Stamp!*

The officer put the entire packet into an envelope, gave it to my father, shook his hand, and said, "Welcome to America, Charlie."

They both smiled. My father had become a legal resident of the United States of America.

Poppa was overwhelmed with this unexpected feeling of joy. He had imagined all kinds of roadblocks and difficult questions to answer. His entry into the United

States was so easy, he thought something was wrong.

"How could they let people into this great land so easily?" he continued to ask years later.

After meeting Aunt Rose, Poppa's next task was to find a job. He did that very quickly. Poppa's first job was as a street hooker. That meant that every day, Poppa would stand in front of the clothing store where he worked, and if he saw a potential customer, Poppa would hook his hand under the customer's arm and gently nudge him into the shop, so that a salesman could take over.

He was paid sixteen dollars a week, working six days each week, including Saturday and Sunday. He was a happy man in America.

≈∂≈

Momma came to the United States through Canada. Her half-sister, Sophie, lived in Toronto.

"Sophie is a bitch," Mom once told me. That was one of only two times I ever heard my mother use a bad word.

My maternal grandfather married three times. His first wife had five children. Aunt Sophie was one of them. There was also Rachel, Minnie, Becky, Solomon, Herschel, and Tevya. My grandmother was his second wife. She had three children, Hilda (my mom), Hanna, and Jack. She died while giving birth to my Uncle Jack. Soon after, Grandpa married a third time, and his wife, Sarah, gave birth to one child, Jennie. The tally was nine children and eighteen grandchildren, which included my three brothers, Earl, Alvin, and Bob, and me.

Momma was unhappy living with Sophie. She told me that she became a maid in that house. She was so depressed in Canada, she begged her half-brother, Tevya, to save her and bring her to New York.

Tevya was a tinsmith. He had his own business, and he also did some work for Uncle Louis's apartment houses. Playing matchmaker, Tevya concocted a plan with Louis for my parents to have an accidental meeting in Prospect Park, in Brooklyn.

Poppa fell in love at first sight. He pursued Momma vigorously for about a month without much success. Momma told me how handsome Poppa was, but he was a little too sure of himself—one of the genes my brothers and I inherited.

Eventually, he stopped his courting and was quickly with another girl who worked in a shirt factory. He liked her very much, but her cousin did not like Poppa.

Again alone, my father went to a *lansleit* singles party. Lansleit means people from the same town or community in Europe. By sheer accident, at this party, Hilda and Charlie met again. This time he was a little softer and more receptive to what Momma had to say.

My dad asked Momma for her address.

That night he wrote her a letter apologizing for his aggressive approach during their first meeting. Charlie asked for a chance for them to become friends. He explained the importance of having trusting friends for those who dared to take the dangerous voyage across the sea to this enormous and wonderful country. He delivered the letter by hand, sliding it under Momma's door. Mom looked out the window, and there was Charlie waiting for his answer.

They were married on July 5th, 1925. My brother Earl was born on June 21, 1926.

# Chapter 4

ఠఙ

**The Love Child**

My thirty-eight-year-old cousin, Max, was the consummate storyteller. I listened, totally absorbed by his version of the tale.

Momma and Poppa separated in November 1930. Mom had been unhappy for a long time. Experiencing persistent depression and headaches, in a fit of anger, she quickly packed two suitcases, left a note for Poppa, gathered Earl under her arms and ran off to her two sisters who lived in Pittsburgh.

At Becky's and Minnie's, Mom suffered two weeks of lectures about the shame of divorce, about not having a man in your life, especially one who earned a good living. Who was going to want a twenty-five-year-old woman with a child?

"Your life will be lonely and bitter," they warned. Carefully planned tears flowed from my aunts' eyes onto the perfectly ironed tablecloth as they urged Mom to rethink her decision.

# A Life of Risks Taken

The two sisters fought with each other every day about the strategy my mom should take with Charlie. They battled about divorce and the waste of money the long-distance phone calls cost. Ignoring my mother's protestations, they argued about how to convince Poppa to come to Pittsburgh and take his loving wife and beautiful son back to New York.

Meanwhile, in New York, Uncles Tevya and Louis tried to convince my dad to come to Pittsburgh. Poppa was adamant, "A woman has to respect her husband and not only provide for his food but for his feelings and his needs as a man. I would rather be alone than live with someone and be lonely."

My uncles were strong and seasoned men. They argued that Hilda was young, away from her parents in Europe. The transition was not easy. They promised him that a new woman would emerge from her experience of moving away from Poppa. They implored him to give Momma a second chance.

My mother had a different view than her brothers-in-law. She was strong and did not want to live with a man who was quick tempered and only thought of his own needs. She resisted her sisters' begging. Still both knew that life could not continue this way. He had to give an inch and Mom would give a yard. A meeting in Pittsburgh was agreed upon.

One Friday evening after work, my father—with a new and slightly more positive attitude—boarded a Greyhound bus at the Union Square Station. As Poppa slept deeply on the bus, Momma tossed and turned in her bed. She quietly wept and planned the changes she would try to make in order to keep her son safe and her life in order.

Charlie arrived in downtown Pittsburgh early on Saturday morning, went to a barber for a shave and a haircut, and then to a florist.

The flowers were not for Momma. Poppa was too smart to make that move. The flowers were for Minnie and Becky. He knew that would please my mother more than buying them for her. However, he was not one to come empty-handed. On the bus he had written a beautiful love letter.

Poppa arrived at the house at nine o'clock with a small suitcase and a big smile. He presented the flowers to my aunts with an actor's bow. He looked at my mom and she instantly began to cry. Earl rushed to Pop's legs and wrapped his arms around them. Dad reached down, picked him up, tossed him in the air, caught him, and did it again.

"He just ate, Charlie," Mom said in a gentle tone.

Still weeping, she fell into Poppa's arms. As strong as he was, he, too, began to cry. My aunts cried and then Earl joined in.

The whole world was in tears, and Momma whispered the magical words, "Are you hungry, Charlie?"

"A little," he said. A little hungry in my family meant that you were starving; you would die any moment if your stomach wasn't filled.

My Uncle Tevya took out a bottle of schnapps, and each of the men had two shots. The women made whiskey sours and joined the celebration. It was only ten in the morning. Who drinks and eats dinner at that time? The answer? Jewish families who are settling issues and celebrating the resolution.

Soon my Aunt Rachel and her son, Max, joined the happy occasion, too. They all sat in oversized, burgundy-velvet chairs around the huge oak dining room table. An embroidered, white-linen cloth that my aunts had brought from Poland covered the table. The spotless, shining sterling came from Germany. All had belonged to Great-Grandmother Malienka.

That part of the family had been in the metal business, exporting and importing from countries all over Europe. On one trip to Dusseldorf, my great-grandfather, Markov, bought the silverware for the equivalent of twenty-three dollars—a small fortune in those days. And much to the joy of Great-Grandmother Malienka, who had reprimanded Great-Grand Poppa for spending so much money, they gave the silverware to Aunt Minnie for her dowry. Three large silver candlesticks from Switzerland, another silly purchase by Markov, lit the room to create a wonderful festive atmosphere.

The family was once again, solid and united. Charlie and Hilda were sitting at the table enjoying the moment, holding hands and touching knees. No marriage counselors, no lawyers, nothing but the powerful source of family.

On Sunday morning, Momma, Poppa, and Earl boarded the big silver Greyhound bus and returned to their apartment on Stone Avenue in Brooklyn.

Max concluded the story and I was silent. I had never heard this from anyone.

Years later, Mom told me that she probably became pregnant on that Saturday night on Coaltart Street. She blamed the whiskey sours.

"And that was you, growing inside me."

She pressed her hand to her heart and shut her eyes as she smiled.

"You were our love child."

# Chapter 5

ഔരഝ

### Growing Up and Learning English

Yiddish was our mother tongue, the language we spoke at home. All the stories in my childhood stories were told to us in Yiddish. My parents spoke Russian, Yiddish and English, although the stories may have been interesting in English, but in Yiddish I found them much warmer and more charming. Yiddish jokes or stories translated to English lose the flavor of the mother tongue. The intonations, the facial expressions all go into the telling. They are some expressions that exist in Yiddish that do not translate at all. For example there is a Yiddish word, *Mechutan*. That word represents the relationship between the parents of the bride and the parents of the groom, or in English, in-laws.

I grew up speaking Yiddish, a bit of Russian, and just a little English, until I was five years old and entered kindergarten. I still have retained some words and sentences in Russian. I remain fluent in Yiddish, and my English is just okay. At home, we played, sang, were read to, and taught in Yiddish. On Sunday we went to Yiddish-speaking *shullas,* or schools. I remember Poppa taking me at nine a.m. Sunday morning, across the trolley tracks, past Church Avenue to Schenectady Avenue, to a house where we went into a finished basement that was like a class room. That basement was our Yiddish-speaking school. We were taught the alef-beys, the "ABCs." We studied Yiddish songs and stories by Shalom Aleichem and Y. L. Perutz, widely read and well-known Jewish folk writers.

Leftist politics were part of the curriculum, stressing the needs of the working class, the second-class citizenship of "Negroes," as well as the importance of education for everyone. We were acquainted with Lenin's words: "From each according to his ability, to each according to his needs." That sounded reasonable to me.

The International Workers Order, a very left-wing Jewish organization, supported all the *shullas.* Probably most of the parents of the kids attending were card-carrying members of the Communist Party. That political point of view was very common and a very acceptable learned point of view to the community of Eastern European Jews.

Earl was five years older than I, and a scholar by the age of ten. My older brother took on the enormous task of teaching me to speak English before I entered public school. He instilled in me a strong intellectual work ethic. He pushed me to the ultimate ends of curiosity, and inspired in me the sense of discovery and enjoyment in learning. He urged me to know more than my friends, to be the best in the classroom.

Earl was an excellent role model. He loved books and

learning and tried daily to raise the level of my interest. It wasn't easy to reach the level of learning my older brother had. I wasn't smart like Earl, a natural, but I was a worker. My effort paid off, and I became a very good student. I was not at the top of the class, but I was in the top ten or maybe twelve. Quite an accomplishment, I thought!

"If you want to be a success in kindergarten," he, as a fifth grader, instructed, "you must learn to speak English." If he said that once, he must have made that pronouncement one hundred times or more.

Our lessons began with numbers and stories. No spelling or writing; we just spoke to each other. He would not permit me to speak in Yiddish. Earl was strict and demanded excellence. He was determined to succeed in his goal. "My kid brother, Seymour, will be speaking English by the time he enters school."

In our darkened room, where we slept together in one bed, he continued with storytelling. I had to learn four new words every day and basic arithmetic. Soon I was able to count to twenty-five, thirty. I mastered arithmetic long before I entered the first grade.

When I was in the third grade, Earl taught me algebra and geometry. In the sixth grade, he induced me to read books by tempting me with the promise of racy parts in them. I devoured book after book, never finding the sexy chapters.

When I confronted Earl about his little lies he smiled and replied, "Good book anyway, right?"

I nodded. "So what else do you suggest?" I asked.

Earl would question me in depth about each book he assigned me to read.

# A Life of Risks Taken

I arrived at the Public School 219 on East Ninety-Second Street in Brooklyn with a strong understanding of English but without a high verbal aptitude. Often my classmates laughed at my accent. Within four months, I was fluent, but the accent remained. They teased me relentlessly. It's something I had to accept. Here I am, seventy-five years later at age eighty-one, still with that slight accent. But I switched from a Yiddish accent to a New York one.

When I started first grade, my family moved to East Forty-Eighth Street and Church Avenue. I attended Public School 135, at Schenectady Avenue and Linden Boulevard, which was a short block away from our new apartment.

Miss Davis, my first grade teacher, was strict but fair. I remember her asking my name, "Shimon?"

"No, no, it's See-more," I responded quickly, my accent betrayed.

The entire class laughed. Miss Davis ordered the room to be quiet.

"Can you spell your name, please?"

"Yes, I can."

"Please stand up and let us hear you." The class continued to chuckle. "Please, everyone, hush, this is your classmate."

I cleared my throat, stood up next to my desk, and began, "S-E-Y-M-O-U-R."

"Yes, that spells Seymour. What a nice name! Very good—you may sit down now."

I was thrilled. I could not wait to tell my parents and Earl of my success at school.

# Chapter 6

৪০০৪

## The Bully

Sonny Tuchman was my next-door neighbor. His father was a taxi driver. He had an older sister, Edith, who was fifteen years old. Unlike my parents, they were not intellectual, nor were they political in any way. They voted for Franklin D. Roosevelt, but that was the extent of it.

Poppa would joke, "They think that FDR is Jewish, that's why they voted for him."

The Tuchmans were always fighting. You could hear the screaming through the walls. "Fuck you!" or "Kiss my ass!" were common phrases.

My parents did not think much of them or their fighting. In Yiddish, they would describe them as "cows, animals, low character, and uneducated."

I did not think much of Sonny either. He and I were the same age and were in the same class. He taunted and bullied me every day. He would pull my hat off my head, knock the books out of my hands, push me when we were in line, and sneak an arm punch when the teacher wasn't looking. If his pencil broke, he would take one from my desk.

In the classroom, we were seated in alphabetical order, so Sonny always sat right in front of me. He was a very difficult kid. He would force a burp or a fart and make everyone in our section laugh. The teacher was always furious at us. One day he burped so loudly the entire class heard, and everyone began to laugh.

Mrs. Hand asked, "Who did that?"

Sonny quickly responded, "Seymour. Seymour," he shouted, "was the one who burped."

Everyone knew otherwise. I vehemently denied being the culprit, but I would not say that Sonny was the guilty party.

I was forced to stay one hour after school and write one hundred times: "I will not burp in class."

When I was finished and handed the pages to the teacher, she asked if I had learned a lesson. I told her that I did not burp. She wanted to know who did. I told her I did not know. I was frightened that if I told her the truth, Sonny would beat me up.

That night, I lay in bed silently. Earl was trying to teach me math. I asked him to stop. I told him about the incident in school.

"I'm not surprised," Earl said. "His sister is the same way with the girls in our grade."

I was surprised. Edith idolized my brother. I would see her gazing at him when he returned home or was across the street buying something in the candy store.

"No one likes her. Only my friend Lionel likes her."

"Why?" I asked.

"She has big tits."

Earl amazed me. I laughed out loud. I never heard him use that word.

"Sonny is a bully. And he is that way because no one challenges him. He's a coward. And if you confront him with intelligence, he will not be able to respond and he'll back down. Also, if he tries to hurt you, one thing is true—he won't kill you. You may have a bloody nose, but you will not be dead. Use your brain and it will work out."

I listened carefully to Earl's advice. In my fantasy, I visualized having a fist-fight with Sonny and beating his brains in. I imagined myself standing over him in front of the whole class like some comic book hero. But I knew in my heart of hearts that it was never going to happen. That boy frightened me, and fear is a powerful deterrent to action. So I did nothing and took the abuse.

As it turned out, Arlene Hoffman, one of the girls in the class spoke up quietly to Mrs. Hand and told her that I did not do the burp. Arlene was one of the smartest girls in the class and I think she liked me.

Because of Arlene, Sonny had to spend two days in detention, one day for lying and another for burping. The teacher came to me and said she was sorry that I had to take a punishment I did not deserve. Nothing happened between Sonny and me for almost five days. He didn't push me or say unkind things to me or do anything that was in any way bullying. I told Earl what was happening; he said that it was a good sign, but he warned me not to be disappointed if Sonny resumed his old tactics. Yet knowing Earl was on my side, I felt a little braver.

To date, no president in my lifetime has received the admiration or the high regard that Franklin Delano Roosevelt enjoyed. He moved in his wheelchair, with a smiling face, a white Stetson hat sitting askew atop his head, with a long cigarette holder between his teeth, smoke floating gently from the tip of his cigarette. He was as strong as any leader can be, elected for four terms with great majorities. F.D.R. was one of a kind, one of the most powerful and most loved and respected presidents of the United States. He sat toe to toe with Churchill and Stalin arranging the globe and the power of western society as we know it today. I remember my father saying that F.D.R. single-handedly saved the United States in World War II by helping Britain, and he saved capitalism during the depression with the W.P.A.

During World War II, we were immersed in collecting junk metal and wastepaper to donate to the war effort. My family bought a twenty-five-dollar war bond every week. At school we bought war stamps that we pasted into a little folder. When we accumulated eighteen dollars and seventy-five cents, we would turn it in for a twenty-five-dollar Victory Bond.

I remember rationing of meat, gas, and other things. We had meatless Tuesdays where we ate fish instead. Getting new shoes was a rarity. We always just repaired soles and heels. We purchased black window shades to keep the lights out of the street. Everything we did was to help win the war against Germany and Japan.

Ironically, it was Hollywood that eventually made

the war tangible to me. I saw a film called, Back to Bataan with John Wayne in 1945. Wayne led his company of men against the Japanese, brutally killing each enemy soldier. The film romanticized war for me, pulled me into the horrors of combat and stirred in me hatred for the enemy. I jumped from my seat, and called out at the top of my eleven-year-old voice, "Kill those fucking Japs!"

The audience applauded. I sank into my seat, embarrassed by my impulsiveness.

Momma found out about the movie incident from a neighbor, who thought it was amusing. Momma did not agree. She cautioned me that using bad words was a reflection on her and Poppa. And she also took a surprise position that never occurred to me. "Many good Japanese people have been put into camps here in America, the same as Jews have been put into camps in Europe. Think twice before you condemn an entire group of people."

"But they are the enemy, Mom!"

"Is it possible for an entire people to be the enemy or for a whole culture to be murderers? I think not. And you should think for yourself; you are smart."

Mom was right. Often a tiny group of terrorists or a few with radical ideas can start a conflagration that has nothing to do with the general population. As Poppa often said, "Most people just want to make a living, educate their children and have a safe and simple life."

Everyone in the school had to stay a little later one day. President Roosevelt was scheduled to make a radio speech to schoolchildren. The program was to be heard in almost every school all over the United States. The teachers told us that the reason the President's talk was on at three-thirty in the afternoon was because kids as far away as California and Oregon and Washington would be listening as well. It would be twelve-thirty in those states.

President Roosevelt's talk was about the importance of education, exercising, fair play, and how lucky we were to be Americans. It was a wonderful talk, reminding me of how my father spoke to us about education, studying and how good it was to live in America.

When F.D.R. finished his talk, all the kids applauded. We liked his voice and the strength his message sent to us. We all left the school auditorium and walked through the school yard.

Suddenly, I heard Sonny call out, "Hey, Ubelly, you are not only yellow, you are also a squealer." A very strong punch on my shoulder followed.

I was caught off guard. "You know something, Sonny? I heard your father changed his name to Tuchman from Fuckman."

Everyone laughed—the older kids used to call his sister Edith Fuckman—I knew that Sonny was not going to let this go. His face turned reddish purple, his eyes bulging in hatred.

Sonny threw a punch to my head. I was lucky. I saw it coming and ducked a second before it landed. Tears flooded my eyes. I was not a fighter.

"My mom says that your mom is a yenta (a gossip), and your father is a Commie," Sonny shouted.

I didn't know what a Commie was, but I did know what a yenta was. No one spoke badly about my mother!

# A Life of Risks Taken

Suddenly I became one of John Wayne's soldiers and Sonny became the enemy.

*I'll kill him.*

I jumped onto Sonny, wrapped my legs around his body, scratched his face, bit him on the cheek, and pulled his hair with all my strength. He was screaming and crying. Two teachers pulled us apart. They wanted to know who started the fight. Sonny accused me.

A crowd of students was around us. One teacher was holding Sonny by the shoulder and Mr. Wall, the gym teache, wrapped his arms around me with all his strength. So much for the intellect that I was supposed to challenge Sonny with.

There was blood on Sonny's cheek and drizzling from my nose.

Selwyn Thorner, who was my friend, told the teacher that he saw the whole thing and that Sonny had started the fight by punching me in the shoulder. Sonny glared at Selwyn with a look that meant trouble would be coming his way sometime soon.

We were both taken to the nurse's office.

That night our doorbell rang. It was Mr. and Mrs. Tuchman and Sonny's sister Edith. The Tuchmans confronted my mother and my father in very loud, threatening voices. Neighbors opened doors. Women assembled in their aprons, their hair in pins or in curlers, men in their undershirts. They looked down the stairs from the higher floors.

"Your Seymour bit my Sonny's cheek so badly, we had to take him to the doctor." Mrs. Tuchman said. "It was lucky he didn't need any stitches. That doctor cost six dollars and we want you to pay us for it." Her voice rose louder. "He bit him like a wild animal for no reason and ripped a patch of hair from his head! And I'll tell you something, Mrs. Know-It-All, to add to his disgusting behavior, that little animal over there," she pointed directly at me, "used a horrible low-life, four-letter word."

Mrs. Tuchman took a breath.

Momma stepped closer, looked her straight in the face and said very calmly, "I have four sons, and they never fight or bully anyone. That is not how we live in our home. I was told that Sonny not only started the fight but he's been pushing Seymour around for a long time. It is time he stopped."

Momma moved another step closer to our neighbor's face. Now they were nose to nose.

"I hope your son learned a lesson today. If he hasn't, the next time he tries to bully Seymour, I will join the fight. You have not seen fighting until someone hurts one of my sons."

A mild sound of applause came from some of the onlookers. The neighbors began voicing their opinions.

Mrs. Rosenfeld: "She is so right. Those Tuchmans are terrible!"

Mr. Ginsburg: "I would never guess Mrs. Ubell had such a strong side."

Mrs. De Blasio: "I would have slapped Tuchman in the face!"

Momma went on, her voice steadily rising and her Yiddish accent becoming even stronger, "As far as using four-letter words, I am surprised that it shocks you. All we ever hear through the walls of our apartment are four-letter words. When you and Mr. Tuchman speak to each other, don't you know how to speak English? If Seymour used a bad word, he learned it from you."

More doors opened in the hallway. Other families heard the commotion and were all standing and listening to my mom read the riot act to Mrs. Tuchman. Mr. Tuchman and my father were silent.

"And one more thing," Mom continued. "Perhaps the six dollars will be a good lesson for your family. The pain of money lost is often more intense that a bite on the cheek."

In one swift move, Mrs. Tuchman and Mr. Tuchman turned around and left for their apartment. Edith remained in the doorway, watching Momma.

Mom turned to me, slapped me in the face.

"If you ever use bad words again, that slap will seem like a stroke of kindness," she said. "I have spoken to you before about bad language."

Our audience of neighbors applauded.

I stood in shock.

Mom said softly, "Edith, darling, is there anything you want?"

"Is Earl home?" she asked.

"Yes, he is. Please come in."

# Chapter 7

ଈୠ

### The Seven-Year Old Business Itch

In the spring of 1938, I began my very first commercial enterprise: a shoeshine box. My simple desire was to go to a busy neighborhood street corner and shine shoes to make money. I was seven years old.

Alas, shining shoes was not to be. My father would not permit it. At the time, I had no idea what his reason was, but when I grew older, it occurred to me that only black boys and men shined shoes in our neighborhood. He must have felt it wasn't nice for a white Jewish boy to take on that work.

Nevertheless he did allow me to shine his shoes, as well as Mom's and Earl's shoes. Not for money, just fun.

ଈୠ

My next venture, in the summer of 1940, was more successful. At the age of nine, I constructed a lemonade stand in front of our apartment house at East Forty-Eighth Street, near Church Avenue. Dad gave me the okay.

# A Life of Risks Taken

Mom was the lemonade expert. My friend Selwyn, who lived next door, did the running back and forth to our kitchen, refilling our pitcher and fetching more cups. Mom gave me smart business advice, which I still use today. Say *"Thank you"* to every customer.

The first day was only a moderate success because we did not have enough people passing in front of our apartment house.

Lying in bed that night, I was thinking about where we could place our lemonade stand so that more people passed it. The next day we made a new logistics plan, though I would not have known to call it that.

On Sunday, the schoolyard was jammed with older boys and their dads playing softball and basketball. We moved our stand right outside the schoolyard gate.

We charged ten cents for each drink, three drinks for a quarter. They were thirsty, and we were a sellout! Pitcher after pitcher was filled and refilled, more than a dozen times. Mom ran out of lemons and substituted oranges. She made orangeade plus iced tea. Everything was sold to the last drop. We were the happiest kids on the block.

That evening we counted and recounted the fourteen dollars and change we had earned. I paid Selwyn four dollars, which was what he wanted. Mom got the rest. We decided that the next Sunday we would bring pretzels and cookies to sell as well.

What a great discovery I made at nine years old: Working hard is fun when you earn money.

ಬಂಚ

At the age of fifteen, I convinced three independent

storekeepers, who shared space under one roof, to hire me as their morning delivery boy. The shopkeepers included Lenny, the fruit and vegetable man, Hairy Hymie, the finger-on-the-scale butcher, and Morris, the dairy man and grocer.

Each shop paid me four dollars a week. I would start at eight a.m. and work until about noon, the time I had to leave for the late session at Tilden High School. During my high school days students attended classes in two sessions because the school had more than five thousand students, but room for half that. The first session was for freshmen and sophomores. Classes began at eight and ended at noon. For juniors and seniors, classes began at one p.m. and ended at five p.m.

Every morning, I arrived at the food shop and swept the place for about thirty minutes. By that time, each vender had at least two orders for delivery.

I hopped on my bike and began my route. In a couple of hours, I returned with some new orders from the places I delivered to and cash for payments—as well as almost seventy-five cents in tips. That was a good morning.

Thursday and Friday were our busiest days. I asked the shopkeepers for permission to hire another boy to help on those two days. I paid him three dollars of my earnings, and we shared the tips. Gary and I worked well as a team. I was able to take care of all of the customers' orders and still maintain a good relationship with the shopkeepers. The lesson was, always take care of your customer and keep your supplier happy.

The time I spent as the delivery boy at the food market was very special to me. It was early spring of 1946. Warm days were approaching. Earning money made me feel older, like an honest laborer, a part of the working class. I was growing up. My body was developing and getting stronger and more muscular from peddling my bike every day. I was never a big kid, just under normal height and weight, but I was fleshing out. I enjoyed the sensation of perspiration on my body.

World War II had just ended. Many of our soldiers were returning home in large numbers. Food at the shop was beginning to appear in larger quantities. I noticed more canned goods, and plenty of vegetables on display. No more shortages. Optimism spread among all my customers.

My brother Earl was still away in the Navy. A small flag with a star in the middle hung in our window, like many others on the block. It designated that a soldier, sailor, or marine lived in that apartment.

Full-street celebrations popped up whenever a son or a father returned from Europe or Asia. On our street, we had four men return in one week. All the families joined together to put on a "Welcome Home" block party. The end of the war and the celebrations that followed gave people perspective. Neighbors who were angry at each other for one reason or another would find themselves shaking hands, wives greeting each other with a kiss.

Irene Lipmann and her baby lived alone in the apartment house directly across the street from where my family lived. Her husband was still overseas. Almost every day I had a delivery to Mrs. Lipmann's apartment— some days, it was milk and bread, on another, fruit, and another, a small chicken for the weekend. This was not unusual. Most customers ordered fresh food every day.

In 1946, not many people had refrigerators, or washers and dryers, or televisions. We had a radio and an icebox. The iceman would come every other day and bring a cake of ice and place it into the icebox for thirty-five cents.

One Wednesday morning, I had an early morning delivery to Mrs. Lipmann. I set the bike down in front of her building, lifted the bag from the basket, and moved quickly up the stairs to her third floor apartment. I rang the bell. I heard the baby crying, so I rang again.

Mrs. Lipmann called out, "Come in, the door is open."

She was holding the crying infant in her arms, trying to comfort him.

"Seymour, put the milk on the table. I will pay you tomorrow."

Her voice was filled with anxiety.

I remember dishes in the sink, clothes scattered all around, a smell of dirty diapers, and newspapers and magazines all over the place. At the time, I didn't really take these things in. I never thought about her distress or what it meant to be a young woman alone during the war. I was just a kid—I cared about the delivery and the ten cent tip.

"Okay, Mrs. Lipmann, see you tomorrow," I called to her, already out the door.

I dashed down the stairs two at a time, jumped onto the bike and sped to my next stop.

Thursday was always a busy day. People began to order for the weekend. Thursday was a warm day. I must have had about twelve deliveries that morning. I took eight and started my routine. I always began with the farthest delivery first so that I could end the morning close to home, where I would shower quickly before leaving for school.

My last delivery was to Mrs. Lipmann. I moved quickly up the stairs, hopping two steps at a time. I arrived at her door out of breath. I rang the bell.

"Coming," she called.

She opened the door.

"Put it on the kitchen table," she instructed.

I did what I was told. Mrs. Lipmann seemed much calmer today.

"Let me get you some change. I also owe you for yesterday," she said.

"Oh, that's all right."

"You want a cold glass of seltzer?" she asked.

"That would be great."

She put two dimes on the table and handed me the cold drink. I stood, gulping the seltzer.

"Sit down and rest," she said.

I sat. We began to chat—more accurately, Mrs. Lipmann did. She asked how old I was, what grade I was in. Did I like my job? She leaned down to pick up a crumpled tissue from the floor, and her bathrobe opened ever so slightly, just enough for me to see her breast.

My body instantly became a furnace. I blushed from my toes to the very top of my head.

She smiled.

"I hope I didn't embarrass you," she said.

I shook my head.

"Have you ever seen a woman's breasts before?" she asked.

Again I shook my head. I could feel my face turning even redder.

Without warning, without fanfare, she opened her robe, and there before me were the first breasts I had ever seen in person. I could not take my eyes off them. I sat frozen.

She closed her robe, and for a moment we sat in silence.

In a daze, I stood and went to the door.

"Seymour, you forgot your twenty cents, and bring back the glass of seltzer," she called out.

She was smiling as I shut the door behind me.

Oy vay, Oy vay! That woman, that woman with those beautiful breasts! Getting her out of my mind was impossible. Those wonderful boobs held firm in my mind on the trolley car going to school, in each class I attended, they were all I thought of. My pants were bursting all day. Oh, how I wished I had had the nerve to reach out and touch Mrs. Lipmann's breasts! I wondered if she would have let me.

The next morning, I rushed to the packages that were waiting to be delivered. It was Friday and there were the usual busy deliveries. The name of each customer was written on the outside of each order. I looked carefully: Levine, Danziger, and Cohen. No Lipmann. Shit!

At 11:45 a.m. I was preparing to leave the market, getting ready to go home and cleanup for school, when

# A Life of Risks Taken

Hairy Hymie the fruit man called out, "Seymour, my boychik. Do me a favor and take a small order to Lipmann on your way home."

I snatched the bag from his hand and ran the two blocks. It was light—just a few pieces of fruit. I double-stepped it up three flights to her door and pressed the buzzer.

The door opened. She smiled when she saw me, took the package, and thanked me.

"You're the best," she said and closed the door.

That was it? I was crushed.

I left for home, washed up, and went to school. On the way, the word for what I was feeling came to me— saddened, hurt or more to the point, heartbroken.

It was only a dream. I would never get to see her bosom again. I began to doubt my own sense of reality. Did I actually see her naked at all? Maybe my desire to see her was so overpowering, that I believed it happened, when it never did. I was consumed with my infatuation, desire and, more than anything, confusion.

The image in my mind partially disappeared when I would see Judy Levine, an absolute beauty of a girl in biology and civics classes. However, Mrs. Lipmann's bosom was never gone for long. The vision of her breasts would swing in and out, in and out of my brain, like an apparition of nude women, one following another through a revolving door.

I didn't work that weekend. We had a family party, and Mom and Dad insisted that I go.

I struggled to get out of bed on Monday. I felt sick, tired. I thought I might sleep late and not go to the store.

# A Life of Risks Taken

"Seymour, you will be late for work," Mom called to me.

I dragged myself out of bed, brushed my teeth, washed my face, dressed, and walked heavy-footed to my job.

There were only two deliveries that morning, one for Thorner on East Forty-Ninth Street, and one for Lipmann on East Forty-Eighth. Suddenly, I woke up.

The Thorner delivery was first. Mrs. Thorner gave me two soda bottles as a tip—each bottle was worth five cents. My heart began to race as I peddled to Mrs. Lipmann's. I tried to push her and her breasts out of my mind. I convinced myself that it would never happen again, if it ever did happen at all.

At Mrs. Lipmann's door, I rang the bell. No answer. I rang again. Still no answer. I knocked. It was quiet. I bent over to leave the package at the door, which I had done many times before. As I turned to leave, the door opened, just slightly. She peeked through the opening, her eyes squinting, a towel wrapped around her, her hair soaking wet.

"Oh, Seymour, it's you. Bring in the package. I was in the shower. I'll go put something on."

Quickly tiptoeing away, water dripping from her body, her entire behind and the sides of her bosom were visible. She dropped the towel and grabbed for a bathrobe. I was instantly aroused and frightened at the same time. It was a strange and pleasurable combination of sensations, like eating ice cream and drinking hot chocolate simultaneously!

# A Life of Risks Taken

Maybe I should not be so obvious, and turn my head away. The feeling of shame dropped into my brain—but it didn't stay for long. My new friend, testosterone, overruled all feelings of decency, embarrassment and dishonor. I hungrily devoured every inch of her beautiful skin from top to bottom. I did my investigation both with interest and intensity. I wanted to be certain this time it was not a hallucination. I wanted to remember every detail.

She returned with her robe on, gave me two dimes, and laughed as she observed my quite obvious response. She touched my trousers where my penis was paying serious attention. It felt like a bolt of lightning. No one, except for me, had ever felt me there. She took my hand and gently placed it on her breast. An electric shock ran from the tip of my fingers, up my arm, directly into my heart, and at lightning speed into my groin. I wasn't sure how I was still standing, dizzy with the pleasure.

I uttered not a single word. The only sound I could hear was my heartbeat.

"I see you're very close to manhood," she said, as she coquettishly opened her robe. "You are going to have to stop calling me Mrs. Lipmann. My name is Irene."

I had envisioned the scene a hundred times, no, a thousand times, alone in my bedroom or in my bath.

When I looked at her, I thought, Is this a movie I'm in? Is this actually happening to me? What was Mrs. Lipmann's first name? She just told me and I couldn't remember.

I left for home, my trousers and underwear soaking wet. What do I do now?

# A Life of Risks Taken

I stepped into my shower with my clothes on. I washed my pants and my underwear. After my shower, I went to the window with some clothespins, and hung them out to dry on the clothesline. I had to prepare an explanation to give Momma for washing my clothes. Not an easy task.

Three glorious months flew by. I was in love.

One day, I brought Irene a bunch of tulips from the shop. Her eyes sparkled when I gave them to her and she began to cry. To this day I cannot figure out why women weep when something happy happens to them. We did not have sex that day. She only wanted to hold me.

Irene always spoke to me softly and explained each and every move she asked me to execute. I listened intently and I obeyed her every command. She was the experienced one. I thought she was quite old, perhaps twenty-two or twenty-three.

Occasionally the baby would wake up, we would stop, and I would return to my bike, but most of the time, it was like living in a dream.

Ejaculating, ejaculating, and ejaculating.

I had never even known that word or what it meant before Irene told me that was what I was doing.

I said to myself, I bet my friends didn't even know the meaning of ejaculating. Not only was I getting a sexual education, my vocabulary was improving. Earl would love that!

During the day at school and at night lying in my bed, I would think that some superpower was being good to me. I had always done my homework, helped at home when asked, worked hard and given the money I earned to my mother. I had been a good son. It is no crime to enjoy a secret life. I was so grateful for this exciting time. I felt I was the luckiest ejaculating kid on the block—maybe in all of Brooklyn. Just thinking about it turned me on.

One late afternoon, I was about to enter the kitchen I overheard my mother and Poppa in the kitchen speaking quietly in Yiddish. When my mother was having a conversation with anyone in our apartment, she never sat down. She had to be doing something—washing the dishes, even clean ones, or just putting things away. In her mind, there was always housework to be done.

"You know the young woman across the street?" Mom whispered, as she was drying some glasses.

My dad shook his head.

"You know the one with the baby and her husband is away in the army."

She touched Dad's shoulder, slightly pushing as if to stir his memory.

My father studied the front page of the *Daily Freiheit*, a left-wing Yiddish newspaper.

"Her husband came home from the army two days ago. He found out she was having an affair with some man. The husband beat her up and said that when he finds this man, he is going to kill him."

I caught my breath. Oy vay! What are they talking about?

My father shook his head and said, "Tsk, tsk, tsk! That is not a nice thing to do, taking advantage of a lonely woman when her husband is risking his life for our country. I don't blame the husband for wanting to kill him."

A cold sweat came to my body. Perspiration seeped through my shirt.

*Poppa don't say that . . . please, please don't say that. The man, that very terrible man is me, me . . . your son, the son you love very much. Do you want me dead?*

I was in a panic. Pain struck my throat and crashed down into my heart.

"Oy vay, oy vay," I moaned quietly. What could I do? What could I do? I would surely be found out. Irene would tell her husband that I was the man she'd been having sex with. She would tell him of my ejaculations. He was going to kill me.

*But I am only a boy—who would want to kill a nice, Jewish, fifteen-and-a half-year-old boy?*

I thought her husband must have had a rifle or a knife that he brought back from war.

*Oh God, what did I do to deserve such a punishment?*

Tears filled my eyes. I could see the headlines in The Daily News:

JEWISH DELIVERY BOY KILLED BY BETRAYED ARMY VETERAN.

My family would be ashamed. Momma, looking at those headlines, would gasp for breath, and strike her head against the wall and scream, "Why did they have to say he was Jewish?"

I was sure my parents would blame themselves. Momma would look at me in revulsion. Her jaw would drop in hatred and anguish at the very sight of me. She will think I am a filthy, disgusting sex fiend, which no doubt I have become.

Death seemed to be my only escape...that would be better than living in my house.

I needed a way out of this mess. I had only one trusted ally, one friend, one person who knew everything about everything—my older brother Earl.

*He'll save me. Or he will tell me where to hide.*

Maybe I could lie about my age and enlist in the Army. The war was over, so it would be safer in the Army than in Brooklyn.

Earl was in the U.S. Navy Air Corps, stationed in Jacksonville, Florida. That night, I put on one of my father's hats, his gray scarf, and an old jacket of mine. Clandestinely, I took the Church Avenue trolley to Nostrand Avenue, purchased a three-cent transfer for the bus. I did not want to chance meeting anyone at Millie's. In particular, I did not want to run into Irene's husband. That crazed, jealous man would finish me on the spot. I could see him holding me by the throat, my feet dangling in the air as he methodically took out his knife or his rifle, pointed either one at me, a smile on his face, hatred in his eyes, and then...

*Sex is not for me, for the rest of my life, I swear.*

I would recant soon. Fifteen blocks later, I arrived at Benny's Pharmacy. I knew about this store from a girlfriend who lived in that area. In the back of the shop, there were four phone booths.

I had a pocket full of change that I took from a small

shoe box I kept hidden in my room. I pocketed three dollars' worth of coins for the long-distance call. Another moan and groan escaped me.

Oy vay! So expensive!

My parents would kill me for wasting my money.

*They will kill me before the lunatic husband has the chance!*

I dialed.

"Number, please?" the operator asked. She instructed me to deposit one dollar and twenty-five cents. One by one I slipped the coins into the phone. I looked around outside the booth to be sure no one had followed me.

The phone rang once, twice, and then the voice I was waiting for, hoping for, answered.

"Hello, Earl. This is Seymour."

Earl asked how I was, how was I doing at school, was I doing my homework, how were my grades. School, school, that is all Earl ever thought about. I had no interest in school at this moment. This expensive long-distance call to Florida was about life and death, my life and my death.

"Earl, I am in big trouble. I may be dead tomorrow or even tonight."

I trembled as I related the entire story to him in detail.

I heard him chuckle. "Don't worry. No one is going to kill you," Earl assured me. "Here is what you have to do. I want you to quit your job first thing tomorrow morning."

"Why should I quit my job?" I asked.

"Are you stupid? You'll get a delivery to Irene's apartment. Her husband will open the door, take one look at your guilty face and shoot you on the spot. Now, stop interrupting me, and do what I say."

# A Life of Risks Taken

I sighed with relief. Earl had taken over. He was now in charge.

He continued, "I want you to go to school a little earlier each day and get involved with the newspaper or some extracurricular activity. After school go directly home, finish your work and go to bed. Study hard and don't worry. This will go away. You're going to be just fine."

Then he said in a strange voice, "I know that girl. She is cute."

As he hung up, a thought struck me: *Did my brother have sex with Irene? I will kill him, I swear, I will kill him.*

Two and a half weeks dragged by. I was a wreck, frightened to walk on the street for fear of meeting Irene's husband. I did nothing but my school work, some errands around the house, and chores for my mother. It was a prison sentence, one I believed that I deserved. I did all that ejaculating. I went back to her time and time again for more of the same. I was addicted to Irene, to her body, her breasts, and her touch.

*I will never be free again!*

My friends Robby and Bernie asked me if something was wrong. They accused me of acting very strangely. I evaded their questions. If I told them my story, they would laugh.

Mom, too, told me she didn't think I was acting right. I was very quiet and appeared to be upset. Almost daily she would place her lips to my forehead to see if I had a temperature. I lied, telling her I was fine and just had a lot of work to do. She insisted that I take a warm bath and go to the toilet. Also, I should eat a banana. My mother's philosophy was that eating, peeing and good bowel movements would cure everything and ensure good physical and mental health.

In the tub, all I could think about was Irene. I loved her and missed her and our daily meetings. As I lay in the warm water, I began to compare my mother's cleanliness to Irene's disorganized apartment. There was no dirt ring around our bathtub. Here the beds were always made. There were never any dishes in the sink or dirty clothes lying around. My mother took care. At Irene's, everything was imperfect, except for Irene.

I pleaded to some greater power. *Please, please free me from this terrible situation, and I will never do anything bad again. I promise.*

I dunked my head under the water and held my breath as long as possible. When I was younger, I used to test how long I could hold my breath. I think I counted to sixty-three once. This time I couldn't keep count. As I brought my head up, I tried to concoct a deal with God. This, of course, was the God I did not believe in. I wanted everything to go away, but I would never consider any arrangement that included giving up Irene. She was mine and I wanted her more than anything.

It was mid-June, close to the end of the term. Returning home from school one afternoon, I heard my parents whispering once again.

As she stirred a pot of borscht, Mom said to Pop, "You remember the woman from across the street, the one that was having an affair?"

Pop nodded.

"The husband found out who that farcockteh,"—shitty—"man was."

What! I gritted my teeth and I shut my eyes. Oy vay, oy vay. I began to tremble.

"You will not believe it in a million years."

"Why the suspense? Who was this terrible person?" Pop asked.

I hovered in the doorway.

Momma put down the ladle, placed her hands on her waist, looked directly into Poppa's eyes, and said, "It was Mr. Schiff, the seltzer man, who lives next door. Can you in your entire life believe such a story?"

Momma picked up a spoon, walked over to her pantry closet, took out a box of Diamond Crystal kosher salt, measured half a tablespoon, poured it into the pot of borscht, and stirred.

So, that's where all those seltzer bottles came from. She was cheating on me! My Irene, how could she do such a thing? How could she cheat on me?

I whispered, "Irene, I loved you. You broke my heart, you broke my heart."

"Sooo, what happened?" Dad asked.

Mom moved quickly to the icebox, took out a small jar of fresh Breakstone's sour cream, and continued, "Mr. Lipmann and Schiff had such a fist fight in the street. The soldier punched Schiff in the nose. There was blood all over the sidewalk. Mrs. Schiff came out of her house screaming. Then somebody must have called the police. They came and dragged the two men away. Can you believe such a nerve?" She chuckled. "In the middle of all the commotion, the husband yelled, 'I am not going to pay you that seltzer bill! Can you believe that?"

"Not paying the seltzer bill? That must have hurt Schiff more than the punch in the nose." Poppa smiled. "So, that's it?"

"No, it's not it. It gets worse."

Momma added a tablespoon of the sour cream to the pot, stirring it into the borscht.

"After the police took the two *meshugenas*,"—crazy dudes—"away, Mrs. Schiff came back into the street. She was wearing a torn housedress—and they are so rich! Can you imagine, with her money she walks around with a torn housedress? She was screaming at the top of her lungs, calling the woman a dirty whore. The police came again, tried to calm Mrs. Schiff. But she would not have any of it. So they put her into their car and took her away also."

Momma tasted the borscht from the spoon and whispered, "Ah, good."

She took another dip into the borscht and offered my father a small taste.

"Delicious!" he said.

My father looked at Momma. He shrugged his shoulders as if he didn't care a single iota about the entire story. And I am sure he didn't. He was worried about Franklin Roosevelt's health.

"Thank God, Earl is away in the service. I know he liked that girl. They went to school together. It would be terrible if it were our son who had been involved with such a girl," she said. "You are going to love this borscht, Charlie," Mom added.

I was distraught. Irene was not a whore. She was a good person!

I could not believe that the woman I loved, the woman I wanted to marry if her husband was killed in the war, could cheat on me. And cheat on me with Mr. Schiff, that dirty old man. He must have been at least thirty-five years old, and probably 4F. That's why he wasn't in the Army.

And my brother Earl—Momma knew that he liked her! I hate him also.

I continued to miss Irene, and I longed for her nakedness, her gentle way with me. I thought of her often, but we never met again. About a month later, Irene and her soldier moved from the neighborhood.

Twenty-seven years later, another woman I loved put me through a similar experience. It was strange that the pain I had as a grown man of forty-two was exactly the same as fifteen-and-a-half years old. Or so I recalled.

# Chapter 8

ഇരൻ

### The Soda Jerk

Each summer my parents rented two rooms with a kitchen in a huge rooming house outside Monticello, New York. Momma called our annual summer resort destination a *kochaleyn*. Translated from the Yiddish, it means a "cook-alone" family facility.

A hacker brought us there. When I was a boy, a hacker was a man with a big black taxi. There were five seats in the back of the car: a bench seat that held three people and two jump seats that folded out in front of the bench. There was also a seat next to the driver that could hold two more people if they were small. Safety belts were nonexistent. A person—even a child—could sit anywhere in the car.

I believe my father paid the hacker twenty-five dollars to drive the six of us up to the *kochaleyn*. We looked like a band of gypsies. A luggage rack was bolted to the roof, where suitcases and large cardboard boxes filled with pots and pans, bedding and towels were all securely tied down. Everything our entire family needed for our annual vacation was stuffed into the trunk of the car. At the rear of the car was another metal shelf to hold more suitcases or cartons.

The trip was a five-hour trek that twisted through small towns from Brooklyn to the little village of Ferndale. I don't remember if the George Washington Bridge or the Lincoln Tunnel existed then. I do recall we boarded a ferry in Manhattan and crossed the Hudson River to Hoboken to begin our journey.

Two hours into the excursion, on Route 17, we stopped at the Big Apple or the Orsek Brothers, roadside restaurants. This was a big treat. We actually did not eat in either of those places. We just made a bathroom and gas filling stop, after which Mom broke out a huge brown shopping bag filled with chicken sandwiches, hamburgers, and an assortment of fruits, cookies, and *mandel* bread.

Boris, the hacker, ate with us as well. Boris was a huge man, with an unmanageable head of gray curly hair. He sang Russian songs as he drove us through each town. Earl and I knew some of them, and we sang along with him.

At lunch, we sat at a picnic table outside the restaurant. Boris would speak to Momma in Russian, telling stories. In detail, he spoke of his three wives and seven children. All girls, he moaned. Mom pretended to be interested in his tales.

For dessert she gave each of us a nickel to buy an ice cream, plus one each for her and the driver.

She continually urged us to take deep breaths and smell the fresh country air. "It makes your lungs healthy."

# A Life of Risks Taken

Boris took the car to the gas pump. I went with him. He filled his tank up with gas. The price? Twenty-eight cents a gallon.

Monticello was a sleepy village in the Catskill Mountains. In the summer, it became alive with vacationers. People filled all the hotels, cottages, and rooming houses—mostly Jewish families from Brooklyn, the Bronx, and other parts of New York City. That was my perception.

Families escaped from the heat of the city to the cool mountains with trees, lakes, rivers, and streams. The Catskills were the 1940 version of the Hamptons for working-class people.

The elite hotels—Brickman's, the Concord, and Grossinger's—featured many famous stars, mostly on Friday and Saturday nights. Performers like Eddy Cantor, Molly Picon, Myron Cohen, Jack Benny, Dean Martin and Jerry Lewis entertained throughout the summer. The Catskill Mountain resort area was called "the Borscht Belt."

Monticello's main street ran for three or four blocks, with food stores, three drug stores, a barber shop with an old fashion spiraling pole in front, a dry cleaners, two hardware shops, a movie house, and a few other assorted shops. There were no malls or shopping centers. Everything took place in town on the village main street.

In July 1946, I was just a month shy of my sixteenth birthday. I did not want to hang out all day at the rooming house. My brother, Earl, was going back to the New York City during the week, where he had a cub reporter job at

# A Life of Risks Taken

The New York Herald Tribune. Though the Tribune was a conservative Republican newspaper, Poppa was very proud of him.

Soon after we settled into the *kochaleyn*, I picked myself up and hitch-hiked into town to find a job. I must have visited every store in the village looking for work. Finally, I got lucky.

Mazur's Pharmacy was a combination drug store, small-accessory shop, soda fountain, luncheonette, and whatever Mr. Mazur could sell for a profit. The shop was a modest destination from our vacation house. Its location was the center of town, next door to the only movie theater. Harry Mazur hired me to be a soda jerk at sixty-five cents an hour, the minimum wage.

I telephoned Mom at the rooming house. Mahlka, the owner, answered the phone.

"Mahlka, would you please call my mother to the phone. Tell her Seymour is calling."

I could hear the landlady scream out, "Hilda, your zindele is calling, cum shnell." I disliked being called a little boy, but I did hope Momma would rush to the phone.

In a frantic voice, Momma said, "Hello, Seymour, is everything all right? What's wrong?"

"Mom, I got a job in the drugstore, sixty-five cents an hour, and I'm starting now."

"This couldn't wait until you got home? You scared me half to death! What time will you be back? Did you eat something? Is the boss nice? What will you be doing?"

"Don't worry, I'm fine. I ate and now I have to go work. I'll tell you everything when I return," I proudly announced.

# A Life of Risks Taken

Irma Held, a girl from high school who I liked very much, was attending a summer camp nearby in Parksville, New York. We wrote to each other on a regular basis. I told her where I was working and invited her to stop by someday.

A few days before the Fourth of July weekend, much to my surprise, Irma came to visit. I was thrilled to see her. I invited her to sit on the last seat at the counter and asked if she would like something to drink. She refused, but I seldom took no for an answer, even at the age of sixteen.

"Since you don't want anything to drink, let me make a sundae for you. It will be fun for both of us."

Irma smiled and nodded her assent.

I was a born show-off. I began with three scoops of ice cream, walnuts on top. I poured on some hot fudge and piled the whip cream three or four inches high. The whipped cream was as tall as the glass. She looked at the sundae and her eyes popped. She laughed her wonderful laugh and her smile made her face so beautiful. I could not take my eyes from her.

I placed the ice cream sculpture before her. With eyes wide open, she pulled a Kodak box camera from her bag and took a photo of me with the sundae. We were both laughing and our heads touched in a moment of affection. A wave of good feeling splashed over me.

At the same time, a customer walked into the shop with his two children. He looked at Irma's sundae with its Mount Everest whipped cream peak. It was a delicious looking dish. He did a double take and without hesitation said, "We'll have that also. Make three of them, all with vanilla and strawberry ice cream."

# A Life of Risks Taken

I moved behind the counter and started to work. As I was preparing the sundaes, Irma asked, "What do you call that sundae?"

I thought for a moment and called out, "The Seymour Special!"

She grinned.

Twenty minutes later, the father asked, "How much do I owe you for the three Seymour Specials, Seymour?"

We all laughed.

"Forty cents each, so that will be one dollar and twenty cents," I replied.

That was fifteen cents higher for each than the regular price.

The man put two one-dollar bills on the counter and said, "Keep the change."

"Thank you very much," I called out to him.

I sat with Irma as she continued to eat the new delight. We gossiped about our friends in school, her camp, and this new job of mine. We promised each other we would be boyfriend and girlfriend when we returned to school in September.

I walked her to the door of the shop to say good-bye. She kissed me on the cheek and said, "Don't forget to write."

I assured her I would write often. I put my hand around her waist and pulled her close to me. I kissed her lips.

"That's the real Seymour Special," she whispered and darted off.

I was in love—again.

# A Life of Risks Taken

From that day forward, the Seymour Special would have a new price. It would be fifteen cents more. Mr. Mazur was worried that we might be overcharging. I told him, the customers we were serving did not seem to care. They were on vacation and having a good time.

"Let's see what happens," I suggested.

When a customer came into the shop and asked for a sundae, I would reply with, "Would you like to try the Seymour Special? It's only fifteen cents more and worth it."

Most of the time, people said yes. It was the beginning of something new in the little town of Monticello. Customers oohed and aahed as I served the Seymour Special with the mile-high whipped cream. It was contagious buying—one person ordered the Seymour Special, and when others saw it, they followed suit. Irma was not the only one to photograph the sundae. Many snapped pictures of the dessert. Our ice cream parlor was becoming a great success.

The fountain was so busy that we had to hire another boy to work with us in the evening. After two weeks of standing-room-only business, including rainy days, Mr. Mazur patted me on the back and said, "You are now promoted to the manager of the soda fountain."

Though the title was fun, it did not feel like enough. I wanted to share in the success I had brought to the shop. Money was on my mind.

☙❧

By mid-July our soda fountain was a must-go for the whole area. People came from everywhere for the special sundae. The shop became a meeting place for friends, both adults and young people. After a movie, one show in the afternoon and one in the evening, we were bursting at the seams. Managers from the other local stores came by to investigate.

One day, a local drugstore competitor, from the first store I had gone into looking for a job, came to see what was happening. I remembered my interview with him. He hardly made time to speak to me. He was not interested in hiring a kid to make sodas. He could do that himself.

He sat down at the counter.

"You're Seymour, aren't you? You came to my store looking for a job."

"Yes, sir," I responded. "I liked your shop. It would have been fun to work there."

"My wife said that I should hire you. I didn't listen."

I smiled and asked, "What flavor ice cream, sir?"

Another time, an attractive, well-dressed woman came into the shop and sat at the counter. I hopped over to her and asked if I could serve her. I was greeted with a warm smile.

"I'll have one of your Seymour Special sundaes I've been hearing about."

I smiled and asked her what flavors she wanted.

"Vanilla and strawberry."

Within minutes, I had the tall concoction in front of her with a small glass of seltzer on the side.

"Where is the cherry on top?" she asked.

I put two cherries at the peak of the whipped cream.

Before she began eating, she took a photo of the sundae with me behind it.

"A souvenir," she said. A spoonful of ice cream in her hand, she looked at me. "You are some piece of work," she said. "What's your name?"

I did not like her saying "You are some piece of work." It felt like a hurtful remark.

"Seymour is my name," I responded in a toned-down voice.

"So you're the inventor of this Seymour Special. It's nice to meet you. I've heard about you. How old are you?"

"I'll be sixteen years old in August." I answered with caution.

That was followed with a slew of questions. What school did I go to? Where was I staying here in the Catskills? Did I have brothers or sisters? Did I have a girlfriend? Seeing she meant no harm, I answered easily. She finished her sundae, paid and left twenty cents on the counter for me.

She asked if she could take a photo of the owner and me. Mr. Mazur ran over quickly, put his arm around me, and she took our picture. She waved good-bye and was gone.

I turned to Mr. Mazur and asked, "Do you know her? I didn't like her at first, but after a while she seemed very nice."

"Never saw her before. She's not from around here."

Three or four days later there was a front-page story in the Monticello Herald about Mazur's Pharmacy and the cute high school soda jerk, as well as the photo of the owner and me. The piece continued on the third page, where there was a quarter-page photo of the sundae with me behind it. I grinned from ear to ear.

Mr. Mazur cut out the article and pasted it on the front window of the store.

The headline read:

Seymour Special is a delicious mountain of fun

The story continued:

*Don't miss the fun at Mazur's Pharmacy. Seymour, an adorable teenager, whose mom and brothers are staying at Mahlka's Boarding House, is serving "The Seymour Special," a not-so-ordinary sundae with a mountain of whipped cream and two cherries on top. It's delicious. Stop by when you are in town.*

From that day forward, we gave two cherries, not one.

The look on my parents' faces when I showed them the newspaper was one of the most memorable sights of the summer. I enjoyed watching them and all of their friends at the rooming house with their faces glued to the story.

Mom said, "Why don't you telephone the woman at her newspaper office and thank her?"

I called and asked for Helen Lathe.

"This is Seymour from Mazur's Pharmacy," I began. "Thank you so very much for the story you wrote about us in your newspaper. And thank you for mentioning my mom, dad, brothers, and the name of the rooming house."

She responded, "That was the most fun story I have ever written in my entire career. My boss loved the story and our newspaper got the most calls they have ever had. More than any other story."

"Why don't you come back to the shop and I'll make you my guest for anything you want."

The newspaper article was a huge boost for Mazur. The store was crowded day and night. People came from as far away as Liberty, Kaimesha Lake, and other towns. Everyone was asking for the Seymour Special.

After a few days passed, Helen, the reporter, returned to the shop with her pretty teenaged daughter, Laura. I had served Laura on other occasions. I learned it was she who suggested the story to her mother. When they finished their sundaes, I told them it was my treat. I took the tip money I had in my pocket and rang it up in the cash register. They thanked me and left.

On top of all that excitement, a few days later, I received a letter from Irma. She wrote that one of her friends had seen the newspaper article and brought it to camp. Irma was very excited for me and so happy to see me when school began. When her friends at camp saw the story, she quietly bragged that I was her boyfriend. Wow! It made me think that perhaps I should have called the sundae The Irma Special because her visit had inspired me.

Mr. Mazur decided to move the newspaper stand from the front of the store to the back. He bought four small tables with four chairs for each table, allowing customers to sit and be served. He asked me to hire another boy to work the counter and the tables.

I hired Laura, Mrs. Lathe's daughter. She was pretty

and wanted to work, and I thought that girls were better than boys in front of the counter.

Everyone loved Laura. She was charming and friendly and fast. If we were too busy behind the counter, she would move in and make the Seymour Special herself.

On the very first evening she worked, after all the customers had gone, I sat down with my assistant, Marvin, and Laura and suggested that from now on, all tips go into one large bowl behind the counter. At the end of the day, we would all divide the money three ways. I wanted it to be fair for everyone. We were now a team.

One evening, I walked Laura home. I liked her very much and she liked me. She put her hand into mine as we walked. When we got to her door, we looked at one another, kissed on the lips, and said good night. I loved and hated that kiss. I had promised Irma that we would be exclusive with each other.

Oh, hell, why did I do that?

Sometime soon I had to tell Laura that I had a girlfriend. But not right away.

At the store, business was booming. Mr. Mazur raised prices on almost everything in the pharmacy—toothpaste, shampoo, combs, brushes, and all sundries. Most people ate their Seymour Special and ended up with a shopping bag full of everything else. The cash register was ringing at the back of the store and at the fountain.

Mr. Mazur had become a great success. Unfortunately, he was a little stingy. With only four weeks to go until Labor Day, I asked for a raise in salary. I tried to persuade Mr. Mazur that, as the manager of the fountain, I should be earning more than Marvin, my assistant, and more than Laura, the waitress. I felt I was the brains behind the new success the shop was having.

I stood in front of him, arms akimbo, a little defiant and said, "Mr. Mazur, I think I deserve a raise."

Mazur's face was grim. "I don't like being held up."

The thought of being fired crossed my mind. I considered that Marvin would be able to take my place. It took Mr. Mazur about thirty seconds for him to respond.

"Seymour, you are like family to me. This shop would be nothing without the joy of your presence every day. I should have come to you and offered you more money. You are the Seymour Special that everyone enjoys. It is not the ice cream or the store. It is your energy and young personality. From the back of the shop I can hear what is going on. People are laughing and having a good time and spending money. The scene here is amazing. So, okay, how does eighty-five cents an hour sound to you?"

I was flabbergasted. I wanted to put my arms around him and give him a hug, but I held back.

"Thank you! Thank you, I said, as I left the shop, and set off for the rooming house to tell my mom the great news.

That summer I earned more than $500. The excitement of that experience surged through my entire body. It was the first time I felt wealthy and smart. I discovered a sense of manliness in my ability to work hard and be rewarded for it.

The bonus of that summer was all the girls who came to the soda fountain. But as much as I liked girls, only working and earning money were on my mind. I made a mistake when I'd kissed Laura. I had promised Irma exclusivity. Laura had to go, and I had to be up front with her.

Once again I reached out to my brother, Earl.

He said, "The truth always works. Tell Laura about Irma, but do not tell Irma about Laura."

I did as Earl suggested, and he was right again. The truth always works. Laura and I remained friends throughout the entire summer. We kissed again. We kissed many times.

My last day at Mazur's shop was just after Labor Day. Most of the people had already left their summer places and returned home to the city. The village streets were empty, still and sad-looking. I felt a little depressed. We were cleaning up and it was very quiet. When I completed my work, I went to the back of the store to say good-bye and collect my pay. The Mazurs were sitting at the table eating sandwiches.

"Well, it's time to say good-bye. I want you both to know that this was the best summer of my life."

Mrs. Mazur began to cry.

"Did I say or do something wrong?" I asked.

"No. You were the nicest young man we have ever had working here. You are a very hard worker and an honest boy," Mr. Mazur replied.

"My wife is crying because you remind her of our son who is still away in Europe. We pray he will be home soon, safe and sound. During the summer, watching you with people and how everyone liked to come here made her happy."

As he spoke, he handed me my salary, in cash, as always.

Mazur told me that he and his wife had been living in Monticello for almost four years. This summer, they had the most fun since moving to that village. When they went to synagogue on Saturday morning, all their friends would gather around him and ask where he had found Seymour. They repeated things I had done in the shop, actions I never remembered.

His friends said, Seymour did this and Seymour said that. And Seymour came out from behind the counter and took a picture with our family and Seymour told us a joke.

"It was like you were a movie or Broadway star. Every Shabbat was an amazing experience. When you were not in the store, customers would ask for you. With your spirit and kind ways with people, you will be very successful," Mrs. Mazur said.

I was so young at the time. I had no idea what they were talking about. I was only a kid who was lucky to get a job for the summer at a place where I was having a great time. Who could ask for more? I earned a great deal of money, I met many people, I kissed a girl who liked me, Irma and I committed to each other, and I enjoyed myself. I was just a happy kid.

# Chapter 9

℘℃

## Working with Poppa

The following summer, I worked for Poppa's company, Heathcliff Clothing Corporation, a men's clothing manufacturer. The company produced reasonably priced men's clothing for *Abraham & Strauss* and *Abe Stark's* in Brooklyn, and *Gimbel's* and *S. Klein* in Union Square. All four of these companies—including my father's—are no longer in business. Poppa's customers also included about twenty other small retail stores in the New York area—probably also gone. I was paid twenty dollars each week, which was really only for spending money.

My mother and my younger brothers, fourteen-year-old Alvin, and nine-year-old Bob, were in Monticello at Mahlka's rooming house. Brother Alvin, like me, was also an ambitious and hardworking kid. He found a job at a local golf course as a caddy. My older brother, Earl, was in the U.S. Navy Air Corps. I had Poppa all to myself, working with him in the city at his factory at 100 Fifth Avenue.

# A Life of Risks Taken

Every Friday afternoon, Poppa and I would board a Short Line bus and ride up to Monticello to visit Mom and the boys. When we arrived, Mom would greet us with one of her great dinners. The weekends were a special treat. After dinner, all the parents and some of the older kids would gather in the recreation hall to play cards, sing songs, tell funny stories and just have a good time. It was good see Momma and Poppa so affectionate. Once I even saw them kiss.

On one Saturday afternoon, I took my brother Bob, to the movies. When Bob and I got out of the movie theater at about five p.m., we walked next door to visit the Mazurs. The shop was practically empty. A skinny kid stood behind the counter. The tables and the chairs formerly in front of the store were now gone. The newspapers were once again at the front of the store.

I looked at the boy standing at the counter with a toothpick in his mouth. He never asked me if I wanted anything.

"Where is Mr. Mazur?" I asked.

He only shrugged his shoulders. I walked to the back of the store and saw no one was there. I could not imagine what had happened.

Then, one day not long after, I was walking on Main Street, when a stranger came up to me and said, "Aren't you the Seymour from Mazur's Seymour Special?"

"That's me."

"We now go across the street to Timothy's Pharmacy to get the Seymour Special, but to tell you the truth, it's not as good."

"Are they getting fifty cents for it?"

"Oh no! It's only thirty cents, but not as much fun."

I never spoke to Mr. or Mrs. Mazur again.

ഔഇ

Poppa and I got up every morning at seven a.m. and off to work we went. We stopped at Harry's Corner Luncheonette. Frieda, the cook and the owner's wife, served Poppa coffee and a bagel with a little butter or cream cheese. I ordered Rice Krispies, milk and a banana every time. Frieda was like my mom during the summer weekdays. She always slipped a cookie or two into my pocket as we left.

Outside the restaurant, at the corner, we boarded the Church Avenue trolley car, which took us to the IRT subway. The train stopped at Fourteenth Street and Union Square in Manhattan, and we walked to 100 Fifth Avenue, at Fifteen Street, where my father's shop was on the fifth floor.

My father never called his office "the office" or his shop "the shop." He called where he worked "The Place."

When Poppa came home from work at the end of the day, my mother would ask him, "How was everything at The Place today?"

When he was about to leave for work in the morning, he would shout out, "Hilda, I'm leaving for The Place."

On a Saturday morning I would say, "Poppa, can I go with you to The Place?"

The Place consisted of an office and the factory workspace with two thirty-foot long cutting tables. In the back of the factory, all the suits hung on metal racks three tiers high after they arrived from the tailor shop. The Heathcliff office was very small. There were three desks, one for Poppa, another for the bookkeeper, and a third for Poppa's assistant.

Riding the subway to work with Poppa one day, I asked him how he started his business. He looked at me, stroked his chin, thought for a few moments, and then began to tell me a story only he, Momma, and Aunt Rose, his oldest sister, knew. He made me promise that I would never tell anyone the secret. So, here goes.

Poppa began his story from the time he followed his sister Rose from Poland to America. He left behind his mother, father, younger sister, Sarah, and his brother Nathan. Sarah was not yet eighteen years old and Nathan was only sixteen. Sarah was very beautiful and had entered the Gymnasium, the same high school Poppa attended. She was a born scholar who loved to read.

Sarah was a member of the Communist Party. At a gathering of young members of the organization, she met a young professor of economics. Poppa thought his name was Peter but was never certain. He was positive that Peter was not Jewish.

After a brief courtship, perhaps a year, Sarah married Peter and left home for a little village outside Kiev. She was just shy of eighteen years old and Peter, Poppa guessed, was about twenty-two. The marriage and her departure almost killed my grandparents. They did not attend the wedding ceremony even though a rabbi performed the service. Marrying a non-Jew was a sin not to be forgiven.

I asked Poppa how he knew all this. He told me his father, Beryl, came to America about this time to see if he and Grandma Hanna could come to the "Golden Land" to live. They were so distraught over Sarah's marriage decision, they wanted to escape from Poland and live close to their older son and daughter.

I remember my Zeyde's (grandpa's) visit very clearly. Earl moved to the couch in the living room and Grandpa slept with me. Brother Alvin was five years old and had just returned from the hospital with what was called a touch of Diphtheria. Our baby brother Bobby was only an infant, perhaps six months old, still in a crib.

I recall sitting at Momma's sewing machine with the lid down, doing my homework. It became my desk when Momma was not sewing. I was about seven or eight years old. My head turned down into the book, when suddenly a quarter fell onto one of the pages. I looked up and there was Zeyde with a big smile.

He said in Yiddish, "Fon sachal cumt gelt," from wisdom comes wealth.

I will never forget his face at that moment.

Grandpa Beryl was a traditional Jewish man from Europe. He always wore a yarmulke and prayed every morning and afternoon. On Saturday, he went to synagogue alone, because his son and grandsons did not believe what he believed. Philosophical discussions always took place at dinner and continued after in the living room. Poppa and Grandpa had totally different points of view about politics, religion, and the way children should be raised. They had tough discussions as we children listened.

Momma always treated Grandpa with enormous respect. She bought special pots and dishes for him and served him only kosher food. She lit a match when he took out a cigarette, made certain his laundry and clothes were always clean. At Shabbat dinners on Friday night, Momma lit the candles and Grandpa did all the prayers. We all sat quietly as he recited the Hebrew.

When Grandpa returned to Europe, I heard him tell Poppa, "You are a fortunate man to have such a fine *baleboste*—an excellent and praiseworthy housekeeper—as a wife. Take good care of her, she is a rare find." When Momma kissed Grandpa Goodbye, tears in her eyes, she gave him an envelope. The envelope had five hundred dollars in it.

Before Zeyde left, he told Poppa about the younger siblings.

Grandpa found America too difficult a place to live. "Work was scarce, but if you had a job, the hours were long and the bosses angry and domineering," he explained. He returned to Poland, where he and my grandmother lost their lives in Buchenwald during World War II.

After that, Poppa remembered getting two letters from his sister Sarah telling him that she was pregnant and was having the baby in a few months. The second letter told him that she had had a little boy who died in his crib one night. I asked him if his sister had other children. He didn't know. He never heard from Sarah again.

I asked him, "Poppa were you as upset as Grandma and Grandpa when Sarah married a man who was not Jewish?"

"At first I said to myself, 'foolish girl, it will never work.' But as I got older, I realized everyone has the right to live his or her own life. Being married is not easy even when backgrounds are the same. Sarah and her Peter will just have to work harder than couples who have the similar backgrounds." Poppa answered.

"Would you be unhappy if I married a Christian girl?" I asked him.

"I'll tell you when it happens," he said.

Around the time of Sarah's second letter, Poppa's brother Nathan wrote to him from Nepal. He was seventeen or eighteen years old at that time. He owned a truck and was doing deliveries of farm produce and some manufactured goods. At the same time he was smuggling contraband for a group of Nepali hoodlums. Another letter informed Poppa that Nathan had acquired three trucks for shipping freight in the daytime and smuggling at night. He told Poppa that he was making a very good living, but it was dangerous.

The next communication Poppa had from Nathan came from Afghanistan. An Asian competitor had stopped his trucks on the road, beaten up two of his drivers, and stolen the trucks and the shipment they were carrying. They also warned him that if they saw his trucks in their territory again, he would suffer much more than losing his vehicles. Nathan picked himself up and boarded a train for China, but couldn't read the signs of the destinations and got off in Afghanistan by mistake.

There, Uncle Nathan took a job as a farmhand. He was young and strong, and he enjoyed working outdoors. He was also handsome—Poppa remembered, even at the age of sixteen, Nathan was a lady's man.

# A Life of Risks Taken

"So what happened?" I asked as we got off the subway at Fourteenth Street and walked to The Place.

"I will tell you the rest of the story on the way home," Poppa replied.

As soon as we got to The Place, my job occupied all my attention. I sewed matching numbered tickets on the sleeves of the jackets and legs of the pants of each suit. I also swept up, ran errands, and helped anyone around the shop or the office who needed an extra hand. A few months before, I offered to help the cutter pull up the cloth on the cutting table, but this was a union job. One telephone call from the cutter to the Amalgamated Clothing Workers of America, Local #4, and I received my first union card. I was a very proud union member.

We followed the same routine daily: the cutter placed each design pattern on top of the piled cloth like the construction of a jigsaw puzzle, using up every inch of fabric. With white wax chalk, the cutter traced the outside of each pattern of both jackets and trousers. When he was through, using a very sharp electric cutting machine he carefully moved the machine along the chalk marks. Then I was ready to sew on the identification tags. We did the same layout with the linings of the jacket. A shipping clerk and I would tie the ticketed bolts of cloth and send them, with their silk linings, canvas, under-collar cloth, and buttons, to the tailoring contractor who sewed the suits and sent them to the pressing machines.

Two weeks later, the suits would be shipped into our factory on rolling racks. Poppa looked at every single one to make certain there were no flaws in either the cloth or the tailoring. Next, the bushel man examined each jacket and each pair of matching pants and flicked off any scattered bits of lint, dirt, or strings of cotton with the tiniest scissors I've ever seen. At that point, the clothing was ready for shipment to the customers.

At six o'clock, Poppa put the cash from the day's sales in the safe, checked to see if the safe was locked and the windows closed, switched off the lights, and locked the door.

As we descended in the elevator, I asked him, "Poppa, what do you do with all that cash you put into the safe?"

"In the morning, I go to the bank and deposit it in the company account."

I remembered Poppa's story.

"So—what happened to Uncle Nathan?" I asked.

"Where was I?"

"Uncle Nathan took a job as a farmer . . . "

"Alzo," he said, which is the Yiddish expression for 'Let's recapitulate.' "Nathan went to work on a farm that grew poppies to make opium and other drugs. The farm also grew marijuana. Nathan worked there for two years. Then he proposed to the owner that with his connections, he could start a business in Nepal. So, Nathan and the farmer made a fifty-fifty deal. By the time he was thirty years old, my little brother was a wealthy man.

"I wrote to him and asked if he could help me start my own business with Sam Sherman and Milton Sawyer, two of my close business friends. They would put up $5,000 each. I would invest $2,500 and run the business. We would be equal partners. They would advise, invest and bring in big customers they knew from big stores, while I managed the day-to-day.

"Two months later, a large carton arrived at our apartment. When I got home, Momma showed me the box, which had been shipped from Kiev. At first, it looked like a gift from Peter and Sarah.

"Carefully, I opened the package. Inside were two beautiful vases. Momma loved them at once. She got a clean cloth, removed all the straw from each vase, and wiped them spotless. I looked carefully inside to see if my brother had sent me something else. Remember, he was a professional smuggler." Poppa laughed. "I was not surprised to find two black envelopes pasted to the bottom of each vase. Each envelope contained $1,800. I had never seen so many fives and tens and twenties.

"Momma was very excited and I started to laugh so hard, I couldn't stop. Instead of sending me the $2,500 I had asked for, he sent two chai, eighteen, the number for good luck. My baby brother all of a sudden had become frum, religious!"

"So what happened to Uncle Nathan?" I asked.

Poppa grew somber. "I never heard from him again. I wrote several letters and got no response. I hope he's alive, but I'm not sure. Maybe someday he will show up."

೩೦೧೪

In the evening after work, Poppa and I would walk over to Fourteenth Street and Fifth Avenue to meet two or three of his friends at Hammer's Kosher Restaurant. The food was plentiful and delicious, and reminded him of his mother's cooking. At sixteen years old, I could eat everything and anything on the table. Poppa said that I could even eat the plates and the table.

Poppa's closest friends, Sam Breg, a shoe manufacturer, and Harry Levine, a tailor from the industry, joined us almost every evening, as their families were up in the Catskills as well. Sam and my Poppa were the entertainers, while Harry and Max Hammer and his wife Lottie, the owners of the restaurant were always a great audience. All were emigrants from Eastern Europe.

Max went to a closet below a table and brought free schnapps each night, which they threw down in one quick swallow. I had seltzer. Lottie, who was also the cook, gave us choices of stuffed cabbage, roasted chicken, grilled steak, sometimes lamb chops, with soup and dessert. Dessert was always fresh strudel, fruit salad, sponge cake, or honey cake, finished with a cup of coffee or a glass of tea. Poppa always had tea, and would take a solid square of sugar, hold it between his teeth, and drink the tea through it. I continued with my seltzer, as no milk was allowed in the kosher restaurant. Price for dinner was Two Dollars and Fifty Cents.

Once a week, we ate at Kramer's Dairy Restaurant. We had borscht with boiled potatoes, cheese blintzes, roasted fish, and latkes—potato pancakes. At Kramer's, I could have my glass of milk. Most times, it was with Ubet's chocolate syrup.

The men entertained themselves speaking in Yiddish, which I could understand, and at times, in Russian, from which I could get the gist of the conversation. But when they spoke in Polish, I was out of it. In Polish, the conversation was about women or sex or it was a dirty joke. Well, that's what I thought, anyway.

When they were laughing and the language was Polish, I laughed with them, though I didn't understand what they were saying. I wondered if someday I would tell Poppa about Irene. I thought we would both enjoy that story when I was a grown man and we could laugh together.

An exciting evening was poker night at our apartment.

Poppa pulled out the kitchen table and placed it in the center of the room. Seven men sat around the table. Everything was in cash, mostly quarters and fifty-cent pieces. The conversation was in four languages, English being the least spoken.

My assignment was to run down to the local delicatessen, Mechick and Halpern, and buy sandwiches, coleslaw, potato salad, sodas, and a few bottles of beer. Poppa's friends always offered me tips, but Poppa shook his head, saying no.

"My son makes a good living at The Place." He winked and everyone laughed.

I often fell asleep before the game ended. When my father won, he usually gave me a dollar. When he lost, he would give me a dollar and a half. He did not want me to know that he lost money. But I knew anyhow, because they spoke about money in Russian. Today, if I go to Las Vegas on business and gamble—which I always do—win or lose, I return with money for my wife. She never asks if I've won or lost. She's kind enough just to take the money, smile, and say thank you with a kiss.

# A Life of Risks Taken

The summer of 1947 was a very special time in my life. I learned so much from and about my father. Poppa had great people skills. Every one of his customers liked him very much. His European Jewish accent was not a handicap, but an endearing part of him. I remember looking at him with such admiration, watching him as he spoke to a customer or the foreman at the tailor shop. To me he was amazing. I did not realize then how young my father was. I was sixteen and Poppa was only forty-three.

In September, I returned to Tilden High School. Immediately, I got into the rhythm of studying, homework, and fun with my friends. I wanted to do that, however, I did miss earning money.

I was chomping at the bit when I went back to work for Poppa in late September during the Jewish holidays, but worked on weekends only.

In order to help my family's new business, I invited my friends' fathers and our neighbors to come to Poppa's factory and buy suits wholesale. Poppa paid me a commission for each and every person I brought to The Place and an additional commission for every sale he or I made from my leads.

I had just passed my sixteenth birthday and was earning forty dollars, more or less, each month. Before Christmas or the Jewish holidays, I earned more than double that amount.

80C3

As I wrote earlier in this story, there are two moments in life a man never forgets: his first time and his last time.

# A Life of Risks Taken

I have never forgotten my very first sale. It was almost as exciting as sex with Mrs. Lipmann. The ability to be able to motivate people to part with money in exchange for a suit of clothing was thrilling. It gave me a sense of worth. I felt I was doing something productive. Making a sale still is a special feeling for me.

"Seymour, show Mr. Bernstein the sharkskin suits that just came in," Poppa ordered.

I knew exactly where everything was and quickly brought down a size forty-two regular, which was my educated guess for his size.

Bernstein tried on the suit and it fit perfectly!

"Hey, Ubell," he called to my father. "You have some kid here. Watch him or you will be out of a job." Today, customers say the same thing to me about my son Edward.

Poppa smiled and nodded.

He called back to me, "Did you take down the charcoal gray flannel worsted with the vest?"

I jumped from where I was standing, picked out the second suit, brought it over to Mr. Bernstein, helped him into the jacket, and led him to a mirror.

"You look great," I said.

He looked at himself in the mirror, looked at the first suit he had tried on, and again at himself.

"I'll take 'em both," he said.

ഇറ

As winter turned to spring, I saw a man carrying a sign that read:

JOE'S BARBER, HAIRCUT $2.50

# A Life of Risks Taken

This looked like a good idea. With Poppa's permission, I hired that same sign carrier to hold our little signboard that read:

IF YOU'RE IRISH,

COME TO THE HEATHCLIFF MEN'S SUIT FACTORY,

BUY WHOLESALE AND SAVE BIG BUCKS!

UNTIL ST. PATRICK'S DAY,

100 FIFTH AVENUE, FIFTH FLOOR

On his first day, my father and I went down to where Cedric, the sign carrier, was walking. Poppa turned to me and suggested that we buy the man a big breakfast. Poppa did not want Cedric to eat alone, so we ate with him. Cedric ate as if he were starving, scrambled eggs, bacon, coffee, and Danish. Poppa had coffee. I had milk with a Yankee Doodle, a little cup cake with cream in the middle. It was always delicious.

Cedric was to begin after breakfast and walk in front of the police station near our office, and then to move to the fire station after two hours. He did that every day for four days, three hours a day. Poppa paid him five dollars a day plus breakfast, which was much more than I had negotiated with him.

On the second day, early in the morning, I took the subway downtown and walked over to the police station to see what was happening with Cedric. He told me that cops were writing down the address of the factory, and it would be a good idea if he had business cards to hand out. Poppa agreed, and I immediately ran back and gave Cedric four-dozen cards.

On the very first Saturday morning, Poppa and I arrived at The Place at nine a.m., where there were eleven customers waiting for us. They were all handsome and strong-looking Irish and Italian men, some with their sons. Several were policemen and three were firemen.

On the elevator, Poppa smiled and hugged and kissed me.

My Poppa usually did business with his Jewish friends and the people they introduced to him. He always had an excellent month of business prior to the Jewish holidays. But these customers were an entirely different clientele. He had to adjust to these new people that were coming to the factory, many who arrived with their wives and children. Poppa negotiated with the coffee shop downstairs to bring food and servers. When the new customers came off the elevator, he immediately offered a drink and a Danish. We were busy all day. I offered help with the refreshments, but he wouldn't permit me. He said he needed me to help with the sales.

One customer, who was Italian, asked my father why we zeroed in on Irish customers.

His quick answer was, "On Columbus Day, we'll target Italians."

Everyone laughed. Poppa pulled out a bottle of Three Feathers Whiskey and offered everyone a drink. No one refused, though it was ten o'clock in the morning.

At the end of the day, we had sold over forty suits, slightly over wholesale.

He was very happy and so was I.

"How did you get the idea to have the man carry the sign to advertise us?" Poppa asked.

"I don't know. I saw the sign carrier and thought it was a great plan. It was just instinct."

"Like your Seymour Special—very good, zer gut, very good."

Because I was supposed to be paid twenty-five cents for every introduction and fifty cents for every sale, Poppa gave me thirty-five dollars. In 1947, that was a fortune! I gave Cedric a five-dollar tip, which made him very happy.

Poppa ordered six brand-new chairs with cushions for the new customers who came with wives and kids. He bought a coffee maker and small electric stove. He filled a huge pail with ice and put Cokes and apple juice in to chill. He hired Cedric on a part-time basis to keep everything clean in the shop and the office.

During the three weeks before St. Patrick's Day, Poppa sold more than 150 suits, much more than he ever sold prior to the Jewish holidays.

I could only be there on the weekends, but when Poppa came home each evening, I asked, "How did we do at The Place today?"

He would smile and in Yiddish answer, "Twenty-three" or "fourteen" and once or twice, "It rained today. Not too good. What's for dinner?"

He sat at the table while my brothers and I watched him eat. Mom served him and they spoke in Yiddish and Russian.

Sam Breg, Poppa's friend, told me Poppa was always bragging about me, saying that I was a natural-born businessman. It made me feel good. I was thankful that my father gave me room to learn and grow.

Working for Poppa held great excitement for me. I couldn't decide whether it was just being connected with my father's work that was exhilarating, or if it was the thrill of bringing Cedric in with the sign and playing a small part in the business success. Or was it the money? I tried not to dwell too much on the reasons. More than anything I loved being in my father's company, watching him as he worked, negotiating or selling or anything. I could not have learned from a better man. I did not know how lucky I was until I had my own son working for me.

# Chapter 10

ഇരു

### Don't Be Afraid to Ask for the Order

I still enjoyed a busy social life during my time at high school. I worked with Poppa on weekends. During the week I spent a lot of time with Irma after school. However I began to notice a change in her, a hairline adjustment. When I kissed her, she gave me her cheek. Only my cousins did that. That may have been the beginning of my inner voice: The cheek. When I kissed her lips, she said that was the Seymour Special. Now I get the cheek.

I remember being unhappy that some of my friends were taller than I was, and I noticed that Irma was getting friendly with another boy. He belonged to a high school club called the Longfellows. You had to be at least five feet ten inches tall to be allowed to join. I was four inches too short. A few weeks into my junior year, Irma broke up with me.

Tilden High had a dance every Friday night. Because of the break up with Irma, I had no one to take to dance.

Judy Levine was a girl in my civics class. She was without a doubt, the prettiest girl in the school. Drop dead gorgeous. I didn't know her too well, but I wondered about her. Wouldn't it be great if Judy would go to the dance with me? Oh, hell, she is so hot that a dozen guys must have asked her to the dance. I let it go from my mind.

Later that day with my friends, I said, "Judy Levine, the prettiest girl in my Civic Class, is someone I would love to take to the dance. It would knock Irma for a loop when Irma sees me with Judy. It might make her a little jealous, like I felt seeing her with the other guy. But I think Judy's so beautiful, a hundred guys must have asked her already."

"Look at Seymour Chicken, he's afraid to ask Judy out. If she says no, you can handle it," said Bob and Bernie. They taunted and laughed at me. Fat Bernie insisted that I go for it.

"Go for it, chicken!" Fat Bernie said. " If she says no this time because she already has a date, perhaps she will go with you the next time."

"Judy is too fantastically beautiful that I can't believe that she's not to be booked for the next decade."

All my friends looked at each other. Who was this beauty that no one knew except for chicken Seymour? They taunted and laughed at me even more.

I thought about Judy seriously. What was the worst that could happen? She would smile and tell me she had a boyfriend, or she already had a date, or didn't go out with boys in her grade, or a hundred other excuses. I was giving myself the no-s even before I got them.

I gathered up all my nerve and took the risk. My heart was beating fast as I dialed her number. I took a couple of deep breaths. The phone rang three times, but as I was about to hang up in relief, I heard a female voice.

"Hello," she said.

"Hi, is this Judy?"

"No, this is Mrs. Levine, Judy's mom. Who is calling?"

"Hi, Mrs. Levine. This is Seymour Ubell. Judy and I are in the same civics class. May I please speak to her?"

"Judy!" her mom called, "Seymour, from your civics class is on the phone."

After a few torturous minutes, I heard a soft voice say, "Hello, Seymour."

"Hi, Judy, do you know who I am?"

"Of course, I know you. You always wear a bowtie. And you're always part of the discussion in class."

*Wow, I must have made some impression!*

"Would you like to go to the dance with me this Friday night?" I blurted out.

There was a five-second period of silence, which felt like a century.

"Yes, I would," she said quietly. I exhaled. "But, let me get my Mom's permission." In a moment Judy returned the phone. "It's okay," she said.

"That's great! The dance is at eight, and I can come and get you about seven-thirty. Does that work for you?"

"It sounds perfect. I am so glad you called. Thank you."

"See you Friday night."

I hung up. What a jerk! I didn't even say good-bye or "look forward to seeing you" or something nice. I had a lot to learn about girls and how to speak to them.

# A Life of Risks Taken

That Friday I wore a new suit that Poppa made especially for me.

As I was getting ready to leave the apartment, Poppa looked at me all dressed up and he smiled. Both he and Mom said I was looking very shane, handsome. Poppa took a ten-dollar bill from his pocket and reached out to give it to me.

"Thanks Poppa. I have my own money. I don't need it. Thanks."

"Take it, take it," he insisted.

"Poppa, I'm okay."

Poppa shook his head at me, still smiling.

Judy lived on Maple Street, about twenty blocks from our apartment. I took the Utica Avenue trolley to within three blocks of her house. I got out of the trolley and hailed a taxi the rest of the way. I told the driver to wait as I walked to her door and rang the bell. Judy's mom came to the door to greet me.

"You must be Seymour. Come in. Judy will be ready in a minute," her mom said.

She looked over my shoulder to see the taxi waiting. She looked pleased, and I was pleased that her mother knew my name.

Judy walked into the living room where I waited. She was very beautiful. Her glistening dark hair, her white and pink dress—I felt as if I was with a movie star. Her mom stood back, looking at her daughter with admiration.

Parents are a strange group of people. They are tough and strict yet loving and proud.

I was dressed in my new suit, my bow tie, one of

# A Life of Risks Taken

Earl's shirts, and a matching pair of socks with only a tiny hole in the right foot.

"Good night, Mrs. Levine, we won't be home too late."

"Have a good time," she responded.

I held the door for Judy as she stepped into the taxi, and I ran to the other side and got in.

*Oh my god! The meter is almost at a dollar!*

I instructed the driver, "Tilden High School on East Fifty-Eighth Street and Tilden Avenue."

In the taxi Judy spoke quietly about school, her friends, she mentioned she had a younger sister. Her parents just recently moved to their new home in Brooklyn and she was a new student at Tilden High School. We continued to chat as I discreetly kept an eye on the meter—almost two dollars!

"Have you ever been to a Tilden dance before?" I asked.

She told me this was her first. I asked why. Much to my surprise she said that no one had ever invited her.

Here you have a very nice and very beautiful girl, and she had never been taken to a school dance. Maybe being too pretty is not a blessing. Guys are too intimidated to ask beautiful girls for a date.

It occurred to me that I was a little apprehensive.

We held hands as we entered the gym. I was excited and could tell Judy was too. It made me feel special. We were a big hit with my friends, who quickly surrounded us with their dates and girlfriends. Judy shone like the brightest star in the sky.

# A Life of Risks Taken

My friend Bernie whispered into Judy's ear, "We are Seymour's best friends, and we're glad we convinced him to call you. Welcome to our group."

She smiled and then burst into happy laughter. "I'm so pleased he did call."

I gave Bernie a stern look.

That night I danced like Fred Astaire and Judy like Ginger Rogers. From time to time, I caught Irma looking at me as she danced with her pimply-faced giant. I still cared about what Irma thought and continued to like her. I was happy to be with Judy and sad not to be with Irma.

Judy discovered that I was part of a terrific group of boys and girls at the school. Most of us were in the same classes, and we were all part of the high school newspaper, called Tilden Topics. None of us were involved in sports, just academics and politics.

We were always laughing, trying to outdo each other with clever remarks. Judy fit in immediately. Everyone liked her. She asked the girls about the school paper—she wanted to join.

Judy was a very quiet person, low-key and a good listener. Although she entered the school at the same time I did, she found it hard to make friends.

"I am shy," she confessed.

She wanted to know why I was reluctant to call her for a date and what convinced me to finally do it.

I told her, "You are so pretty that I thought you would've had boys calling you all the time. Finally, I found the courage to call you, for two separate reasons. First, my friends didn't know who you were or what you looked like. You were a mystery, and they wanted to see what I was talking about. We are an outgoing group. We're all comfortable in our skins, as well as our friendships, and each one of us can hold our own. The guys were surprised at my nervousness. They urged me and encouraged me. That helped a lot."

She stopped me for a moment. "Thank you for all these wonderful compliments."

"What also convinced me was something my Poppa tells his salesmen. My Poppa says 'the word no has no place in your vocabulary if you want an order. A good salesman always asks for the order. Let the customer say no to you, you should not be the deliverer of the 'no'. The 'no' the customer gives you is only temporary. Judy," I said softly, "Now you know where I'm coming from. How I had the courage to tell you any of this is more of a surprise to me than you realize!"

I mustered up a little more courage and said, "It would be nice to do another evening, or a Saturday afternoon, like this again."

Judy said that she felt the same way. Now I was wondering if that was an invitation to kiss her good night. At her door, to my surprise, Judy kissed me! She followed with a thank you for being her brave knight and for telling her what I was thinking. It all added up to having a great time. I kissed her back. And then we kissed each other.

As I walked down the street to the corner to get the trolley home, I said out loud, "Irma? Irma who?" grinning from ear to ear. It didn't help, though. I still liked Irma. And I liked Judy. Oy vay!

# A Life of Risks Taken

&#8500;&#8500;

One day we were all together, our whole crowd, including Judy. We were discussing a story for Tilden Topics. Our managing editor, Margaret, suggested a story about the issues that black students had in an almost all-white, almost all-Jewish school.

"Why is that an important story? There are only four or five black students in the school." Judy said.

The room went silent.

"Will the other 5,000 students find it interesting?" Judy asked.

I said, "The real question is how anyone can know how it feels to be a minority, unless we inform them. It has to be difficult for Alisha and Eutemy to be surrounded by all-white students, mostly Jewish student body? And don't you think that it may be important for the students to have sensitivity about this situation?"

There was a pause. Judy rose to the occasion, "I would like to volunteer to write the story." I was feeling very proud of her.

Bernie said, "Margaret and I write it with you."

&#8500;&#8500;

For the next Tilden dance for juniors, I asked Alisha to go with me. She was one of two black girls in the school. I was being a wise guy when I asked Alisha to the dance. I wanted to be above racial prejudice. Alisha was a nice girl, but that was not why I asked her out.

Judy went with Billy Shapiro, quarterback of the football team. I could not stand it. I was so jealous.

# A Life of Risks Taken

Alisha said she would go with me, but she suggested it would be better if she and I met in front of the school at 7:45 p.m. on Friday night. I agreed, but I did not like it. It felt strange to me.

I arrived early. I wore a sports jacket, slacks and my usual bow tie.

At the corner, I waited until I saw Alisha get out of a car. She looked at me, but she didn't wave. The car pulled away, I walked over to her.

"Hi, Alisha," I called to her.

Suddenly she looked more animated. She waved and we walked toward each other.

"You look great!" I said.

She thanked me. We didn't hold hands as I had with Judy. We were both quiet as we entered the building. I started to notice that kids from the school, as well as parents dropping off students going to the dance, were staring at us.

I asked Alisha if she had ever been to a Tilden dance before. She told me she hadn't. I mentioned that she looked distracted when she got out of the car. "Was anything wrong?"

She was quiet for a while and then she nodded.

"My parents were so pleased that I was going to the dance. They asked me who I was going with. I told them, 'with Seymour.' They asked me for your last name. I didn't know it."

"My last name is Ubell." I interrupted.

"They got upset that I didn't know your last name. They asked me if you were colored. I said you weren't. They were furious that I was going to the dance with a white boy. They were frightened that it could only lead to trouble."

"What kind of trouble could we get into at a high school dance?" I asked.

"I don't know. But they said I was naïve. They almost didn't let me go."

"Why?"

"They said whites and blacks don't mix."

"Nothing is going to happen. Let's go into the dance and have a great time. We will not get into trouble. There are teacher chaperones." And jokingly, "I will protect you."

The band was already playing a *Lindy Hop* when we arrived at the gymnasium. Alisha was a very good dancer. We danced together very well and ignored that everyone was watching us.

At first, no one else was dancing. My friend Bernie cut in on Alisha and me. I left the floor and asked Bunny, Bernie's girlfriend, to dance with me. After that, everyone got on the floor and danced.

My friend Eutemy, one of the few black male students at Tilden, came over to me and said, "Seymour, you're crazy. But I really like you."

We both smiled. I knew what he was talking about, but I still didn't see what all the fuss was about.

I bought Alisha a Coke and joined her at a table. We sat and talked for a while, and then Bunny and Bernie came over to us and joined the conversation. They wanted to know if Alisha was having a good time.

Around ten p.m., the dance ended and Alisha said, "I

have to go now."

"I'll walk you to where you are being picked up," I said.

"Please don't," she answered. "I can do it."

I said, "It's much nicer if I take you to your pick-up spot."

"Okay, let's go."

I walked Alisha to the corner where she was to meet her Poppa. We waited for about five minutes, and the car came to the corner. Alisha said good night to me and darted off to the car. I walked quickly behind her.

"Hello, Mr. Dallinger," I said. "I'm Seymour Ubell, one of Alisha's classmates. We were together at the dance."

"Good to meet you, young man," he replied.

"If you don't mind, sir," I said. "I live on East Forty-Eighth Street and Church Avenue. If that's the same direction you're going, can you give me a lift?"

"Absolutely. Alisha, get into the backseat. Seymour will sit next to me."

"What make of car is this?" I asked.

"A Chevy Impala. What does your Poppa drive?"

"We don't have a car."

"What work does your Poppa do?"

"Poppa's a men's clothing manufacturer," I said as we pulled up to my apartment house. "This is where I live. Thank you very much."

I got out of the car, turned to say good night to Alisha, and noticed Mr. Dallinger looking at my building. He seemed to be as puzzled as I was.

Alisha came up to me outside the cafeteria on the

Monday after the dance.

"Daddy liked you."

I smiled in silence.

"He was sorry that he frightened me with the black and white stuff. He said I had to grow up and go out into the world as the woman I am, work it out for myself."

I couldn't fathom what Alisha or her Daddy were talking about. Discrimination was unfamiliar to me. I had never thought about it. But it was a fact that the Dallinger family lived with every day of their lives.

"The main thing about Friday night was not that I am white and you aren't. The important thing is that we had a great time together. Your description of your Daddy had frightened me. That's why I asked for a ride. I wanted to see who this guy was. He's okay."

She had a huge smile on her face. She reached up to me and kissed my cheek before darting off.

&#x8480;

Judy was mine after that dance.

"I didn't have a good time, and I was a little jealous seeing you with Alisha."

I said, "You want a laugh? I was also a little jealous seeing you with The Jock."

"Judy, would you like to go to the Paramount Theater on Saturday afternoon to see a movie and Tommy Dorsey's band with Frank Sinatra," I blurted out.

The movie we saw that afternoon was The Road to Singapore with Bob Hope and Bing Crosby. In the theater we held hands and moved close, shoulder-to-shoulder.

# A Life of Risks Taken

When the film was over, she turned her head to look at me and smiled. I kissed her.

Then the Tommy Dorsey band began their show. The band leader began his performance with one of my all-time favorites, *"Begin the Beguine."* The newly famous Sinatra was introduced and the audience went wild. He sang about six songs, all love songs. In the midst of all this I was surprised when Judy said, "I think I like you very much."

I felt my heart beating fast. I kissed her again.

We were both dressed up, Judy in a navy suit with a white blouse and medium-high heels, which made her taller than me. She also had a little lipstick on. I wore a sports jacket and slacks, a white shirt, and a tie. That kind of a date and dressing in a formal way, is history. I think today's young people are missing out on the fun it is to get dressed up and go on a date.

We went to Child's Restaurant after the show. We both had open, hot turkey sandwiches with Cokes. It was a wonderful afternoon. Those were the days. We had such good time for less than five dollars for both of us: $1.25 for each ticket, 40 cents for bus and subway fares, 65 cents each for the sandwiches, and 10 cents each for the Cokes. One Hershey bar to share, 10 Cents Total:  $4.50 for the entire date.

On the following Saturday night, Judy's parents had planned to go to a movie. They asked her to baby-sit for her younger sister. She asked her mother if it was okay if I kept her company. Her mom said yes.

I arrived on Saturday evening a little late. Judy's parents had left, and her little sister was already asleep.

# A Life of Risks Taken

Judy and I sat on the couch and watched TV on a very small black-and-white screen. It didn't take long before we began to neck.

We kissed and kissed, and Judy said to me, "Is that the only way you know how to kiss?"

I did not have a clue as to what she was talking about.

Kissing is kissing, what other way is there?

And that is exactly what I asked her: "What other way is there?"

She put her lips to mine and slowly stuck her tongue into my mouth. I pulled my head back. That was disgusting.

But I said nothing. We did it again and again, until I got the hang of it. It wasn't great, but she liked it, and I didn't mind. Judy told me that they call this French kissing.

Why didn't Irene tell me about this kind of kissing? Or Earl? Where was Earl in all this? He should have taught me about French kissing!

# Chapter 11

ഇൽൽ

**Business Ideas**

"How was your date?" Poppa asked, riding the subway to The Place on the Sunday morning after I took Judy out.

"We had a great time. We saw a funny movie with Bob Hope and heard Frank Sinatra."

"Who is Frank Sinatra?"

"He is a new young singer—very good."

"I heard you also went to the dance at school with a Negro girl."

"Yes, I did." Surprised at the comment.

"How was that?"

"It was just okay."

"How come?"

"Alisha's parents made such a mishmash over our date, she was not having a good time."

"What was the problem?"

"They were upset that she did not know my last name and that I was white. The parents frightened her with a story about how whites and blacks don't mix, and it was possible that a fight would start and someone might get hurt."

"Her parents were absolutely right to be worried."

I could not believe my ears. Was Poppa a bigot? His statement went against everything he ever taught me.

"Sometimes there is a *meshuggener*, a crazy person, out there who might see you and the girl together. And in an act of *mishegas* do something crazy. We live in a strange world. When I was a boy in Poland, I saw many incidents of bigotry in our *shtetle*, village. Once—and I will never forget this—Jewish and Polish boys where playing soccer. There was a tiny, meaningless confrontation, and two Jewish boys and one gentile were killed. For absolutely nothing, the parents of three children suffered their entire lives, their children gone forever. I want you to understand this: I hate all bigots and their twisted ideology, but I cannot and will not sacrifice my son for those beliefs."

I listened to Poppa and tried to understand where he was coming from. It was beyond my comprehension that I could be hurt just going on a date with Alisha. I had neither seen, nor experienced anything close to the stories I heard about racism and anti-Semitism.

The subway ride was taking longer than usual that morning. I wanted to change the subject. My father's face was stern, and I could tell he was upset by our discussion.

"You know, Poppa, a couple of customers who bought some suits last week asked if we carried shirts. Maybe we could take some of the money I have in my bank account and buy a dozen shirts or so."

His facial expression changed.

# A Life of Risks Taken

"That's an idea," he responded. "My friend Morris is a peddler on Essex Street. He sells shirts and ties. I'll call him as soon as we get to The Place. Maybe he'll give us a special price."

Poppa ordered two-dozen shirts and one-dozen ties. I took ownership over my ideas and invested $160. The haberdashery became my business.

Shirts were a good business, we discovered.

Before late afternoon on the first day, Poppa had called Morris and ordered four-dozen more shirts and ties. I grinned. I was very deep in the shirt and tie business.

"Look up in the telephone book the number of Arrow Shirt Company—that was the name in the shirts we bought from Morris."

"Why?" I questioned.

"If we're going to be in the shirt business, let's buy directly from the shirt maker—better prices, better margins."

"Poppa," I asked, "Will your partners Sam and Milton be my partner in the new shirts and ties we're selling?"

He smiled. "You talk too much."

On the way home that evening in the subway, I asked, "Poppa, why don't we bring in some socks and hats?"

He gave a gentle slap to the side of my head and said, "Someday you will be a millionaire. But don't be in such a rush. You will only get there if you save your money."

He put his arm around me and hugged me to his chest. I loved his smell of Turkish Blend Camel cigarettes. Even as I write, I am taking a deep breath through my nose searching once again for that memory of smell.

# Chapter 12

ဆာ

### Careful with Money

"You've earned a great deal of money in the last four weeks. You used to give all the money you made to the house. Why did you change?" Mom asked in Yiddish.

I was not prepared for that question, nor did I have an immediate answer.

"What are you going to do with it?" she continued.

I never once thought of what to do with all that money. I had a savings account at the Lincoln Saving Bank that was opened in elementary school. I made a twenty-five cent deposit every week. My account totaled twelve dollars.

"I'm older now and it's a good thing for a guy to have a little of his own money. Now that you ask, I think I'll put most of it into my savings account and the rest keep for spending money," I answered in English.

My voice was a little firmer than my usual tone.

I had earned more than four hundred dollars, which was a fortune in those days. My parents looked at each other.

# A Life of Risks Taken

My mother asked, "How much do you actually have?"

I went to my room and opened my hiding place shoebox.

"I counted $486," I proudly reported.

"It would be wise for you to put three hundred and fifty into the bank. We would like you to contribute one hundred dollars for household expenses. Remember you live here as well, that means you have a responsibility to the family. And if you like, you may keep thirty-two dollars for yourself. We also suggest that you donate fifteen dollars to the polio fund, in honor of your friend Irwin."

My friend Irwin Silverman had contracted polio during the summer epidemic.

Tears filled my eyes, I clenched my teeth. I was silent. Not a peep from my lips but my mind thundered, *It's my money, my money! Why should I give anything to the house? I will put into the bank what I say I will put into the bank.*

I looked pleadingly at my father for help. He knew my hard work and knew my contribution. He responded with a look that told me he agreed with Momma. This was a battle that I was not going to win.

I counter-offered in a non-belligerent voice, "Can I give the house fifty dollars, give twenty dollars to the polio fund, put four hundred into the bank, and keep the rest for spending money?"

My voice had a pleading tone.

Mom looked straight into my eyes. Poppa turned his head a little. These two were a tough team. They knew what they wanted, and it was going to be their way.

Both said firmly, in one voice, "No!"

"And when you're finished doing exactly what we want you to do, go to your room and finish your homework. School is more important than spending money at this time in your life," Momma said.

"Okay, okay," I answered, exasperated.

"You watch that tone of voice when you speak to your mother, or you will hear from me!" Poppa scolded.

I was standing in the path of a disaster.

"Sorry, Mom," I said. I would never attempt or risk offending my parents.

She reached out and gently touched me. "Doo bist mein shayner gooten zindel." You are my beautiful and good son.

With my head down, peering into my books as I was doing my homework, I could hear my mother and father continue speaking in Yiddish.

"That's a good boy," Mom said.

"Zayer goot," Poppa answered. Very good.

It was worth every cent to witness the caring my parents expressed for me.

With maturity, I realized they were teaching me the important lesson of responsibility and the value of saving money. Someday an emergency will come, and if you save, you will be better prepared. That time of need always comes, in everyone's life.

For me, that day of need came sooner than I had ever dreamed. A month after Poppa died, I went to the Lincoln Savings Bank where I had more than seven hundred dollars saved. I requested a check made out to Momma for the entire amount and closed the account.

# Chapter 13

ഓരു

### Facing the Truth

Earning money is not an easy task. Although I'd had income from the time I was eleven years old, I still didn't have a clue about how to create real cash flow. I questioned my ability to be able to go out into the world and have enough income for food, rent and expenses. This was a skill I had to learn. Earning income when you don't need it is one thing. When one is desperate that is entirely different.

Listening to my father's phone conversations, watching him as a seller and businessman, overhearing him negotiate with customers and suppliers sank quietly into my subconscious, but I didn't know it yet. I would soon be put to the test

ഓരു

September in New York City was more often than not, hot and humid. In 1948, I was out every day looking for work. I needed a job that paid for household bills.

# A Life of Risks Taken

My brother Earl married his girlfriend, Shirley, and now had his own responsibilities. He contributed what he could, but the real weight of supporting the family fell to me.

I was seventeen and angry.

The top-paying jobs for a high school graduate required becoming a member of a union. In my father's factory, the union workers were all the best paid. This idea brought me to the offices of the Amalgamated Clothing Workers of America, which was the union where my father's company got its skilled employees.

My visit was brief. By chance there was an opening as a stock clerk at the Rose Brothers Men's Clothing Company, one of the largest companies in the United States at that time.

This giant organization dominated six floors, comprised of offices and a warehouse, at 275 Seventh Avenue in Manhattan. The receptionist directed me to the sixth floor where Mr. Handwerger, the tough foreman of the firm, would interview me. I was warned at the union office that Handwerger took no guff from anyone, even if you were a union employee.

The door to his office was open. I stood outside waiting for an invitation to enter. He looked at me, said nothing, and then waved me in. I stood close to his desk. He continued working. He paused, moved only his eyes up again, a small cigar clenched in his teeth. A Mona Lisa smile crossed my lips. I thought he could hear my heart beating as he sat across the desk.

Handwerger had an image that was more like a mobster than a shop foreman. His jowls hung from his cheeks as well as from his neck. His voice was gruff. The half-smoked, half-chewed cigar drooped from his lips. A black fedora sat slanted on his head. His face was shaggy as if he hadn't shaved in a week.

He stared up at me. I flinched and moved back an inch.

Whoa, hold steady there, I ordered myself.

"What the hell do you want?" Handwerger growled.

"The union sent me here for a stock clerk job," I squeaked.

Handwerger snarled again, "Where have ya worked before?"

Turning his head to the side, he spat into a trash can at his feet.

Could I say delivery boy, magazine seller, lemonade stand? No, that would never do. I couldn't say any of those things.

"What's a matter, boy, didn't you hear my question? I'm busy, goddamn it!"

I blurted in as deep a voice as I could muster, "My father owned a men's clothing company. I worked for him as a stock clerk, hanging suits, sewing tickets on sleeves, and weekend sales."

"Why the hell are you here, why don't you work for him now?" he grumbled.

"He died," I whispered, trembling.

Handwerger looked me over. "Sorry, kid," he said. "I just hired someone for the job. I can't use ya."

He was finished with me. He had no time to waste on a know-nothing nobody like this pipsqueak of a kid. His head twisted away from me as he spat again into the trash can. He waved me off with his two fingers dancing in the air and returned to his paperwork.

Is this what they call an interview? I am never going to survive doing this again and again.

My heart was bursting, but I would not, I could not cry. I could feel the sweat creeping up my clinging shirt.

In a moment of desperation and with failure about to engulf me, I took a risk. An explosion of words sprang from my lips at full speed: "Excuse me, sir, Mr. Handwerger, the union sent me down here for the job that you just gave away. I really need this job! Please," I pleaded, "I promise you, I will work hard. I'll go for coffee, lick stamps, run errands, sweep up, whatever it takes. I am not lazy."

Tears flooded my eyes. I tried to hold them back. My teeth crushed against one another. I turned my face ever so slightly away from his view. I didn't ask to be in this situation. It was not my choice. It was thrust upon me. I let my head fall.

Handwerger stood up from behind his desk, his eyeballs bulging with fire. He reminded me of Sonny Tuchman, my childhood bully, in a rage. He narrowed his look, pushed his head right into my face. I thought he could swallow me whole.

"Look at me!" he thundered. His voice was furious. My head remained down. "Look at me!" he shouted. "What kind of a wise ass, piece-of-shit kid are you? I never heard any son-of-a- bitch talk to me that way." His face moved closer to mine. My head inched back. I could smell the tobacco on his breath.

# A Life of Risks Taken

He tapped his pencil on his desk, scratched his crotch, and shook his head in a moment of consideration. He put his cigar down and grinned—an ugly grin, a frightening grin.

Oh my, he is going to enjoy my death.

"The 'going for coffee' sold me," he said. "I like it black, hot, and lots of sugar. Start at eight a.m. tomorrow and don't be late. You screw up and you're out on your ass."

"I promise you I will not screw up, and I can start now, this very minute, if you want me to."

In the rush of adrenaline, a tiny surge of vomit tickled my throat. I swallowed.

"I like your attitude, but don't get too pushy. Okay! Okay. Mike!" he bellowed.

Another young man came running. Handwerger turned to me, "What da fuck is your name?"

"Seymour, sir."

"Seymour Sir, what kind of a pussy name is that? Mike, take Seymour Sir to aisle twelve and show him what we do around here."

Mike whispered to me, "Let's move it."

Life is strange, because on that miserable hot day in midtown Manhattan, I began my career. I was a pants-piling-and-pants-picking stock clerk with a salary of $42.50 a week.

To this day, I believe it was there in that small office, frightened to death, that I made my most important sale. I sold myself to one of the toughest S.O.B.s in the men's clothing industry.

# A Life of Risks Taken

The euphoria of getting a job engulfed me. I could not wait to get to a pay phone, to call Millie's candy store and tell Momma.

The next morning, I arrived at seven a.m with a large container of black coffee, plenty of sugar and very hot. Handwerger was not there. I left it on his desk.

Two minutes later, I heard the loudspeaker with the lion's voice, "Will the kid I hired yesterday come to my office A.S.A.P." I did not know what A.S.A.P. meant, but I ran at full speed.

I dashed from my position and stepped into his office.

"Thanks kid," he said quietly. "Take the money, and fill out this form and take it to the seventh floor to Miriam."

He never lifted his head.

I didn't take the money. Just for the record, a large cup of coffee cost twelve cents. But I took the form and went to the seventh floor. I had my first job, but unbeknownst to me at that moment in time, it was the place where I was to receive my real education. I learned more at Rose Brothers Men's Clothing Company than I could have acquired at any college. It would take more than a decade for me to be able to stand on my own two feet. But then I would be prepared, totally confident and ready for my life.

Life has a strange way of leading you in the right direction. I did not realize that my natural instinct to show up would lead me to the road I was to take.

# Chapter 14

### ഩറ

**Momma Falls in Love**

No one expected Momma to fall in love one year after Poppa died.

The truth is, my conservative, quiet mother did not fall at all—she plunged into love. And Philip Segall, the man she chose, did not fall in love with Mom—he tumbled head over heels into the affair. They were like two young lovebirds in a relationship filled with passion and respect.

Mom never called her new husband by his first name. She addressed him in an esteemed and respectful manner that was quite formal, but warm and loving.

"Mr. Segall, would you like a drink? Mr. Segall, would you like your dinner?"

Now these two young lovers, ages forty-three (Mom) and fifty (Philip), were bound together in a secret nuptial agreement called the *Katuba*, a Jewish contract committing husband and wife to each other with honesty and loyalty. It was not a union ordained by the State of New York. Mom did not want to lose her Social Security payments for herself and her sons under the age of eighteen. Money was always a very thoughtful priority.

The seven of us—Philip's three daughters and Momma's four sons—were along for the ride. It was going to be bumpy, filled with tears and laughs, but most of all, jam-packed with love. We would become one tight-knit family.

Before their marriage, Mom and Philip had arranged a day when the two families were to meet for the first time. Mom invited Philip's three daughters to our apartment for dinner. It was a very exciting day. I discovered that Evie, the middle sister, was one of my classmates. We were taking a Spanish class together. Evie sat right in front of me. She was pretty and smart. I had even asked her for a date, months before we knew that our parents were going to be married. But alas, she turned me down. To this day, many years later, I still tease her about how she rejected me.

I only saw photos of Clara, Philip's first wife. She was a very beautiful woman. She died at a very young age from cancer.

The folks moved all seven of us into a large apartment with a finished basement. Fortunately for everyone, Momma's and Philip's oldest children, Earl and Anna, were already married.

We didn't have much money, but we had lots of room, plus the excitement and new siblings.

Philip was a hardworking man who earned his living as a contract laundry agent. He had his own customers whose laundry he collected on a given day of the week at their homes. He delivered it all to a wholesale laundry and cleaning factory and picked up the washed and ironed laundry a week later. He then delivered it to his customers and got paid for his service.

Mom and Philip's marriage relieved me of some responsibility. I did not have to give my entire salary at home. I could keep at least half of it to spend on an occasional date. Those were the few years that I remember feeling completely free. I was a real man, strong, independent and able to take care of myself.

Our new home on East Fifty-First Street in Brooklyn had three bedrooms. One was for the boys, Alvin, Bob, and me. Another was for my new sisters, Evie and Esty.

Nightly we would sit on the beds in the girls' room and talk and laugh and tease. Finally, just before eleven p.m, Evie would say something about going to sleep and how the guys should scoot off into our own room. We resisted. Having sisters was such a new thing and a big treat.

Evie would say something like, "If you don't leave so we can get to bed, we're getting undressed."

I'd retort, "Go ahead, we won't bother you."

"Okay," she'd say, "Have it your way."

And slowly Evie would begin to unbutton her blouse. Before she got to the third button, the three of us scrambled out of the room screaming and laughing, closing the door behind us.

It didn't take long for the children in our newly formed family to discover that we were crowding the recently married couple. They wanted and needed privacy. Of course, all the kids thought our forty-three-year-old mother and her fifty-year-old husband were very old people. They couldn't be in love or have sex! We were kids, what did we know about adults getting a second chance to enjoy love and happiness? The folks, as it turned out, had a twenty-six-year relationship that changed all of our lives.

About a year or two after Momma and Philip married, a mass exodus began. At that time, it was a Jewish custom that an adult child never moved out of his or her parents' house unless they were married.

My sister Evie married Bert. Evie went on to become a successful and happy schoolteacher with a master's degree in child education.

Estella moved to Argentina to marry Ernesto. In Havana, Etsy honed her skills as a documentarian, producing, filming, and writing many films about Cuba and South America. She has been the recipient of many awards for her work.

Sister Ann became a wife and mommy, and at midlife went to college, and then developed a successful career as a therapist focusing on women's issues.

A year or two after I moved out, my brother Alvin married Estelle.

Then only our youngest brother, Bob, was left at home. Mom and Philip could handle that quite well.

Bob was more independent than his older siblings. He just glided into manhood, doing anything that pleased him. He was the youngest and, of course, got whatever he wanted. Bob was intelligent, educated and very handsome.

## A Life of Risks Taken

It would not take long for him to meet someone similar.

As for me, I married Sabina. I was in love. She was beautiful, very smart, the type of person I thought I wanted to spend the rest of my life with. What did I know? I was just shy of twenty-one years old and ready to fly the coop.

# Chapter 15

ౠౠ

### The Craps Game and the Mob

East of Utica Avenue on Clarkson Avenue and East Fifty-First Street stood the infamous Funzie's Billiard Parlor, a place where I would have my first major entrepreneurial success.

Shooting pool and playing billiards had become a weekend pastime. Funzie's wasn't a down-and-dirty place with shady hustlers and bookies. It was an under-the-radar pool hall and gambling spot in midtown Brooklyn. Most wagers were placed on ballgames. Once or twice on the weekend, a large craps game was held in the basement. Funzie, the resident bookmaker, would not allow me into the game, nor would he take any bets from me. I was still only about eighteen years old and the word was out that I had just lost my dad. There must have been some unwritten law that orphans were banned from the game. Not a single person in the pool hall would place a bet with me on anything. If I wanted to play a game of billiards for fifty cents a game, I was refused.

# A Life of Risks Taken

"Ya wanna shoot pool wid da kid and have fun, dats okay, but no gambling wid him. You guys hear me?" Funzie announced.

When the craps game was on, I was upstairs shooting pool by myself. I was able to make some extra change running for drinks and sandwiches for the players downstairs. I earned about fifteen to twenty dollars on a Sunday afternoon. My pool shooting upstairs, on Sundays only was always on the house.

Stefano Tetari, the landlord of the pool hall building, was a grouchy Italian immigrant. He spent his days sweeping the sidewalk in front of his property.

If a person walked by the pool hall and threw a cigarette butt on the sidewalk, Stefano would leap from his folding chair, grab his broom, and sweep the butt into the gutter, simultaneously swinging his arm in the air and cursing the offender. It got to be that Mr. Tetari became the subject of teasing by the men in the neighborhood. A few of the guys held on to their finished cigarettes until they walked in front of the pool hall, where they would toss the butt onto the sidewalk in front Stefano.

The other young fellas in the pool hall could see a regular coming and knew that he had at least three cigarette butts to discard on the sidewalk as he walked into the billiard room. Everyone moved to the window to watch the scene. In a single swift movement, the butts landed on the ground and the regular made a quick dash into the pool hall.

"You sum-ina-bitch," Stefano would attack the butts in one wild stroke with the broom, sweeping them past the curb. Everyone inside the poolroom exploded in laughter. Stefano would turn to the window and place his hand into the crook of his elbow with his middle finger up in the air, cursing the crew.

I felt sad for the old guy, but I knew if he would ignore these jerks, they probably would stop their harassing.

The real reason Stefano sat outside every day was to keep his son from going inside the pool hall. Stefano owned five similar buildings in the neighborhood. His son Dominic swept the sidewalks in front of the other buildings. He also took care of the maintenance of each property. Dominic was a gambler. He bet on all the baseball games and gambled in the craps game in the basement on the weekend. Dominic was always a loser. His markers with Funzie ran so high that the bookie did not have to pay rent for two months.

Stefano was so furious. He sat all day in front of the pool hall swearing and cursing at anyone who entered.

"You bigga bum, low life! Da mal occhio on you! Ah fungool!"

No one was ever offended. To the young lions of our neighborhood, he was only a source of laughter.

Stefano wanted to evict Funzie from his building, but, was afraid. He knew that the pool hall was connected to one of the five New York Mafia families.

That did not stop Stefano completely. One night he walked into the pool hall and lambasted the bookie for allowing his twenty-five-year-old son to lose so much money. He screamed at him that the basement of the pool hall could no longer be used for the craps game. This was going to be his revenge, and it would take place at once, on that very day, when players from all over Brooklyn would be coming to Funzie's craps game.

A light went on in my head. At home we had a finished basement, a place that no one was using. I took a calculated gamble and suggested to Funzie that perhaps he could use my basement for the weekend game. He nodded.

I asked, "How much would you pay me?"

He put his arm around my shoulder, looked at me and smiled. He told me that I could charge two dollars per man to play in our basement. I would get to keep all the money. The only condition was that I couldn't gamble. This was an opportunity I could not resist. We could get at least fifty dollars for the day. That was real money.

Momma, Philip and I sat in the kitchen as I began my sales presentation. I offered the possibility of using our basement and likely getting at least fifty dollars for the afternoon.

"Some of the men from the pool hall would like a place to play cards or even poker on Sunday afternoons." Momma loved to play poker, and I thought she might see the value in my suggestion if I changed the game.

My mother was reluctant, but Philip, not quick to pass judgment, said, "Let's discuss it. We could certainly use an extra fifty dollars."

A brief conversation went on between them and they finally agreed. Momma and Philip would be out for the afternoon visiting some friends on Long Island and would not be back until seven p.m.

I returned to the pool hall and told Funzie that it was okay—the game could take place in my basement. The game could begin at two p.m and everyone had to be out by six-thirty. We were in agreement. We shook hands. Funzie looked straight into my eyes. Once again he put his arm around my shoulder, walked me over to the corner and told me that he, too, lost his father as a boy. His father was killed in car accident when Funzie was very young. He, too, did what he could to help his family.

The basement had to be cleaned up. I thanked Funzie and dashed off to our house.

I began by sweeping and putting some things against the wall. I opened an old dining room table and put all the leaves in so there was a big enough place to play. Funzie had given me a green cloth, similar to the ones used on pool tables, which I put on top of the dining room table. I pushed the table against the wall. When the dice were thrown, they would hit the wall and bounce back and the players could view the number. I opened the windows to let in some fresh air. We had about ten folding chairs downstairs. I wiped them down and placed them up against the walls.

When Funzie and the players began to arrive, promptly at two p.m., many commented about how nice and clean the basement was. It was a big change from the one at the poolroom basement.

As each man arrived, Funzie pointed to me and instructed each one to give me two dollars. During the entire afternoon more than a hundred players showed up. They came from all over Brooklyn and a few from Queens and Manhattan. Word must have gotten out that a new game was opening up. Some played for an hour or less, others for the entire afternoon.

As the day progressed some of the men called to me, "Hey, kid, you got a Coke here or a beer?" I ran to the corner store and got a dozen bottles of Coke. Each cost ten cents.

"How much I owe ya?" the man asked. I looked a Funzie.

"A buck," Funzie responded.

In three minutes, I had twelve dollars in my hand and ran to the store again and asked the grocer to send over a case of Coke and a bucket of ice. I started to leave and then turned on my heel. I asked Max, the grocer, to send a case of beer for Funzie. In fifteen minutes, the delivery was made. Funzie paid for everything

"Charge two bucks for beer and one buck for the cokes."

By the end of the game we sold four cases of beer and six cases of Cokes. Total revenue was $168 dollars. The last shooter took the dice at seven p.m. The first craps game at Seymour's basement was over. Two of the winners each gave me a twenty-dollar tip.

That afternoon Momma, Philip and I earned $220 in admissions, $168 for cokes and beers and $40 in tips—$428. I could not believe it. It was a miracle. If I could do this every Saturday and Sunday, I would never have to work again.

Nevertheless, my instincts told me this was not what I should be doing, and although I was earning serious money, I felt ashamed. I was uncomfortable getting money that was not from labor but from wheeling and dealing. And I had lied to my mother. If caught, I might create unhappiness for my family.

I greeted Momma and Philip upon their return home, saying, "Let's sit down in the kitchen. I have something to discuss with you."

Momma put her hands to her head and moaned, "What happened? Was there a fight? I knew this was a mistake. Who got hurt? Was he Jewish?"

"No one was hurt. Everybody is fine. I have good news and bad news."

"So tell us already before I drop dead here in the kitchen! This was your idea, Mr. Segall!" She shot him a stern look. She began to shake her head and rocked in her seat.

"The men did not play poker as I told you, they played another game."

My mother asked, "What game did they play? Gin rummy?"

"No, they did not play gin rummy. They played craps. And each man who came to play, gave me two dollars to be allowed to come into the game," I confessed quickly and with regret. "Here is $428 that we collected for the use of the basement plus some Cokes and some beer I got from the corner store."

My mother looked at me, puzzled. "What is a craps game?"

She turned to Philip. He also didn't know. The folks took the money and gave me the forty dollars I had gotten in tips. It seemed that the money we earned made up for the fib, but I was sorry I did that.

"If you sold bottles and bottles of drinks, do you think the men would also like something to eat?" she suggested.

I could not believe my ears. Momma wanted a piece of the action.

"What's your idea?" I asked.

"A few weeks ago I was looking downstairs for an old ironing board and found an old electric stove in the basement. If it works, we can boil a large pot of water and cook about two dozen frankfurters with some rolls on the side, and mustard, and napkins, and sell them for fifty cents each. What do you think"? A wave of love came over me. Not only did Momma approve of the venture, she was thinking of a way to improve it.

"I think it is a good idea, but I will ask Funzie."

"Who is Funzie?"

"He is the boss of the game."

"Believe me, he will love the idea. What man can stand around and play crabs—what do you call it?"

"Craps."

"Play karps from two to six and not get hungry. It is not possible."

Funzie had a smile from ear to ear when I told him of Momma's idea to sell hot dogs at his 'crabs' game. He told me to buy the kosher specials and charge two dollars each. He knew that when people gambled, money was never an issue.

"Don't buy two dozen, buy four dozen," he said. "The guys will love it. They will think they are in Las Vegas."

The next Sunday we sold eight cases of beer, four cases of Cokes and seven dozen hot dog specials. I was exhausted from all the running around, even though Funzie brought another kid, his nephew Benny, to help me.

# A Life of Risks Taken

"Your Momma is some smart girl," he said. "I see where you get your smarts from."

The craps games went on every Sunday for months.

We were getting rich, earning five hundred to seven hundred dollars every weekend. My stepfather, Philip, sold his laundry truck and bought a beautiful brand new red Ford station wagon. During the week he had signs on both windows that read, "Erasmus Laundry." Every Friday, he would go to the gas station and have the car washed for the weekend. He took the signs down when he and Momma visited friends, and it appeared like it was just a family car.

At the game everyone was always polite. There was never an argument or a fight.

"Hey kid, gimme a dog and a Coke."

"Right away, Allie.'

"Thanks, buddy. How much?"

"Three bucks."

Here's a finsky, gimme a buck change."

Looking around the room, I had noticed two tough-looking men in their forties, who were helping Funzie: Punchie Paulie, a former prize fighter with a flattened nose and bleary eyes, and Vinnie the Vig, who had a tobacco shop in Hoboken. Vinnie, in particular, took a liking to me.

One Saturday afternoon, Funzie asked me to go to Hoboken to Vinnie's shop and pick something up for him. He gave me directions and ten dollars for fare and lunch. The tobacco store was amazing. In the front all you could see was cigarettes, cigars, pipes, lighters, ash trays and anything that had to do with smoking. In the back, a sliding door opened to a huge room filled with leather lounges, a bar, two craps tables, three poker tables, and four black jack tables. There was a windowed office, like a teller's window, where players exchanged bills for playing chips.

Vinnie showed me to another room beyond the casino, where there were several huge humidors where he kept all the Havana cigars. He put three cigar boxes into a shopping bag, which I was to bring to Funzie. Funzie smoked Monte Cristo. They were the best you could get from Havana.

Vinnie asked me to sit down. "Margarita!" he called out. A beautiful young girl walked in and greeted him, "Yes, Grandpa?"

"You wanna a drink, kid?" he asked.

"Water or a Coke works for me." He offered me a pack of Newport cigarettes. I took it, opened the package and lit up. I took a deep drag and exhaled with relief.

Margarita brought a Coke for me and a glass of wine for Vinnie.

"You're Jewish, ain't ya, kid?

"I am, but we are not religious."

"You should be more religious. It's good for you. The reason Funzie asked you to do him this favor is because you're a Jew boy. They are always smart and they keep their mouths shut."

I never heard anyone speak like this. I had no a clue what being Jewish had to do with running an errand.

# A Life of Risks Taken

"Running that craps game is a dream come true for you. If you work hard you will be very rich someday. We always take care of our own."

What was this guy talking about? Funzie is running the craps game. I am just renting my parent's basement.

"You are an unplanned, no overhead money maker for a great organization. It's quiet, no one knows about it, and best of all, no one knows who you are. It works. Using your mom and dad's basement was an act of genius."

I still did not know what this man was talking about. My act of genius was trying to earn an extra fifty dollars a week for the folks. It would make their life easier. That we were making more was just luck.

I took the shopping bag with the three boxes of Havana cigars, thanked Vinnie for the cigarettes and the Coke, and boarded the bus from Hoboken to the Thirty-fourth Street station in Manhattan. I hopped on the New Lots Avenue subway to Utica Avenue. From there I took the trolley to Funzie's place on Clarkson Avenue.

Funzie was on the phone when I walked into the pool hall. He held up his hand for me to wait. He got off the phone and waved me into his private office.

I gave him the shopping bag. He took out the three cigar boxes, each wrapped in white paper with a white string holding them together. He took a pocket knife from his jacket, clicked the blade out and cut the strings. The three boxes read Corona/Corona cigars. I wondered when he had switched from Monte Cristo. With the knife he pried open the three lids. He opened the top wrapping paper and beneath were stacks of hundred dollar bills.

Each box must have had at least five thousand dollars. I could not believe it. I had walked through the subway with fifteen thousand dollars.

Standing right in front of me, Funzie opened the safe behind a photo of Betty Grable. He put all the cash into the safe, shut the door and spun the dials. He looked at me, went into his pocket and pulled out a huge wad of bills tightly tied with a large rubber band. He peeled off five twenties and gave them to me.

I was stunned. I said nothing. The bills lay in my hand.

"What is this for?" I asked.

"That is for being a smart and honest Jewish boy. I knew I could trust ya."

What is this Jew boy shit? What is it with these guys? Goyim, goyim, I could never understand them.

No one ever told me who Vinnie or Paulie were, but I soon began to understand the roles they played in the gambling scenario. Paulie was there to ensure the house cut of the game for the syndicate. Vinnie collected interest on the loans he made to some of the players in the game. They misinterpreted my silence as smart and shrewd behavior. They did not understand that I was just being young and ignorant.

Punchy would come over to me and say in a very quiet and polite voice, "Hey kid, gimme a dog and a Coke." He was no different than the other guys. I did what he asked. He took three dollars from his pocket to pay me.

I told him it was my treat.

"Nuttin doin', kid, we all woikin' for a livin' here.

You get yours, and I get mine." Vinnie was the same way. He paid for whatever he ate or drank.

On my regular job at Rose Brothers, they always saw me as a kid. Here at the craps game the players who came in on a regular basis knew I was young, but there was a level of respect. They imagined that I was part of a quartet.

One fateful Sunday, the police came to the basement.

Funzie took them aside, whispered something to them and they went away. I never heard what he said and I did not care. My hand was shaking, stuffed into my pocket, fingering the money I had collected.

I didn't understand who sent the police. I did not know what they wanted. But for the first time I was frightened. The two policemen had been staring at me, like they were trying to memorize my face. I told Funzie what I was feeling.

He said, "Don't worry. Those guys are on the payroll. Trust me, they think you are important. They know me. They know Vinnie and Paulie. They know we are just working men. You're a new face, and young. You are a puzzle to them. You could be the son or nephew of someone big. They are not going to mess with you."

Momma heard of the police incident and the craps games ended. The mob, Funzie, Vinnie and Paulie did not know it was Momma who was the Boss of Bosses. She alone was Capo di Tutti in our family. Our sudden riches had to disappear. Philip and I pleaded with her, but she was adamant. And she was right. It was the wrong place for me to be.

As my poppa always advised, "You never know when

a good run is going to end. Save your money, it will keep you safe." After clearing out my savings account when he died, I now had $450 in the bank.

# Chapter 16

ഔര

**My First Real Paying Job**

I left home at six-fifteen each morning, arriving at my stock clerk job at the Rose Brothers Men's Clothing Company at seven-thirty. I would get coffee for Handwerger and go to my position. I finished at five p.m., a half hour later than the rest of the staff. After work, I took the subway uptown to City College where I had enrolled in three courses: Accounting, English Literature, and Marketing. It was not easy going to work every day and going to school every night. I did my homework on the subway and more than once fell asleep on the train. I was awakened by the conductor at the last stop. With a book on my lap, my head hanging from neck and shoulders, eyes shut tight, I felt a nudge on my shoulder. It did not wake me. A second stronger push got my attention. Finally,

"Wake up young man. You are at the last stop. I cannot leave you in this car—it is too dangerous," he shouted into my ear.

I did not know where I was, or what time it was. I eked out an "Oh shit, I missed my stop again."

"You will have to go up the stairs to the other side to get back to—Utica Avenue?" he questioned.

"How did you know my stop?"

"I have seen you before, dashing off the train in a last desperate effort not to miss your station. And I have—let me see—awakened you at least three other times at this last stop."

ഇരു

I was on the job about four months when a deranged-looking red-haired man came charging into the stock room screaming for a special trouser style number in a size thirty-six waist.

I was on a ladder a few aisles away. I jumped swiftly from my rung and dashed to the location of the style the lunatic was yelling for.

I whipped out three sizes, just in case I may have misunderstood him. I hustled at full speed to the chubby, red-haired maniac and placed the pants into his hand. He looked at all three and threw two back in my face. Then, he left, gone as quickly as he had come.

A month passed after this frightening episode. Handwerger called me into his office first thing on a Monday morning.

Handwerger did not just say, "Seymour, please see me in my office as soon as possible." That was not his style. He bellowed. The sound of his voice was like a gorilla beating his chest after a victorious battle. It was loud and ominous, and never ceased to scare me half to death.

At the top of his lungs, over the loudspeaker he shouted, "Seymour! Get your goddamn lazy ass into my office this second!"

"Oh my God, I'm going to be fired! Please, please, don't fire me." I whispered to myself.

I was trembling as I ran into Handwerger's office.

"Yes, sir?"

"Don't 'yes, sir' me, you ass-kissing piece of shit! Get your brown nose upstairs to the seventh floor. Mr. Silverstein wants to talk with you."

I stammered, "Wha—what could he want?"

"He is probably going to fire your ass for bringing him the wrong pants last month."

Oh, no, oh, no. I went into the locker room and washed my face and combed my hair. I wish I had worn a better shirt. No, the shabby shirt was better. It made me look poor. Maybe he would have sympathy.

Up in the showroom, Silverstein sat me down and asked me my age. He wanted to know about my family, my schooling, where I lived, what I liked to do, if could I drive a car. I was puzzled. Finally, he explained that he was leaving on a three-to-four week business trip, and he needed a young man to accompany him and help with samples, swatches, luggage, appointments, writing orders, mailing orders. There would be no overtime, no extra salary. Was I interested?

Was I interested? You bet I was! Traveling to Harrisburg, Pottsville, Cincinnati, Cleveland, Toledo, Columbus, Chicago, South Bend—I was going to see the world! I was thrilled.

What I learned from working with Poppa was that having a good teacher in business is more important than a good salary. Working closely, side by side, with the best of the best is more important than an extra five hundred dollars a week on your paycheck. On second thought, make it better than two hundred a week in your paycheck.

"You know, Mr. Handwerger recommended you. He said you're a hardworking, no-nonsense young man."

I sat there stunned by the revelation.

Son of a bitch, that fat prick, really likes me. I guess his bark is stronger than his bite.

I responded quietly, "I'm going to have to get permission from my mother. My dad died about eight months ago. I'm the breadwinner, the head of the family, sort of."

"Do that. Call me at home tonight."

Jack gave me his phone number. I could not admit that we did not have a telephone.

That evening, at home, I sat down with Momma and told her the whole story of how my foreman had recommended me for a new job in the company. Momma was no fool. She knew how excited I was to get this opportunity.

Momma said, "You'll have to leave night school. Is that what you really want to do?

"Momma," I answered, "I know school is important. This is an important break and it is a chance I must take. If in one year it does not work out, I can always go back to school."

Momma was strong. She heard my case, but she insisted on meeting Mr. Silverstein.

I went downstairs to the candy store and made the call. I told Mr. Silverstein that my mother wanted to meet him.

He said, "I understand. I have two children myself. Let me speak to her."

# A Life of Risks Taken

"We don't have a phone in our apartment," I said quietly. "I'm calling you from a candy store across the street. Would you come here to our apartment after work?"

Thankfully, Silverstein agreed.

The next day, we drove in his car to my apartment. It was a cordial meeting. Momma and Mr. Silverstein spoke for about ten minutes and my mother agreed to let me go. Silverstein gave my mother his business card and home phone number. Momma and I looked at each other. She smiled.

"You be careful on this business trip. We all depend on you now."

"I know, Momma, I know."

# Chapter 17

ಬಂಡ

**My Mentor**

Jack Silverstein was an unusual man. He was five foot seven inches tall, yet I thought he was a giant when I first met him. He never smiled. He always kept a non-lit cigar to his lips. He never smoked. He only chewed it. He was consumed by his job and his business. He added many lifelong touches to my early business education, continuing where Poppa had left off.

Jack's sales approach was brilliant. He arranged his sales meetings only with chief executives of companies—he made his sales pitch to "the people who pulled the trigger." To me he was fearless.

He had the ability to turn a small order into a large order, a huge order into something spectacular. As he showed our collection, I watched him as the buyer turned him down on a specific style or color, time and again. It did not take long for him to convince the customer to place the order with our firm by extolling the virtues of Rose Brothers, the best men's clothing company in the country. He consistently took business from our competitors.

# A Life of Risks Taken

The word "no" was not in his vocabulary. He never heard it. When he showed a sample to a customer and the client waved it off with a sign of dismissal, Jack quietly put the sample aside and continued with his presentation. A few minutes later, he would show the exact same sample again and finally the buyer would say, "Okay, okay, Jack give me two dozen of those."

A smile and a wink of success to me followed.

This style of salesmanship takes a special talent, extraordinary memory, and careful planning. You need confidence in your product or service, as well as excellent people skills. Jack's best attribute was his charm. All the customers loved him. He became their friend.

When the business meeting was over, we would return to our hotel, I would write up the orders and get them ready for mailing to our New York Office. In the evening, it was dinner with the customer—drinks, salty stories, and laughter. The talk was always about women, families, and the trends in business. I smiled. Poppa was exactly the same way.

This was the man who laid the foundation for my sales education and my entrepreneurial approach to business. Jack Silverstein instilled in me the concept that an entrepreneur is, without a doubt, "a lunatic with a vision." I have often felt that way about myself, being just slightly insane pushing myself to the limit.

Jack's mentoring and my father's training were the two most fortunate learning experiences of my life. Although Poppa affectionately passed his skills on to me with a sense of pride, Jack's schooling, only occasionally awarded me words of support. He offered mostly tough lectures of admonishment. In the end, they made me stronger, hardening my sense of security. I could listen to his ranting about a minor error without a tremor. I was always confident that I was the best man for the job.

Serious errors were different.

An incident in Harrisburg, Pennsylvania, showing the new fall collection of men's suits and sports jackets to a clothing store called Doutrich's, was a horror for me, and a turning point in my relationship with Jack. At the time, I thought it was the end.

Doutrich's was one of fifty-five hundred independent men's retailers operating in our country during the 1940's thru the 1960's. Those mom-and-pop stores are mostly all gone now, swallowed up by Wal-Mart, Macy's, Kmart, Sears and Target.

Showing our collection at the hotel, Jack turned to me and asked for one of our new style sports jackets. I looked on the rack we had in the room, but the jacket wasn't there. I knew I brought it. I was certain I brought all three new jackets. I remembered placing them on the clothing rack.

Looking at the rack before me, I became dizzy with fear.

Holy shit, this is going to be my death. He will surely kill me. Not with a gun or a knife, but with relentless screaming and name-calling.

"Jack the jackets look like they are not here." I had forgotten the samples, probably left in the New York Showroom.

He glared at me and shouted, "I already have one

asshole. I don't need two!"

Still shrieking at me, in front of the customer, he ordered me to go to the train station at once. I recall not feeling any sense of embarrassment. Fear had immunized me from any sensation whatsoever.

I was married with two children, being fired and not having enough money to support my family is like death.

"Take the next fucking train to New York, get the goddamn jackets and be back first thing in the morning," Jack screamed. "Are you listening to me?"

"Yes, sir," I whispered.

I moved quickly and quietly. I felt inefficient. I couldn't believe I'd ever live down this mistake. I had failed at my job. I boarded an eight p.m. train to Penn Station and crashed down into my seat, the back of my hand crossing my forehead. I welcomed sleep.

I arrived in New York at one o'clock in the morning. The taxi pulled up to our office building on Seventh Avenue and Twenty-Fifth Street at about one-twenty. The night watchman didn't know who I was. Impatiently, I showed him my business card and driver's license plus the key to the office. I strongly urged him that this was a serious emergency and said I had to pick up some samples for one of the owners of the company.

A five dollar bill persuaded him to accompany me to the seventh floor. I calmed down a little as I opened the door to the office. I went to disengage the alarm, but strangely it wasn't on. I entered the showroom and there they were, the three jackets hanging in the sample closet. I rushed for the three samples and turned to leave.

# A Life of Risks Taken

Suddenly, I heard a noise coming from the private showroom, murmuring voices. I wondered if someone had left a radio on, or if someone was working late.

I instructed the watchman to take the jackets downstairs to the lobby and said I would join him there in a few minutes. I quietly walked towards to the private showroom, where now I was sure I heard people speaking. I knocked and simultaneously opened the door. I was surprised and embarrassed to see the company sales manager, Bernie, having sex with Alice, the C.E.O.'s secretary.

I excused myself, closed the door and took the elevator down to the lobby. I went straight to Penn Station and boarded the next train to Harrisburg.

The express train to Pittsburgh departed at five-fifty a.m., with a stop in Harrisburg. I met Jack at the hotel at ten-thirty in the morning. He already had the car. We were going to drive to Pottsville, and then on to Pittsburgh. I didn't change my clothes, wash or brush my teeth. I was still a mess from yesterday's beating.

I chose not to tell Jack what I had seen in the private showroom at the office. What I did tell Jack was my analysis of why the jackets were missing. "I put all the samples we were taking for our trip on our sample rack. One of the salesmen must have taken them off the rack to show to a customer and forgot to put them back on our rack."

Jack looked at me, eyes squinting, and said, "What the hell are you talking about?" He had moved on.

∞∞

# A Life of Risks Taken

Jack and I survived many business trips together. Four years later, in the fall of 1958, we were on the road in Fort Wayne, Indiana. Our customer in that city was a retailer called Patterson-Fletcher, a major department store. When we left the office of the buyer, I noticed Jack was pale as a ghost. He was perspiring. He felt ill and decided, after only four days on the road, to terminate the business trip.

I was frightened as I rushed him to the airport. I suggested he leave his suitcase with me. That way he could get off the plane and go straight home. I asked if he had called Ida, his wife, to meet him at the airport. He had not. It would make her worry unnecessarily, he said. I thought he was making a mistake.

His final words to me as he boarded the plane were, "That's a good idea to leave my luggage with you. You're a good kid."

Wow, that is the first nice thing he has ever said to me.

Before he left, he gave me three hundred dollars for expenses to get home.

As he left to board, he said, "Try to get home as quickly as you can."

"I will," I answered. "Don't worry. I'll be all right. Please take care of yourself."

I sat in the car, concerned for Jack. He looked awful.

I considered my choices. Should I take the sleeper car, relax with a good dinner, and have a comfortable night's sleep, or should I keep the money and take the bus? Then I had another thought.

Jack always said, "No risk, no reward. No guts, no glory." I was twenty-six years old. This was my chance to demonstrate that I was the consummate seller. I could get fired, but that was a gamble I wanted to take. I had done crazier things in my life.

With $360 in my pocket—three hundred of Jack's money and sixty of my own—I thought I had enough money to finish this trip and visit all the customers that we were scheduled to meet. I had a rented car. All the samples were packed. I had everything I needed. I was excited and feeling strong—and nervous too. I was, for the first time in my career, totally and unequivocally in control.

Before I began, I telephoned Ida and told her about Jack.

"I don't want to frighten you, but I think he's very ill," I said.

I suggested she meet him at the airport and gave her his flight number and time of arrival at LaGuardia. She thanked me profusely for not listening to her husband.

We all learned later that Jack was having a heart attack. My decision to call Ida may have saved his life. Ida met him at the airport and quickly drove him to the hospital, where the emergency room doctors immediately attended to him.

Next, I telephoned Sabina and told her what I was doing.

She questioned my decision, but finally said, "Good luck! I know you'll do well."

I drove to Indianapolis, where my first visit was with Mr. Paul Mode, the menswear merchandising vice president at a store called the William H. Block Company. Block's was one of the largest department stores in Indiana, most likely one of the ten largest stores in the country.

# A Life of Risks Taken

A uniformed elderly elevator operator took me to the third floor in an old-fashioned elevator. As I stepped off the lift, I saw that each office was constructed of half window and half oak-paneled base. You could see the people working inside. Large-pillowed, dark brown leather chairs surrounded the waiting area. A huge ashtray filled with cigarette butts lay in the center of a dark oak coffee table. There were three large paintings of businessmen on the wall—C.E.O.s from different periods in the history of the firm. Esquire, Time, Look, and Life magazines were also on the table, as was the Men's Wear weekly newspaper, a publication I had never seen in our New York office.

I found Mr. Mode's office and told his secretary who I was.

I was stunned when I heard Mr. Mode say, "Send him in immediately."

Mode was a man of about forty-five, graying slightly at the sideburns, dressed in a navy striped suit with a vest, a white cuff-linked shirt, and a very clean striped red tie. I wore a gray worsted flannel Rose Brothers suit. We looked each other over and smiled.

"Sit down, Seymour," he beckoned me in. "Welcome to Block's and to Indianapolis."

"Thank you, sir. I am sorry I don't have a business card. However, I do thank you for seeing me without an appointment. I work for Rose Brothers and my boss, Jack Silverstein, took ill on our trip out here. I am pinch hitting for him now."

After a brief chat, I learned that he knew all about our company. At one point, the store had been a major client.

It had purchased thousands of suits from Rose Brothers more than two decades ago.

I told him about myself, my background and the training I had working with Jack over the past eight years. He smiled broadly. He knew Jack and Louis Rose, the founder, very well.

"Well let's see what you have learned. Show us your collection."

He instructed me to bring all my samples up to his office. My heart was pounding. My first true on-the-road solo selling experience—and it was with one of the largest department stores in the United States, a store that Rose Brothers had not done business with since the end of World War II!

When I arrived at his office with my samples, Mode apologized and told me he had changed his mind. He had reserved the conference room on the fifth floor and had invited his sportswear buyer to join us. He instructed his secretary to help me with the samples and show me to the conference room.

I did exactly what I would do if Jack were with me. Neatly I laid out the swatches of our summer suits in price lines, followed by sports jackets, slacks, and some shorts. It was a beautiful sight.

Ten minutes later, Mode and three other people came in together. They were all grown men of about thirty-five or forty. Each one gave me his business card. A flood of nervousness washed over me.

"I'm so sorry, I don't have a card yet," I said. "I just got this job yesterday."

# A Life of Risks Taken

They all smiled and congratulated me and wished me good luck.

I said, "If we do business this morning, that, gentlemen, will be the best luck a new salesman can have."

They laughed and encouraged me to relax. One of Mode's associates asked if I wanted a cup of coffee.

I said, "A double Scotch would be better—if I drank."

Their laughter put me at ease. I began to show them our summer suit collection. This was followed by sport jackets, slacks and finally our white dinner jackets.

Three-and-a-half hours later, I had written the second largest order the Rose Brothers Company had ever received. I thanked Mr. Mode and his colleagues. My head was swimming. I was not sure what I had on all those sheets of paper.

As I left, Mode said, "Seymour, it's almost one, perhaps you could hang around for a while and join us for lunch?"

"Thank you, but my plan is to get moving on to South Bend. It's about three hours away."

Mode smiled through tight lips. He had not expected a refusal. I should have accepted his invitation, but I was young and chomping at the bit for the next order. I had much to learn.

"You're going to be a very successful young man," Mr. Mode said, shaking my hand. "You know your product, you understand retail and you've been most accommodating. Thank you. Next time you come to visit, we'll have Chivas Regal for you."

I replied, "No, sir, I won't need a drink. I know I'll be

with friends. Please let me thank you and your team. With this order, I'll be the new wunderkind of Rose Brothers, I assure you."

In a serious tone, Mode said, "Make certain you take extra care of this business you have from us. I'm depending on you." He went on to say, "The number one road to success is Showing Up. The second is Follow Up. You got that?

"Yes, sir."

I took his advice seriously. A thought came to my mind. I remembered something that Jack would do when he had a large order.

I asked Mr. Mode if I could use his phone and call the order in to Meyer Greenberg, the chairman of the company.

"Let's reserve all the piece goods."

"Now that's good thinking," Mode said.

I dialed the number. "Hello. It's Seymour. Is Mr. Greenberg in?"

"Seymour?" Margie said. "Where are you? Everyone is worried. They want to speak to you urgently."

"Is Jack all right?"

"Yes, he is. He called yesterday and wanted to know if you had returned home yet."

"Thanks, Margie, I'm okay. Please put Mr. Greenberg on."

I could hear Margie telling the big boss that I was on the phone and I wanted to speak to him.

As he approached the phone, I heard him say, "Vere is dat little shit calling from?"

"Hello, Mr. Greenberg, how are you?"

"Vere da fuck are you?"

"I just finished showing the line to Paul Mode at Block's."

"Dat no good son of a bitch! Vee gave him so many goods during the war and when it was over, he dropped us like a fuckin' hot potato!"

"Mr. Greenberg, that was so nice of you to say. Mr. Mode suggested I call in the order so you can reserve the piece goods."

"Vot kind of an order?"

"Yes, sir, do you have pencil and paper? Okay. The Airgora suits, Style 2334, 250 suits, and Style 2336, 250 suits."

On and on, until the order came to 2,500 suits, 3,000 pairs of pants, 750 pairs of dress shorts, 1,500 white dinner jackets, and, finally, 800 summer sports jackets. The total was more than $150,000. In today's money, in excess of $1,000,000.

There was silence over the line.

"Mr. Greenberg?"

"You sold him fifteen hundred white dinner jackets. Right? Did you sell him the tuxedo pants to go with the white dinner jackets? You are such a schmuck, how I keep you in dis company is impossible to think about.

"I will look into it, sir."

"Mr. Mode, the boss said I forgot to write the black tuxedo pants for the white jackets."

"That sly, old Jewish fox. Put in fifteen hundred pairs of tux pants."

"Did that goddamn anti-Semite piece of shit say something about being Jewish?"

"Yes, sir."

"Tell him to go fuck himself!"

"I will do that before I leave, Mr. Greenberg. Good-bye, sir. And thank you very much."

I hung up.

Unbeknownst to me at the time, Mr. Mode had been having problems with our competitor, the Palm Beach Company. He was eliminating their clothing from the store. Timing is a good thing. If I had not gone there, perhaps another company might have gotten the order. Luck is good. Smart is better. And I remembered for the rest of my career, Show up and Follow up. That was a very important lesson.

The rest of the trip was equally successful. In store after store, I increased the previous orders that Jack had taken by thirty percent or more. The reason for that was that Jack only showed the customer what was bought the previous year. It's not a bad way to sell, because it saves time and cuts to the chase, but I didn't know any better. I couldn't understand the previous year's purchase codes on the history cards. I let the buyer see everything we produced.

With each day of sales, I became more and more confident.

My most immediate problem was, running out of money. That was a telephone call I did not want to make. But make it I did.

"Hello, Mr. Greenberg. This is Seymour."

"Vere da fuck are you?" he screamed into the phone.

"I'm in Detroit at Benson and Rixon."

"Those sons of bitches. They used to be a big customer, but they got rich during the war. And they don't give a fuck for anyone."

"I am with them now, sir. I sold them 800 suits, 250 summer jackets, and 600 pairs of trousers."

"Hmmm." Greenberg was momentarily silent. "So vot da hell do you vant?"

"I need some money. I only have twenty dollars left."

"How much do you need?"

"I need $250."

"You crazy little putz, vot do you tink, I am made of money? You must tink I am a Rockefeller."

"That is very nice of you, Mr. Greenberg. Mr. Benson is standing next to me. He would like to speak to you."

"Hello, Meyer, you old son of a bitch. This kid is terrific. I'd like to steal him from you. I'm going to give him the $250. You can have your bookkeeper send me a check. Good. You're absolutely right. It is good to be back with your company again, Meyer. Take care. I'll see you when we come to New York. Bye."

Upon my return one week later, everyone, including Jack and his partners, congratulated me.

Greenberg called me into his office, a huge Havana cigar in his teeth.

"Sit down, my boy. I vant to have a void wid you."

"Yes, sir," I said as I stood before him at his desk.

"How old are you?"

"Twenty-six."

"Sit," he commanded. "Ven I vas your age, I vas just like you. I could kill a lion with my bare hands." He shook his head. "It was not easy for me, like it is for you. Louis Rose vas my uncle, he should rest in pieces. He vas a killa."

*You believe working for you and your partners is easy? How could you think that? Every person here is scared to death.*

"Ven I came off the road and gave him a big order, it vas never enough. He vas tough. You, my boychik, did a good job and everyone is proud of you, and you will make a lot of money here. But, and dat is a big but, you must be honest and always tell the truth. Jack told me he gave you $300, and then you called me to get another $250. What did you do with all that money?"

I could not believe my ears. He was questioning my expenses. I spent $550 in just shy of three weeks of traveling. Most of the time I ate two meals a day. Lunch very often was a Hershey's candy bar. In Detroit and Chicago, I slept at the Y.M.C.A. for two dollars a night. In the Chicago Y I bunked with a two hundred and fifty pound man who snored like a gorilla.

Moreover, this was the first time I was on the road alone, and I had brought back the largest advance sale in the history of the company!

 Prick.

"Mr. Greenberg, I was very careful with the money. I spent sixty dollars of my own money, but I never put in an expense slip for it."

A huge puff of smoke came from his lips.

I continued, "I was actually thinking about the expenses. I came up with a plan. Here is my proposal."

# A Life of Risks Taken

Greenberg leaned back in his huge leather seat, an unfamiliar smile on his face. I could tell he was toying with me, but I didn't care. I was in my zone, about to give a sales pitch he'd never heard.

"Give me a two percent commission on all the sales I brought in during this trip and deduct my expenses, and we will be even. You owe me $8,460."

Greenberg burst out laughing. He laughed so loud, he started to choke.

I grabbed a silver pitcher of water from his desk, poured a glassful and handed it to him. He tried to drink, but he could not stop laughing.

"How da fuck did you come up wid such a number? You must be a *meshuggener*, a real lunatic."

"If you don't mind, sir, I must confess to you..." Now came the time to shoot craps with the boss. I was improvising, but I was not afraid.

"You are going to tell me what you really did with all that cash, you little *gonif*."

"I'm not a thief! I'm an honest person, and I loved selling and getting orders. I had the best time of my life! I enjoyed speaking to you on the phone and reading off the quantities. Meeting customers made feel so happy. The truth is I don't want a commission. I don't want any money. I just want you to let me go anywhere in the country and sell. Money is not my goal. Being the best salesman in this company is my dream. Let me do that and I'll be a happy person."

Greenberg's eyes narrowed, a half smile exited his tightened lips. The smile grew into a grin, and he laughed again. He reached into his pocket, pulled out a huge wad of bills tied with a rubber band. He peeled off four twenties and placed them on the desk. "Here is your sixty dollars of your own money that you spent and an extra *tsvantsik*"—twenty—"for yourself. Take your wife to dinner."

At twenty-six years old, I possessed the instincts to make a good presentation. I knew how greedy Greenberg was. He hated to part with money. His idea of a raise in salary was four dollars a week. And he felt generous doing that. The fact that he gave me all that money right out of his pocket made me the original miracle worker.

He stood up, came from behind his desk and put his hand on my shoulder so I couldn't budge from that position. Then he passed a huge blast of wind. There was no escape. I held my breath.

"I am going to give you a thirty, I mean, a twenty-five-dollar-a-week raise. But you must promise me not to tell anyone. And one more thing, if you hear of anything bad that anyone is doing, you tell me—even if it's Mr. Silverstein."

*Jack is your partner, you don't even trust him. Who do you trust?*

I gasped for air as I stood up from my seat. A hint of the aroma reached me, making me cough. But I was smiling. Twenty-five dollars a week was not a raise in salary—it was a conquest. Greenberg liked me because I told him I did not want money. All I wanted was to become the best seller in the company.

The phone rang and he waved me off. I started to leave and then dashed back to his desk. I scooped up the eighty dollars that lay there and crushed the bills into my pocket. I couldn't believe what had just happened. This tough old guy was not so tough.

Two weeks went by and I didn't see the new money in my paycheck. I went into his office.

"Vot da hell do you vant now?"

I reminded him of his promise.

"I don't believe it," he shouted. "I told that moron Manny the same day we spoke. How much did I say you would get?"

"You started to say thirty dollars a week and then you switched to twenty-five dollars a week."

He picked up the phone and dialed, "Manny, didn't I tell you about the kid that was on the road with Jack? He wants the boy to get thirty dollars a week more. Start the first of next month."

That was two weeks away. He had saved four weeks' pay by his manipulative procrastination. The comptroller, Manny Wasserstraum, told me that the boss never said anything to him about my increase.

Nonetheless, we both won. I got my raise. In those days it was serious money.

Jack invited me into his office and asked me to sit down.

"I'm very proud of you. You did a good job, and Greenberg told me about your raise. I want you to know I was upset that you didn't do what I told you to do. You were supposed to return home and you didn't. Why?"

" 'No risk, no reward. No guts, no glory.'"

He smiled, "You're a natural, but I want you to

175

remember I taught you everything you know. What I didn't teach you, is everything I know."

I grinned. Would I ever know everything that went through his head? I thought not.

Jack told me that he got several telephone calls from our customers asking him how he was feeling.

"They also told me that I taught you well. I know I was harsh with you at times, but I knew you could to take it. My partners and I have very big plans for you in the future. Greenberg thinks that you have courage. He said you were a kid from the old school."

*Maybe, just maybe, they are planning a partnership.*

Jack continued, "What was the key to getting so much business? It's been a difficult time. You ran against the flow of what our other salesmen are doing, including the sales manager."

Poor Jack didn't have a clue what a loser Bernie was.

"Wow!" I said.

"So, what did you do?" asked Jack

I had rehearsed this conversation in my head many times. I knew exactly what I was going to say.

"Jack, it was all you. You are loved and respected by every customer you call on. They admire you, and they feel that you are their friend." It was the truth.

He smiled the best smile I ever saw, yellow teeth and all. "That's nice to hear."

"Each and every account I saw, I told them that Jack was counting on their friendship in this difficult time with his health. I was only your messenger. They had known me over the years. I reminded them that I had always been, and remained, your assistant."

# A Life of Risks Taken

Jack smiled and said he knew it would be something like that. "I knew you couldn't be that good," he said.

He could think or say whatever he wanted, but that sales trip taught me something important: I was better than I thought. My self-esteem blossomed. I was, at last, confident that I could always earn a good living for my family.

From that day forward, Jack's attitude toward me totally changed. It was a 180-degree turn around. No shouting, no calling me asshole. Our relationship became quiet and respectful. All the important sales tasks for the company kept coming my way. Jack knew that he was good, but he also knew that I was going to be better. He believed that if the pupil did not do better than the teacher, the world would go backwards. He lived all his life with the knowledge that Louis Rose, the founder of the company, was a great seller. Jack was his assistant and ultimately emerged as the top salesperson in the company. He knew what would come next.

# Chapter 18

ಶೋಗ

## Crisis

My sudden success, and my bursting in on his late night escapade, made my relationship with Bernie, the sales manager, difficult. Two years had passed since I discovered Bernie and Alice. For me it was almost forgotten, but for him, every time he saw me, he saw the moment that I walked in on him in the private showroom. To say he disliked me was a given. The truth was he also feared me. I was the new fair-haired boy of the firm, and he was determined to stick it to me every chance he got.

I took little notice. I was moving quickly. I had been assigned all the firm's fix-it sales jobs throughout the country. I was asked to help seasoned salesmen in their territories when they were ill or could not break into a store that Greenberg wanted. When Greenberg wanted something, he got it. Almost every time a problem came up, he called on me—his new *boychik*—to fix it.

As well as being the Mr. Fix-It-All for the firm, I was accused of being Mr. Know-It-All. Once I heard someone say, "Here comes the ass-kisser." I was also called a wise guy, a big shot, and though I let these things pass, however painful. I was so very young and did not have the experience to handle the success. The truth was at twenty-eight years old, I was a baby, a know-nothing-do-everything baby—an ass-kissing-Mr.-Know-It-All-wise-guy kid.

The wake up call came soon enough.

I started on the road early each Monday morning, visiting my customers in New Jersey, Pennsylvania, West Virginia, and occasionally in Connecticut. Typically, I'd written about ten orders by Wednesday afternoon.

One evening, returning to the city, I decided to stop off to see Hong Kong Tailors on Canal Street. They were always open until nine p.m.

It was about six p.m when Mr. Yu acknowledged me with his usual bow. His wife offered me a cup of tea and we all sat. Our conversation was warm. He politely asked about my wife and my two daughters. I asked about his son, who was attending Princeton.

"Jason is doing very well." She nodded.

I asked Mr. Yu, "How is your business this month?" He shook his head from side to side. His closed her eyes and bowed her head from her neck down. This Asian conversation of wordless movements was "It's not bad. It's not great, but okay."

"With your permission I would like to help you," I suggested to Mr. Yu. "I have a wonderful opportunity for you here in New York and for your partners in Hong Kong. Our firm—much to the regret of our boss—has about 1,600 navy blue suits. All small sizes that would be just right for his customers." Mr. Yu exported men's and women's clothing for his small-sized Asian customers in China, Taiwan and Hong Kong.

Mr. Yu's head bowed slightly. His wife once again closed both eyes in consideration. We continued with our tea.

After about ten minutes I suggested, "May I go to my car outside and bring the blue suit in for you to see." He bowed his head in assent.

I returned with the sample. I put the jacket on to show him how it looked and went to the mirror to look at myself. "Looks good, No?"

Mr. Yu bowed his head again. I walked over to Mrs. Yu.

"Nice, isn't it?" She nodded silently, touching the cloth with her thumb and the pointer finger of her right hand.

The only hurdle left was the price. Mr. Yu's silence was his way of negotiating for a better price, though I hadn't offered it yet. Dave Askenase, one of the major partners, asked me to try to sell these suits. Even if I got just the piece goods at cost, he would be happy. That would make the selling price about ten dollars each suit.

"Can you please show me your stock sheet?" Mr. Yu asked.

I went into my briefcase, extracted the sheet and showed it to him. He looked at it with great care. "I can use all the small sizes, but I cannot use sizes thirty-seven and thirty-eight."

# A Life of Risks Taken

*Oh my God, he is going to take all those suits. Here I go again pushing the envelope.*

"Mr. Yu, we have been friends for a long time, let me make you an offer. All the small sizes are $32.50. If you take all the suits, including the size thirty-seven and thirty-eight, I will sell those two sizes to you at twenty-five dollars each. That is a saving of about eight hundred dollars. I think you will have an excellent buy."

He looked at me, thought for a minute and suggested I call him on Friday. I told him I would and I offered to leave the sample for him to look at again. We shook hands and bowed.

"Thank you for the tea, Mrs. Yu. Good night." I knew Mr. Yu would be telephoning his partner that evening in Hong Kong.

When I reached home in Laurelton, Queens, Sabina told me that I looked haggard. I was out of it. She suggested, or should I say she ordered me to take a few days off. For a change, I listened to her. I must have been very tired. Most of the time I never listened to anyone when it came to my business. For me, I was only happy with the next order and the next. It was endless.

While resting at home the following day, I continued to make telephone calls to customers most of the day. On Friday, Mr. Yu confirmed the order, but negotiated the large sizes from $25 to $23.50. I agreed.

Soon after I said goodbye to Mr. Yu, the phone rang again.

"Hello, hello?" No response.

That was strange. I felt my inner voice ping.

# A Life of Risks Taken

As I stepped from the elevator on Monday, the receptionist told me that Meyer B. Greenberg, Dave Askenase, and Jack wanted to see me the minute I arrived. I could not even imagine what they wanted. Perhaps there was a problem and they wanted me to help one of our sales reps with some customers. I went to my desk and put the batch orders I had written into the booking basket.

One of the men working nearby asked, "How did our star do this week?" I knew in my head that the blue suit order was about forty thousand dollars and the other orders were at least seventy thousand.

I whispered to him, "About a hundred and ten give or take."

He rolled his eyes and punched his desk. I continued on to Greenberg's office.

Greenberg had a beautiful oval desk with photos of his wife, his daughter and his grandchildren scattered about. Behind him hung a painting of Louis Rose, his uncle and the founder of the company. A huge leather couch reclined against the wall with a map of the United States above it. An antique coffee table stood centered between two brown leather chairs. On the table copies of Esquire magazine fanned out in front of a box of Havana cigars.

The three partners sat in a semicircle around the desk. They looked serious, Greenberg with a big cigar and Askenase with a cigarette dangling from his lips.

Greenberg was first up at bat. "Look who has finally arrived—the big shot. Are you such a rich man that you don't have to work anymore, you just stay home and collect money?"

# A Life of Risks Taken

I was caught off guard. What was going on here?

Askenase delivered the second blast. "Your presence in the company has been hurting the morale of the sales staff. You think you're the cock of the walk, and we're told that you're a wise guy." Wise guy was not new, but "cock of the walk" surprised me.

Are they planning to fire me? No, they're not planning to fire me—they are firing me.

I couldn't believe what was happening. Smoke rose all around us. The office reeked of tobacco. Jack remained silent.

Who in the company would say I was a prima donna? Who would say I was not working? Not Larry, our New England salesman. I helped him in his territory when he was ill and refused to take any part of his commissions. Not Mr. Barnett, our senior salesman. Aaron Barnett was a mentor. Not anyone in the company would bad mouth me, with the exception of Bernie, Greenberg's nephew and a royal prick.

I stood frozen and silent. If I were going to be fired, it would not be without a fight. I was twenty-eight years old. This kid shit was over. These bastards were not going to intimidate me when I had a briefcase filled with orders lying on my desk. I was in a rage. "For someone to say I am not working, that is a fucking lie!"

"We don't like that kind of language around here," Greenberg said. Fuck and cocksucker were Greenberg's favorite words.

I began shouting. I knew everyone in the outer office could hear my voice. I turned my back on them and walked quickly to the door.

# A Life of Risks Taken

As I walked out, Greenberg shouted, "Don't you walk out on us, we are not finished with you yet, you little shit." He often called me "little shit" when he was angry. Now the time had come to tell him that I was not a "little shit," but "big shit."

I did not respond. I went to my desk and pulled out the eleven large orders that I had written during the week, plus the one from Mr. Yu that I had taken over the phone on Friday.

When I returned two minutes later, I said, "You can tell your nephew Bernie that he is a fucking liar and an asshole. He has started a war with the wrong person. I will expose him as the putz he really is."

I knew Bernie could hear me. Everyone could.

"I have worked hard for this company every damn fucking day of my life, from the first day I arrived as a stock clerk. You want to know how much I don't work. Let me show you."

I held up in the air the eleven orders. "Here is a bunch of orders—they total about $120,000, including 1,600 closeout suits that I got regular price for. You, Dave, said I could sell them at cost."

I dropped the orders in front of Greenberg on his desk. My face was red hot, my heart pumping. I had nothing to lose. I was about to put all my cards on the table and take my best shot. Win or lose, I took their dare.

"Meyer," I shouted. I had never called Mr. Greenberg by his first name. Only Dave Askenase called him by his first name. "Your asshole nephew is a low life. He is envious of me and of you. You think he would appreciate what you have done for him. Someday you'll find out the kind of man he really is."

I grabbed the orders off Greenberg's desk and began to walk out with them.

"Vere are you going vid doze orders?" he demanded.

"I am going to burn them," I shouted back.

Jack moved from his seat with athletic speed and pulled the orders from under my arm. "Stop being an asshole," he said through gritted yellow teeth.

He had not called me an asshole in more than a year.

He must still like me.

Greenberg started laughing. He hadn't heard what I had said about his nephew. Only the orders were important.

"This kid is meshuga! But he is a seller from the old school. Sit down in that seat," he commanded, pointing to one of the leather chairs.

"I vant to see those fuckin' orders."

Jack handed them over. Greenberg looked at them and nodded. He leaned over to Askenase and pointed to the sixteen hundred closeout suits I sold, which I knew had been a thorn in their sides for a long time.

"I see you sold all those goddamn old blue suits and at regular price." He looked up at me. He was not angry, he was proud of me. "Did you know we have about three hundred sport jackets in those small sizes as well?" I made no comment.

"I took that suit order over the phone on Friday from home. I had gone to his store on Canal Street on Wednesday night. I worked with the buyer until ten and then drove home. That's how much I'm not working." It hadn't really been that late, but it felt the moment to embellish.

"Stop shouting, please. Mr. Greenberg is still the chairman. Have some respect." Jack winked at me. "What were you doing home on Friday?"

"I was resting from overwork. Unlike you and your partners, I like to get laid once in a while."

All three laughed. I'd never seen that before. No one said anything for a few moments.

"Only one person could have said these dreadful things about me," I said. "That's Bernie, our no-sales-tomorrow-or-yesterday sales manager, who earns $25,000 a year while I, one of the largest sales producers in the company, second only to you, Mr. Askenase, and to you, Jack…"

Both nodded in agreement.

" …I earn only $12,000 a year busting my balls."

I really earned $15,500, but I thought they would never know the difference.

I continued, "And do you know why your nephew is not producing as he should? You should ask him."

My face was cooling down. I was in control of this meeting. They had been trying to fire me, now they were trying to figure out how to pacify me. Greenberg got up from behind his desk. He placed his cigar into a large crystal ashtray. He walked over to me and looked down. I looked up.

In his soft, fatherly voice, Greenberg said, "Seymour my *boychik*, if you need a few days off, all you have to do is ask me or Dave or Jack. We're not tyrants."

# A Life of Risks Taken

I wondered if he knew that the entire staff worked in fear each and every day.

"When I vas your age and Louis vas the boss, ve vorked six days a veek. Sometimes a half day on Sunday. A day off was unheard of. Uncle Louis used to have a joke," Greenberg said. "If you don't come in on Saturday, don't bother to come in on Sunday."

Once again he placed his hand on my shoulder, and as was his custom, he farted. I could have fainted. I almost burst out laughing.

Jack shut his eyes and grimaced.

Perhaps I was the cock of the walk. And true, maybe I did act like a big shot. Maybe I was a little arrogant. But I was always kind and polite to everyone. More important, I was a selling fool. I had become an addict. I was never satisfied by the orders I took. I wanted the next and the next. It was an endless parade of desire. Selling was my marijuana. Taking orders was my cocaine. I needed my fix every day. More than fifty years later, I have not changed.

Jack said, "Do we have anything more to discuss with Seymour?"

Both Greenberg and Askenase shook their heads.

Dave said, "Moving those blue suits was well done, young man, well done."

"What? A compliment from Askenase—unheard in anyone's lifetime."

Finally, I had the upper hand. It was a place I had never been in my entire life. I was twenty-eight years old and felt the power of controlling my own destiny.

I turned to Askenase and Greenberg. "Since today is my last day, I would like to leave on a good note. I would like to have a check for all my commissions and six-weeks severance pay."

Greenberg got up from behind his desk with all the orders in his left hand and he continued to look at them. Once again he put his right hand on my shoulder. I prepared for another fart.

Instead he said, "Jack taught you well, my boychik."

I returned to my desk, dropped into my chair and almost started to cry. I looked down at myself and saw my shirt was soaking wet.

Later that day, Jack called me into his office.

"I saved your ass today. They were set to fire you."

"Why would they fire someone who loves his job and the company, and to top it off, I make money for them? Dave was ready to take ten dollars a suit just to get his piece goods out, I got him $32.50." I looked my mentor in the eyes. "Jack, I have had it. I'm ready to leave today, right now. All I want is my check."

"Stop talking like a shmuck! No one is going to fire you, and you are not going to quit. I'm not going to allow them to do that. Bernie hates you. Can you tell me why?"

"I have no idea why Bernie hates me—maybe because I'm happily married and he is not. I cannot guess. I never did anything to hurt him."

I almost told Jack what I knew about Bernie and Alice, but I decided to keep my mouth shut. For some unknown reason I was thinking that my father never earned the kind of money I was getting.

In the afternoon of that confrontational day, I was sitting in the lunchroom when Alice walked in. She watched me as she crossed the room. Everyone in the company had been looking at me all day, mostly from afar. No one dared to come over to me or speak to me—with the exception of Irwin Askenase, Dave's son. He was a nice kid but frightened of his father.

He sat down next to me and said, "Not to worry. Greenberg likes you, Jack loves you, and my father . . . I'm not sure. I don't even think my father likes me." We both smiled.

I wasn't worried. I knew I wasn't getting fired. But one thing I was absolutely certain about: I'd be out of there sometime soon.

After Irwin left, Alice caught my eye again. We were alone in the lunch room. She whispered to me, "I want to tell you something. The whole office heard every word you said. You're the staff's new hero. No one ever spoke to those three like you did." She looked me in the eyes. "And thank you. You've been very discreet concerning the incident you walked in on. I very much appreciate it."

"It was none of my business," I replied. "But you should know that Bernie is a bad person. He will break your heart."

"He already has." Alice took a last sip of coffee. "And after you walked out of Mr. Greenberg's office, the three of them were laughing. They're all bullies and they respect people who can't be pushed around. They complimented Jack on his good training of you." She shook her head, also laughing.

"I'll tell you something you are never to repeat. Promise me?"

"I promise."

"I sounded strong and on top of my game. Right?"

"Right."

"I was shitting in my pants."

We both laughed.

Another person walked into the room, and the conversation ended. I got up and left.

Three months later, Alice resigned because she was pregnant. One of the other girls in the office went to Greenberg and told him that Bernie was the father. Bernie was dismissed that very day by an angry, screaming uncle.

In January, my bonus was six thousand dollars, an amount equal to more than one third of my annual earnings. It was the first year I earned over twenty thousand dollars.

At twenty-eight, in 1959, I was the highest grossing salesman in the company. Yet, I was still "the kid," and the lowest paid. I knew I had to make a change sometime soon.

# Chapter 19

ജ‍ന

## Making a Move

Harry Friedman, our neighbor in Laurelton, Queens, was a printing broker. He and I drove into Manhattan most mornings in his Cadillac. One morning, I was bragging about my success as a seller. I told Harry that I could sell anything. I asked if he thought I could sell printing. He advised me that selling printing wasn't easy.

"It's not like selling suits. When you make a clothing sale, the item has already been produced. It's ready for the customer to buy. Printing is an altogether different product. You start with nothing, just a blank sheet of paper. If you're lucky you get a print order. Then the work first begins. First it's layout followed by design. Approval by the customer of artwork, mechanicals, blueprints, color keys is essential. This is followed by production which may include color okay on press. It takes serious attention to all the details."

I was not paying attention. All I wanted was to give it a shot. We made a deal. I would moonlight for his company and sell printing orders on a sixty-forty split of the profits. He would get the sixty percent. With two dozen business cards—on which I crossed out his name and wrote mine, I entered the sales world of printing. I knew zero about the graphic arts industry.

As I left he said, "You say you're the best salesman in your firm? Okay. Now it's time to put up or shut up." It reminded me of one summer day, when my brother Earl took me to the Erasmus Hall High School swimming pool. Earl was with his girlfriend at the time. I was ten. We entered the pool area and, being a show off, I jumped right into the pool. Did I know how to swim? Of course not. There was a girl to impress. Bravery and risk go hand-in-hand.

Now here I was, seventeen years later, jumping in with both feet. I continued to work as a clothing salesman and in my free time sold printing.

What I loved most about the printing business was that everyone you met could be a customer. In the first month of my graphics career, I opened sixteen accounts and earned five hundred dollars in commission. I almost doubled that in the second month. I was excited. I was flying!

"Hey, kid," Harry said, "you're doing good, but it's just a living. Show me some real business. Then I'll know you're a great seller."

He never ceased to challenge me.

Four months later, my wife and I went to a resort up in the Catskills which I could now easily afford. At lunch, I met a man who eventually became my lifelong friend, Sam Kreiengold. Sam started by asking me what I did for a living. I told him I was a printing and clothing salesman. He was very interested in my printing sales. Sam owned an old-fashioned letterpress printing shop called Altum Press. I told him all about Harry.

"Why do you want to work for someone else and share your profits?" he asked. "Come to my office, and I'll show you how you can be in your own printing business and keep all the earnings."

The following Monday, Sam helped me give birth to Sabine Press & Advertising.

As my young printing business flourished, I hesitated to move from the company that had been my home for almost a third of my life. I was working two jobs simultaneously, putting in fourteen to fifteen hours a day.

Change is a challenge many people fear more than anything else. I was no exception. I was frightened of failure. Planning my exit was a stressful experience that I hadn't expected. I pondered for three weeks what I was going to say and to whom.

On the eve of making a serious decision, I opened two new printing accounts for my fledgling company— the Sunshine Biscuit and the Silvercup Bread companies. These were two of the largest organizations in their field and both only a few blocks away from each other in Long Island City. I needed help. I hired a bookkeeper and a production clerk. My firm was actually a real company now—a company with a staff of three. Now the time had come to pull the trigger of the next step in life. Jack taught me , 'No risk, no reward, No guts, no glory,' so here I go.

Monday morning, October 11, 1962, I arrived at the Rose Brothers office where everyone greeted me warmly.

I felt like a stranger. I did not belong here anymore.

Could they read my mind? Did they know from somewhere that I was ending everything that I had built during the last twelve years? Was I paranoid? Who cared? The time had come. I was about to say good-bye to $20,000-plus a year.

Confronting Jack Silverstein and Meyer Greenberg felt like walking into a pool of fire. I pinched my fingers to my nose and jumped right in. I strode to Silverstein's office.

His secretary greeted me with her usual, "Good morning, big guy. How's Seymour today?"

I hardly smiled. I asked if Jack was in.

"Yes," she said.

As I had done a thousand times, I walked right into his office.

Jack was alone and working on some production issues. Without picking up his head or missing a beat, he asked me what progress I had made with the Shillito's and Schottenstein's orders. And had I worked with Lazarus in Columbus? These were three of the company's largest accounts—customers that I had cultivated over the years.

"I just returned from Cincinnati and finished with both Shillito's and Schottenstein's," I answered. "I've written up the orders and given them to production. The Lazarus group is still working on their order and advised me that we will be giving us a substantial increase in business." I looked at Jack. "Thanks to my attention to their business," I added. "That is a quote from Bill Hipple, the boss."

He gave me a rare smile.

"So what are your plans for next week?" he asked.

"Next week?" I said nonchalantly, "I will be leaving the company."

There it was on the table. I bit the bullet. I was finally free. I was floating in midair, with no safety net—only my own talent, skills and determination. Was it enough? Only time would tell.

The room was silent. Jack's head stayed down. He continued to look through his papers. I waited a moment or two, then turned around and began walking out.

"Where the fuck are you going?" he demanded.

I wondered what question he was asking. Was I going to the toilet to throw up? Or what company was I going to work for? I gave the answer I thought he wanted.

"I'm going to work for my own company. It's a printing company and in no way will I compete with you."

"What the hell do you know about printing?"

"I know enough to make a living and you taught me to be the best seller anyone could be and I am grateful."

"Is that the appreciation you show, after all the years I invested in you?"

That caught me off guard.

"Are you sure you're doing the right thing? What will it take for you to stay?"

I grimaced. Where was the firm yesterday, or last year, or the year before that? It was a question that came too late and too little.

"Jack," I said in a gentle voice, "it's time for me to move on. I appreciate your gesture, but I want to be on my own."

"Is there anything I can say?"

"Yes," I said. "A kind word, 'good luck, kid' and 'drop by and see us once in a while.' Or even better," I added, "you could offer to give me all of your printing business."

"I don't get involved in that," he answered coldly.

Such an alien response, without feeling. I loved that man, but it was time to get out of the company.

We shook hands. I walked out and went into Greenberg's office. He was truly sorry to learn I was leaving. He wished me good luck and said, "If it doesn't work out, I will always make a place for you."

I said good-bye to all of my colleagues, who were in shock, and it was over. I never returned to the office.

&Oacute;&Ccedil;&Ograve;

A few months later, my wife and I were invited to a former colleague's celebration. Many of the Rose Brothers' salespeople and executives were there. Everyone was pleased to see us and offered congratulations and well wishes for my success.

I asked Ida, Jack's beautiful wife, to dance with me. We quietly moved around the dance floor, and she told me how proud Jack was of my success. Then she told me that no matter how good I was, Jack was still the best.

"Ida, that's not true. I must insist that I'm a much better seller than Jack is."

"How can you say that?"

"If the pupil did not exceed the talent of the teacher, the world would go backwards."

A smile curled up her lips.

"You're right, you're right."

# A Life of Risks Taken

I led her to her seat next to Jack. He touched my hand.

When Jack passed away about eight years later, Ida called me to speak at his funeral. She told me that Jack always spoke about me, even after I left Rose Brothers. I was the son he never had, and he'd been proud of the huge company I built on my own.

Only three people spoke at Jack's funeral: a Rabbi, a relative, and me. I related the real story of Jack, his work ethic, his love for his wife and family. I told everyone how he tutored me, tortured me, helped me and pushed me around. I told them of the first day I met him in the stockroom, and how he went to visit my mother. How he never walked, he only ran, with me, the puppy, chasing behind him. Everyone laughed at the familiar tales.

Later, the whole family gathered around me and asked if I had written my speech. They all wanted a copy, but I didn't have one. I had spoken from the heart.

# Chapter 20

ഇൗങ

### Sabine Press & Advertising

I named Sabine Press & Advertising in honor of my wife Sabina. I had no business strategy or any financial plan. All I knew was how to sell with honesty and thoughtfulness. Starting out, I was more determined than ever to succeed. I put up a brave front to the world, but I was very frightened.

Print customers are everywhere, in all walks of life. There isn't a single individual that does not require some kind of printed product at some point in his or her lifetime—whether it is a letterhead or a business card or an invitation to send to friends and relatives.

I attacked building after building in Manhattan, Long Island City, and Nassau County. From the top floor of each building down to the basement, I climbed flight after flight, walking through each and every company's door. I announced my name to anyone who would speak to me.

Getting a new account was thrilling. Finding a new customer felt as good as sex. I seldom struck out. Usually I ended up with some piece of business and on a good day, many new customers. On a bad day, I wasn't discouraged. On a very good day, I was dissatisfied. I wanted more and more.

Still the reward for my efforts was mostly small-to-medium size print jobs—my only significant customers were Silvercup Bread and Sunshine Biscuit Company. They were the nucleus of the firm—until one fateful day.

A new office building had just been completed on Queens Boulevard. I parked my car, entered the building to find only one tenant in the entire fourth floor. The name on the door was Unicard. Three young men were setting up desks and unpacking furniture, filing cabinets and other office equipment.

I quietly asked who was in charge, and one of them volunteered that he was. I presented my business card. I told him I was a printer and had come by to introduce myself. He was interested in discussing my services and asked me to see him the next morning, a Saturday. I said that I would be there.

Dressed in jeans and a casual shirt, I arrived at eight-thirty a.m. with two containers of coffee, one with milk, the other black, and two danishes. John Roukes said he took his coffee with milk—that was lucky, because I always had mine black.

We sat down in his disorganized office and talked for a while. I learned that he had two children, that he had been married for ten years and now had this new job, which he felt was a great opportunity. I told him all about my life with Sabina, my daughters, my old job and that

# A Life of Risks Taken

Sabine Press was a new business. He told me Unicard was a new credit card company, and they would need a strong supplier of print materials. "I am your man," I replied with confidence.

His first request for pricing that day was for 5,000,000 envelopes, 250,000 four-color letterheads, and 10,000,000 I.B.M. computer cards. We sat for a while, finishing our coffee. He gave me the company's artwork on boards and I assured him I would give him prices by midweek.

I left his office exhilarated and frightened to death. How could I find the suppliers to make all the envelopes and all the punch cards he needed in time?

When I arrived at home I told Sabina I have good news and bad news.

She paled. "Tell me the good news first."

"I got a new customer who has ordered 5,000,000 envelopes, 250,000 four-color letterheads, and 10 million I.B.M. computer cards."

"Okay, so what's the bad news?"

"I got a new customer who ordered 5,000,000 envelopes, 250,000 four-color letterheads, and 10 million I.B.M. computer cards."

We both laughed.

We hugged each other and she opened a split of champagne that had been in the refrigerator for months and we drank to our good fortune. It was 11a.m.

My friend Sam from the print shop gave me some pointers as to where I could place this business. I telephoned I.B.M. to find the card producer. Then I called the vice president of sales of an envelope company about the order I had and asked if he could give me a quote. The very next day this vice president of the U.S. Envelope Company—the largest in New York at the time, came to visit me. I showed him the envelope samples. He took out a pricing chart and in fifteen minutes gave me prices for the envelopes. His pricing sounded good. I had no clue. I also had no credit standing. He said he would need a deposit. I asked if a one thousand dollar deposit would suffice. He said that would be acceptable.

Oy vay! Where am I going to get a thousand dollars?

I called my mother. I asked her to lend me eight hundred dollars. I told her I was able to repay her with interest. But she refused it. The money she lent me became a gift. That was a learning thing. I too never lend money to relatives in need. We give the money as a gift.

The card manufacturer telephoned me with prices and said delivery could be made in ten days. His terms were net thirty days *EOM*—this meant that I was required to pay the bill within thirty days from the end of the month that the invoice was dated.

With a great new customer, suppliers and pricing under my belt, I was prepared to go forward.

I telephoned Mr. Roukes, gave him the prices and advised him that our credit department would require a one-third deposit to begin producing his order, the second third on delivery and the final payment net thirty days after delivery of the merchandise. All future orders would have regular terms of net thirty days.

There was a moment of silence.

John said, "No problem. Pick up the first check

tomorrow. And please bring a written quote with you. I want to get started at once."

The next day, I delivered the quotation, a deposit invoice with the payment schedule and terms.

A check for $65,000 was placed in my hand. I'd never seen such a number in my life. I was absolutely stunned. At home I showed Sabina the check, who stared at it in a daze.

"I hope it doesn't bounce," she said.

About a week later, Roukes called me, and said, "I have bad news."

I almost dropped dead on the spot. I could feel the surge of my heart beating at full speed.

He said he discovered that he didn't have the space to hold all that paper in his storage room. He would like to have it shipped as needed. As space opened up, he would take more of the paper into his warehouse.

I worked out the logistics with both companies, confirming that they had bona fide orders but would have to ship as needed. Then I telephoned John and told him we could meet his needs, but he would have to pay the bill in full, since everything was already produced and in inventory, and there would be an extra charge for shipping. He agreed to the terms and asked me to submit my invoice.

Now I had a ton of money—more than $250,000—and a huge profit. I could barely believe it. Jack's philosophy about taking risks, floated through my mind.

By 1964, Sabine Press and Advertising flourished beyond our expectations. Sabina and I decided to move from Laurelton to Great Neck, Long Island, an affluent community with good schools for our daughters. We purchased a beautiful Pennsylvania Dutch farmhouse. It was built on a huge lot. Our new home had a fireplace, beamed ceilings, four bedrooms, a two car garage and plenty of space for all of us to live comfortably. The house cost $37,500.

On the day of the sale, I telephoned my mother to tell her the good news.

Her first question was, "How much was the house?"

I told her. She asked if I had bought an apartment house. To Mom that amount was astronomical and to me as well.

Three years later in 1967, Chase Manhattan Bank eventually purchased Unicard. The company moved its headquarters to Great Neck, New York—just another lucky break. The Unicard Company was my biggest and most profitable account. The proximity of the new offices to our new home and my good relationships with the staff gave me an inside position to garner new work within Chase Bank.

Eventually, John Roukes left his position. I worked with John's replacement with great ease. Every morning, I would stop by Franklin's office and pick up an envelope with thousands of dollars' worth of business. More than once a month there was an order with a selling price of more than $100,000. I was always careful with my rates. Both Franklin and John trusted me and I never ever wanted to abuse that. I would rather have a customer for ten years with fair and competitive prices, than have a customer for one order with a huge profit.

Franklin and I worked together for close to ten years before he decided to retire at sixty-two years old. A farewell party was arranged for him. Since I was the firm's main supplier at that office, I was asked to be the toastmaster. I had a reputation as a humorous person. I always had a good joke and a smile on my face.

Four limos arrived from midtown Manhattan on the afternoon of the party. The cars were filled with senior executives and the chairman of Chase, David Rockefeller.

Cocktails and hors d'oeuvres were served in an anteroom of the office building, after which everyone entered a conference room that had been converted into a dining room for lunch.

I sat at the head of the table. On my left was Franklin the honoree. On my right sat David Rockefeller.

The room quieted. Everyone was seated as I looked around at the eleven men and a single woman, all in charcoal gray flannel three-button suits. I stood up and, to their astonishment and delight, welcomed each person by name.

Mr. Rockefeller smiled and nodded in appreciation. I told them how honored I was to be the designated speaker of the day. I invited everyone to remain comfortable and whoever wished to speak was welcome.

I thanked them for coming out to the Great Neck office in order to honor Franklin. We were especially honored to have the chairman of Chase Manhattan with us, Mr. David Rockefeller. I applauded and everyone followed.

I cleared my throat, sipped a little water and began: "Gentlemen and ma'am, I have an interesting story to tell.

# A Life of Risks Taken

I never thought in my wildest dreams I would be here today."

*Here I stand, about to speak to the financial giants of the world. They are all brilliant, the high priests of capitalism sitting front of me. Do I have the balls to tell the story I had in mind. Like the Erasmus Hall swimming pool, I decided to jump in.*

I took a breath and turned to the chairman.

"Mr. Rockefeller, I am of the Jewish faith, and the language we spoke at home was Yiddish. I grew up believing that the word Rockefeller was a Jewish word."

There was an immediate silence in the room at the mention of the word Jewish. The charcoal gray vests were about to explode. I wondered if someone would faint. My lips touched the water glass and slowly took more water. I cleared my throat again to assuage the tiny bit of fear that lurked within. The others silently sipped their cocktails. I continued,

"When I was a boy, for my thirteenth birthday I wanted a new bicycle." I went on, "My father took me to a bicycle shop in our neighborhood in Brooklyn to buy one for me. My father picked out a fifteen dollar refurbished bike. It was a nice bike, but I didn't like it. I wanted a different one. My eyes were fixed on the beautiful, shining, red, white and blue Schwinn, a White Wall Balloon Tire bike. I told my dad, that was the only bicycle I wanted and no other. It cost thirty-nine dollars. Well, like most fathers who were used to being the final word of the family, my father looked at me and in commanding Yiddish said, 'No, that one is too much money. This one here is the one you can have. Make a choice—this one or nothing.

''But Poppa please, I want the Schwinn bike, I love it.' I whined.

Poppa reared back, his eyes glaring at me, he shouted, "Who do you think I am, a Rockefeller?"

The room was stone silent. I wanted to crawl under the table.

David Rockefeller laughed. He stood up, looked around, shook my hand and put his arm around my shoulder. As a photographer snapped our picture, he said, "Seymour, when I was a boy and I wanted something expensive, my father always said to me, 'Who do you think I am, J. P. Morgan?'"

The whole room burst into laughter.

A few months later, two of the V.P.s at that table invited me to their offices on Park Avenue and offered me all the printing business of their Chase wealth management accounts. They also told me a story. On the way back to Manhattan after the party, David turned to the other three people in the limo and announced that he planned to tell my story that weekend at his brother Nelson's birthday party. Nelson Rockefeller was the governor of New York.

# Chapter 21

ೞೞ

**Another Market**

Three years had passed since I opened the doors of my own company. In the winter, Sabina persuaded me that the family should take a much needed vacation. She argued that from the day I began the printing business I had worked nonstop with hardly a weekend to rest. It would be good for all of us to reconnect in a quiet and warm climate.

She was right. I was consumed with my work and the company. I was having a great time at the office. The action was so stimulating and exciting, still I agreed it was time for a break.

Sabine Press grew from a one-man operation to a staff of twenty-two-plus people. I had a secretary, a production man, a bookkeeper and an entire art staff of twenty professionals. At thirty-three years old I thought some powerful magician had waved a magical wand over me for all the good fortune I was experiencing. I recall someone saying to me, how lucky I was. Followed by a business man I knew, adding to that phrase, "I find the luckiest people are always the hardest workers." True, true, true.

It was exciting to go on vacation and not worry about the cost. We were doing well. Sabina was able to buy new things for our daughters, Lynn and Jane, to wear in Puerto Rico.

Landing at San Juan Airport, I saw a new adventure before us—palm trees, warm weather, a small band playing island music at the baggage claim. The girls giggled. As we walked down the ramp, stepping onto the sun-filled tarmac, Lynn asked, "Am I tan yet, Daddy?"

That phrase became the motto of that holiday, as well as the many beach vacations that followed.

Sitting on a lounge chair at the hotel pool, I stared at the pages of The New York Times in a trance. It was indeed a miracle, this feeling of safety and satisfaction.

"How's the weather in New York?" a man sitting close by called to me.

"Thirty-eight and dropping to twenty-four," I replied.

"Where are you from?" he asked.

"I'm from Great Neck," I said. "And you?"

"Westchester," he answered.

We introduced ourselves and struck up a conversation about our jobs, children, how long we'd been married, and do you know so and so who lives in Scarsdale or who lives in Great Neck?

Bruce Zenkel was an executive vice president in a women's clothing company. I shared the particulars of my printing business and told him about my coming from the men's clothing business. He was impressed that I led my own firm at such a young age. He worked for a company called Act III, a division of a much larger conglomerate that included ten different women's apparel firms.

During our stay we had drinks and lunch with Bruce and his wife, Lois, several times. My newly found friend invited me to come to his office at 498 Seventh Avenue, in the very heart of the apparel industry, when we all returned to New York.

We exchanged business cards and Bruce said, "Let's see if we can do some business together."

Back home a few weeks later, I stepped out of a cab and into the bosom of the fast-paced women's apparel industry. Racks of clothing on hangers were pushed swiftly through the streets. Men and women rushed in every direction with designs and patterns strapped to their shoulders. It was a montage of action that felt exciting. I strode through the neighborhood with a fresh realization that another opportunity was tapping gently at my door.

The possibility of a new business relationship was invigorating. The feeling always got under my skin. I felt powerful and questioned once again, "Is this my life?" A deep sigh followed as I said out loud, "Let's go." And I walked into the offices of ACT III.

Bruce's office was the epitome of style and comfort. His secretary led me into a beautifully designed showroom and offered me coffee.

He and I sat down together as he explained in detail all about his firm and the other ten sister companies in the conglomerate. I told him about my life and how I began

Sabine Press & Advertising. We easily maintained the rapport we had on vacation. Bruce gave me the opportunity to quote on several print products his firm needed.

A few days later, I submitted my prices and he was impressed with the competitive cost I offered. We began to work together. Bruce's business introduced me to the gigantic world of the women's apparel industry. As the weeks and months passed, this wonderful new friend recommended my company to all ten divisions of this vast organization, called Jonathan Logan Corporation. I received orders from their production branches throughout the country.

I began an advertising campaign in Women's Wear Daily, the industry newspaper. Quarter-page ads ran each month for our company.

The response was startling. Before the six-month contract was completed, we moved to full-page ads. The ads had a headshot of me and a statement that became the icon and logo of our firm. In bold letters, the ad read:

IF YOU LOVE YOUR BUSINESS

CALL

SABINE PRESS & ADVERTISING

TODAY

The ad went on to describe how our firm offered creative marketing ideas as well as high-fashion ads and brochures—and always the most competitive pricing. Each ad cost about seven thousand dollars. Our competitors thought we were insane to gamble so much money. My reasoning was that I only needed one response to make back my cost—and usually we received inquiries from three or four interested companies.

Our firm became the printing arm of almost every key apparel company in the industry. Our list of customers included, *Leslie Fay, Jonathan Logan, Ralph Lauren, Donkenny, Abe Schrader, Liz Claiborne, Jones Apparel, Michael Forrest Furs*, plus thirty other major and mid-sized firms.

My photo in the monthly ads created a 'superstar.' The power players of the women's fashion industry became my friends and colleagues, inviting me to industry functions. Whether they were charity balls or meetings, people would greet me and say, "I know you, 'You love your business.'"

"I sure do," was my response.

I lived, dreamed, and breathed Sabine Press & Advertising almost all of my waking hours.

Sunday evenings were the most stressful times for me. I felt the pressure of going back to the office on Monday. I worried about getting all the new projects done correctly and on a timely basis. Yet, the moment I stepped into my office on Monday morning and started the engines running, the pressure diminished. Sunday, I was the race horse at the starting gate, chomping at the bit. Monday morning, I was running the race.

The Sabine Press & Advertising account base and sales grew, as did the staff. We outgrew our offices and moved to a new space at 111 Eighth Avenue. We had tripled our space, emerging as a tightly knit organization of forty talented people.

§⃝℞

# A Life of Risks Taken

Six in the morning was wake up time. Lying in bed, eyes wide open and alert, I dreamed up a new concept the apparel industry was ripe for—a deep-discount advertising agency. We were in the right position, at the right time and were able to offer this service to all the clients. This time I was not taking a risk or a gamble. It was a no brainer. The idea stemmed from a single creative person on the Sabine team. She was brilliant, smart, a very hard worker and insane. She could come to work at 5 p.m. and work until 3 a.m. I would find her asleep on the sofa as I walked into my office at 8:30 a.m. On my desk were fabulous layouts for ads and a catalogue for the Goddess swimwear company.

"Good morning, Emily," I whispered.

"What time is it?"

"8:30. Want a cup of coffee?"

"No. I will get it myself. I want to finish the layouts for Goddess."

"They look great to me."

"They are not finished and you keep your hands off them. I will wash my face get a cup of coffee and finish them in about an hour or two."

Two hours later this extraordinary, creative woman was absolutely correct. They were not finished—now they were perfect. I shook my head in wonderment at the depth of Emily's talent.

That morning I rushed to the Goddess showroom with all these excellent full color ideas. It did not take more than ten minutes for the owner of the company to say, "These look great, let's do it, but I want one or two changes."

*No, no, no. Emily will never allow it.*

The next day Emily arrived at the office early, about 4 p.m. "How did that bitch like the layout?"

"She loved it."

"You are a fucking liar,"

"No, I swear, she truly thought it was the most creative swimsuit campaign she had ever seen."

"You're kidding me, aren't you?

"I lie not your highness. Let me show you something. She loved page four, six and twelve. She shook her head in admiration. That's the good news. But—and it is a small but—she just wants this suit here and the other over there, pointing to a center fold.

"Go fuck yourself. I will not allow it. She is a moron."

"Think about it for a moment. It is just two suits switching locations."

"NO!"

"Emily, she is paying us a great deal of money for this project. She, too, is a creative person like you. She respects your genius. She understands creativity, and like you, she will fight like a tiger to make her designs unchangeable. But she is selectively flexible, and I have seen her compromise often." This was a sales pitch to an employee. I, too, was nuts.

"Compromise? She is whore."

"Emily, please be reasonable. You are brilliant. There is no one like you. You are my Degas, my VanGogh, please work with me. We will turn this industry upside down. And you will sit on top of the heap. On the next Sabine ad of 'If you Love Your Business' your photo in place of mine. The copy will read, "If you love your business, visit our studio and meet Emily Latine our exclusive creative director."

Silence.

"Okay, I will let this go by for now. But no other changes."

"Thanks, you are my star and my sweetheart. Love you."

"Up yours!"

We did run the ad as promised. The phone rang all day. Emily spoke to about ten companies. Many wanted to hire her. She loved the attention, but she could not handle the pressure. She stormed into my office, and begged never to put her photo or her name in the paper again. She said she would have a nervous breakdown. I smiled and said, "Whatever you want, my love. I just sign the checks around here."

∞∞

Emily worked for Sabine for almost four years. The longest she remained at any company. She moved to Los Angeles to work at a large ad agency. She was there for six months, called me and asked if she could return to our firm. She promised she would be good. We worked together for another six years creating some of the most exciting new catalogues, brochures, ads, bill enclosures, and other point of sale materials. It was fun, she was nuts, she made the staff crazy, teaching the young people in our firm with patience and kindness. Switching her personality on and off almost made me insane. Our creative firm, because of Emily, became the sought after agency in the women's apparel industry. We were lucky to find a good fit between her creativity and my people skills with her, and the sales ability I developed with my customers.

Emily did not come into work one day. No phone call, no message, just gone. She never showed up again. I put $8500 in cash into our office safe, in hopes she would turn up to collect her bonus. I never saw her again. It was a strange love/hate relationship. I knew, and respected the fact that I was working with genius. It was a rare experience.

ଅଠଈ

Our clients used famous name agencies. These large advertising company's production and creative rates were very high. Our cost and subsequent charges were very low. Our new business plan included minimum charges for creative talent and slightly higher margins on the printing of catalogues, brochures, and newspaper ads. We did not do television work, which was a major mistake. Television commercials and advertising were the future. I saw it, but didn't have the knowledge or the experience to adapt.

I never priced by percentage of margin. The result was that we consistently outbid the competition. We could count on getting ten projects or more each month based on my dollar profit way of pricing. It was fair to the customers and we and the customer were benefiting by the large volume of business flowing into our shop.

Eventually our business changed. It did not take long for all the major apparel companies to seek us out to develop campaigns for their brochures for swimwear, evening gowns, sportswear, women's suits, and men's suits and shirts. We offered model selection from the best agencies, the best photographers, and a team of high-powered designers. The end product was sophisticated, well accepted and very profitable. We grew to be one of the largest hybrid printing-broker/advertising-agencies in New York.

Yet, with myriad business opportunities circling me, I lacked many basic, down-to-earth business skills. My most serious deficiency was not allowing some of the qualified people in the company take over customer relationships. Those connections were my inventory, my possessions. Mimicking my old boss, Jack Silverstien's style of business, I would not permit anyone but myself to negotiate with, or even speak to, the dozens of clients I nurtured and befriended.

I did not push myself on hiring talented managers and, therefore, I struggled with my inability to make Sabine Press into a diversified, multitasking organization. I did not have the background to interview, to select and to hire top executive talent to help me run the business, perhaps because I didn't want them interfering. My demand for uncompromising total control was the company's biggest weakness.

My constant quest for quality led to many dismissals of suppliers and employees. I stressed the need for perfection and excellence down to the most minor detail, which caused many an incident with my contractors.

Once, I held back payment for a brochure because of poor quality. My production man and an art director had been on press watching the print job. They saw color deviations, called it to the attention of the owner of the factory. He convinced them that he would correct the color and it would be perfect at completion. They left before seeing the final sheets come off the press. This was unacceptable, as both were highly paid professionals. I fired them both.

In an effort to assuage the anger of my client, whose disappointment in the brochure was evident, I offered a thirty percent discount, plus a twenty percent reduction on the next project. The customer agreed. Unfortunately, the printer wouldn't cooperate and accept my offer to pay him thirty percent less. As much as I tried to convince him to take my offer, he refused. He was a tough and angry old country Italian. He told me that my staff signed an okay. I countered he did not make the correction as specified.

A few weeks passed, and as hard as I tried, the printer would not budge. He still wanted his payment in full—or else.

On an early Monday morning, a giant of a man walked past my receptionist, past my secretary and came directly into my office. He was six feet, six inches tall, weighing about three hundred and fifty pounds. He was dressed in suit and tie, a very fine hat and shined shoes.

"How can I help you?" I asked as I stood up, frightened. I came up to roughly his belly button.

He told he came from Sal's, the printer I had the dispute with, and expected to pick up a check.

"What's your name?" I asked.

"Frigg."

"Like the football player?"

"No, his name is spelled differently. He spells his name F-R-I-D-G-E. Mine is spelled F-R-I-G-G. And the names are pronounced differently," he explained amusingly "When I go out to collect for a company, if they don't pay, they are fuckin' frigged. Get my meaning?"

I smiled and nodded. I gave him my business card and asked him to take a seat.

"Do you work for Sal the printer?"

"No, I work for a specialty collection organization."

"For whom do you work?"

"My boss is Vinnie TV."

Could this possibly be Vinnie from the crap game? Keeping my cool, I quietly asked, "Do you happen to work for my old friend, Vinnie the Vig?"

"How da fuck do you know Vinnie?" Mount Everest responded. I rose from my seat and with a huge pair of cojones gave the Frigg a startling command, "Call him right now."

Vinnie and I hadn't seen each other since I was eighteen years old.

Mr. Frigg lifted the cradle of the phone on my desk and made the call. "Mr. Vinnie I am in the office of an old friend and he wants to speak to you."

I took the phone in my hand. "Vinnie," I said. "This is Seymour, the kid from the craps game in Brooklyn, from Funzie's poolroom."

He didn't remember me. I kept talking.

"Don't you remember? I was in your shop in Hoboken, your granddaughter brought us drinks. I came to pick up some things for Funzie. I was getting two dollars a guy to come to the game, until the cops came and my mother stopped us from playing?" I could tell I was blabbering.

Vinnie started laughing. "You were the kid with the bowtie and the Sinatra pompadour?" He did remember, but only vaguely.

"That's right, that's right."

He asked what the Frigg was doing with me. I explained to him my dispute with Sal.

"Vinnie, sweetheart," I said, trying to be like one of the mob. "Could you help settle this? I would appreciate it."

"Gimme your number," Vinnie said.

About ten minutes later, Sal called me, very apologetic.

"Hey, Seymour, I didn't know you wuz one of us. Give Frigg the check for thirty off and we're okay."

It was as simple as that. What power that was!

Our bookkeeper wrote a check, and I asked Frigg if he would like to work for me on a couple of collections. He called Vinnie and we made a deal.

I gave Frigg three customers' invoices that I was having a difficult time collecting. Within a week, I had all my money. Two of the three customers continued to do business with me and even asked if they could use the Frigg. I gave them Vinnie's number. I never saw Frigg again.

I told this story many times to my children, and they loved it. Somehow people love Mob-connected stories. It's very strange.

# Chapter 22

୧୭୦୫

## The Tennis Racket
### 6-love, 6-love

My brother, Earl, had a friend, Julie, who invented a new tennis racket with an ingenious string design. It helped players hit closer to the sweet spot of the racket.

I was a regular tennis player in the 1970's and 1980's. I used this new racket, as did many of my friends. Everyone enjoyed playing with it. I thought if I could find a manufacturer to produce this new piece of equipment, it might be an interesting business. Tennis has always been a hot sport in America.

I found the supplier, set the price and now the question was how to proceed. A friend suggested that having a famous name on the racket would give it authenticity. He came up with the name of Pancho Segura, a renowned amateur champion who lived and worked at a tennis club in Southern California. What made Segura the perfect sponsor? He was also the coach to Jimmy Connors, the number-one-ranked player in the world. During that time, whenever Connors played, Pancho was in the front row. His name was often mentioned as Jimmy's coach.

I contacted Segura and found he was receptive to our idea of putting his name on the racket. Norman Menell, my attorney, and I made an appointment to meet him at his club.

A little research informed me that Pancho loved food as much as the game. Before we left New York, I ordered bagels, lox, sturgeon, herring, cream cheese and the works for the trip.

When Norman and I arrived, we arranged for one of the waiters to set up a table in a conference room. We gave the waiter all the food we had brought and he laid everything out with coffee and juice.

When Pancho entered the room, he laughed and said, "Just the food I love."

He moved right to the table and started eating. We joined in. After, we introduced ourselves and showed Pancho the tennis racket with his name on it.

After a quick bite, we went to the tennis courts, rackets in hand, and began hitting balls back and forth. Pancho made some suggestions, which we assured him we would make to his wishes. We offered him ten thousand dollars a year for his name and appearances at three conventions. Before we left, the deal was made. Norman and I left excited.

Now we had a product, a supplier and Pancho Segura.

The Pancho Segura Sweet-Spot was an instant success. Our new company sold eighty thousand rackets in four months, an unheard of accomplishment in the sporting goods industry.

# A Life of Risks Taken

But you can't be in business if you don't know your customer and his needs. Our customers were mostly pros at tennis clubs and country clubs. They were transients. They moved from job to job, club to club, taking our rackets with them. We could never find where they were from one month to another, and as a result we never got paid.

Our other customers were sporting goods retailers. Again, I knew nothing about the retail business. The rackets cost me about twenty-two dollars each, and my selling price had a sixty percent margin. Our company appeared to be very profitable on the books. Unfortunately, we only collected about a third of the money. It was a costly error, but a great learning experience.

We closed down in ten months. 6-love, 6-love. We lost the set. That huge loss taught me that I was getting too cocky. Too sure of myself. I had to spin the dial downward just a bit to 'Hey asshole, be careful, a little more conservative.'

# Chapter 23

ജ⭕ര

## The Tall Ships

During the Sabine Press & Advertising period of my career, one of our employees met an artist who was an expert in recreating historic sailing ships. The artist came to visit my office and showed me fourteen wonderful drawings of tall sailing ships from the 18th and 19th centuries.

I looked at the drawings and was fascinated by the detail of the ships. I asked the artist if he would leave the drawings with me for a few days. He must have thought I was interested in buying one or two from the collection, but my interest was not in one or two of his renderings. I wanted all of them.

The drawings laid on my desk for several days. I was intrigued.

*How could I take these wonderful pictures and convert them into a profit?*

Something in my head was swirling around but I couldn't grasp it. My inner voice was telling me not to ignore this situation.

# A Life of Risks Taken

Finally, the idea came to me while I was visiting the dentist. Leafing through a sailing magazine, I saw a story about the "Operation Sail." A fleet of tall ships, were sailing up the East Coast of the United States, arriving in New York City the first week in July. A bi-centennial celebration was going to take place on July 4, 1976. I thought of producing signed copies of the artist's drawings, arranging them in a beautiful portfolio and selling them to sailing enthusiasts all over the United States. It would be a keepsake for sailing hobbyists commemorating the two hundredth year of the founding of the United States.

I contacted the artist and laid out the plan step by step. At first, he had no interest and did not want any part of it. I pursued him for several weeks, finally convincing him to allow me to take this chance. We signed a contract and we were off to the races. We thought we would sell about a thousand sets at one hundred dollars each.

That's not what happened.

My staff and I spent a week or two creating the portfolio. We lithographed six hundred sets as a test, and then we were ready. The recreated fourteen illustrations were beautiful in their glossy folder with its gold embossed title. But now it was important to learn the lesson of the tennis racket business. I did not place a full page ad.

On a Sunday in April, 1976, we placed a quarter-page ad in *The New York Times*. The ad had a photo of one of the tall ships, some historic copy, the price for the collection and where and how it could be purchased—at our offices at 71 Murray Street, New York City, 6th floor.

On Monday the very the next day, when I arrived at my office in Manhattan, four hundred people were in a line waiting for our office to open. The police were there to manage the crowd. I was stunned. I rushed up to my office and found my staff in turmoil. Some people had cash, but most had credit cards. We didn't have credit card capability. It was a mess! We allowed fifteen people at a time to come up the freight elevator to the office and buy the portfolio. Customers begged us to put aside a portfolio so they could run for cash. Husbands called wives to bring checks. Buyers would give us all the cash they had as a deposit and would return with the balance. It was exciting and profitable. We sold out completely in one day.

Now we began to rethink this situation. It was an enormous opportunity. We decided to make a new limited edition, hand-signed by the artist. The new edition would have improved paper, a better portfolio cover and gold hot stamping plus embossed logo, a photo of the artist and his history. It took a week for all the materials to arrive at our print shop. The edition would be limited to one thousand sets. Each set would sell for $250. We had the artist come in and sign each and every lithographed drawing including the inside of the portfolio cover. Poor guy, he was exhausted. I encouraged him by saying, "You're going to be a very rich man." Magical words.

Besides signing his name, he had to write the print number—1/1,000, 2/1,000, et cetera—on each drawing. We hired six women to collate and insert the printed drawings into the portfolio. I hired my mother, a natural leader, to be the forelady.

A serious dispute arose between my partner and me as we pushed ahead. It was my strategy to place another ad in the *New York Times*. He argued for a quarter-page ad, and for us to be conservative. I wanted to take the risk and go for a full page. The cost difference was about $5,500. Eventually we settled our differences; we placed a full-page ad in both *The New York Times* and *Sailing* magazine. It was now two weeks before Memorial Day 1976. "Operation Sail," the nautical parade of the tall ships, would arrive in New York Harbor in less than six weeks.

The *Times* ad ran that Sunday, and by coincidence there was a brief news story about the coming celebration of the 200th anniversary of the United States of America.

The *Times* ad displayed the actual portfolio, the drawings of each tall ship in miniature size, as well as a brief, but informative history of the tall ships and the artist. We included instructions to purchase by mail or phone with American Express, Diner's Club or check.

Everything was perfect. We were ready for the onslaught.

On the Monday morning after the ad appeared, I was at the office early, ready for the madness. We also hired extra staff to help.

That day, however, only a dozen people came to buy the new portfolio. During the day, we had about forty phone calls with credit card purchases. Everyone in the company was very disappointed. Morale was at a new low.

*Oh my, what have I done? Have I been overly optimistic? This was not a casino in Las Vegas. This was our company.*

I failed myself, my partner and our staff. So much time and a great deal of money appeared to have been lost.

# A Life of Risks Taken

My partner gave me an I-told-you-so look. "We sold the first five hundred and made a good profit. Now we'll end up losing money," he said. "You should have listened to me, but you never do." Ted complained.

Under my breath, I said, "Fuck you!" But he was right.

I couldn't sleep that night. I felt ashamed, greedy— the same greediness I had accused my old boss, Myer Greenberg, of having.

The next day we got another twenty-five phone orders and about fifteen people came to the office to buy the limited edition portfolio.

"Perhaps the ad was too aggressive. Possibly it was too showy. Maybe our price was too high," I said to my staff.

One of the young art directors said that everyone who came to buy the portfolio loved them and could not wait to bring them home and frame them. It was nice to hear, a fake smile crossed my lips, but it failed to uplift me. My partner sat in his glass-enclosed office on the phone, probably cursing me to his friends. I went home early, had a martini, watched television and fell asleep in my chair.

Day three, I arrived to work a little late. I asked if we had received any phone orders. Yes, we had, I was told, about three or four. My partner had not arrived yet. Alone in my office, I sat bemoaning my business error. "I am not a direct mail expert. I am a seller. That is what I do best." I tortured myself. "Stick to your own last." I thought.

Then out of the clear blue sky, Daryl, our mail clerk, rushed into my office.

"Mr. Ubell, we just got three mailbags filled with those picture orders!"

I couldn't believe my ears.

Everyone ran to the mail room. It was true. We had received approximately twenty-five hundred orders in the mail. Orders came from almost every state in the union. It was exciting, overwhelming and beyond belief.

Someone said, "Looks like we really are in the *Tall Ships Portfolio* mail-order business."

More bags of orders followed the next day, and another bag the day after that. Bags of orders were delivered every day for almost a week. Sixty-five hundred orders for portfolios sat in our laps. We hadn't realized that it takes a day or two for *The New York Times* to reach subscribers in different parts of the country and the rest of the world.

It was a bonanza.

There were many problems that had to be solved in order to expedite this exciting piece of business windfall. For example, how could we justify a limited edition of one thousand and fill sixty-five hundred orders? It took a week to find a solution—not a great idea, but it was all we had. We asked the artist to draw two antique lifeboats from different periods of the tall ship era that would become part of the portfolio.

Then we hired a professional writer to prepare a letter of explanation to our customers, saying that they were free to return the set if they were not satisfied and their money would be refunded. We told them that the response to our advertisement had been unprecedented, and we had been forced to increase the limited edition to sixty-five hundred. We included the two lifeboat drawings in the package as a bonus at the same price. The letter was included with each order shipped.

One hundred and ten customers complained and returned the portfolio. Within twenty-four hours, each received a refund. We repackaged the returns and sold them all to a photo shop dealer in one day.

Our company was not finished exploiting the tall ships just yet. We produced still another batch of the original one-hundred-dollar edition and another smaller superior collection in a leather-bound portfolio. We profited highly and by July fourth it was all over.

Today, I have only two drawings left, which hang in my office.

The tall ships investment—and gamble—was one of the most exciting ventures I have ever made, or so I thought at that time. If this had happened in the twenty-first century, with the exposure one can get from television and the internet, who knows what the profits might have been? We probably could have sold millions of copies.

Here again, I cannot stress strongly enough, I honestly believe that the true slogan of the entrepreneur should be: "No risk, no reward. No guts, no glory." I have lived my life by those guidelines with reasonable success. I found that whenever I hesitated, as I have on several occasions, the hesitation was a mistake. I never regretted any undertaking, whether I've won or lost. The only regrets I've had in my business career are those risks that I did not take. A good entrepreneur sees an idea, seizes the moment and turns the idea into reality.

# A Life of Risks Taken

For the next decade, Sabine Press and Advertising enjoyed a very profitable existence. We had excellent cash flow, good profits each year, which I shared happily with my staff, as I do today. But nothing is forever.

Somewhere in late 1989 to about 1992, the printing and advertising business, as well as many other businesses, experienced a serious downturn. It was the beginning of a difficult recession. Three or four of our major customers filed for Chapter Eleven bankruptcies. Simultaneously, other accounts paid very slowly, and some, not at all. Our firm lost several million dollars.

I was sixty-one years old. The energy needed to carry on was more than I could handle at the time. I decided to retire. I had been working with all of my strength for almost thirty years. Enough was enough.

I turned the company over to my sister-in-law and son-in-law, who both worked for the company, and included my production supervisor as well. There was still enough business for the three of them to earn a very good living. I told all three, if they did well, they could pay me something. If not, that was okay, too. Soon Sabine Press & Advertising closed its doors. After three decades of running a profitable business, the company I gave birth to was gone.

# Chapter 24

ॐ

**An Affair**

In the winter of 1971, as a forty-year-old man, my career and the business were exhilarating to the point that it was all I ever thought about. I could barely acknowledge what was going on around me personally with my daughters and my wife. Each success I experienced seduced me into my addiction of wanting more of the same.

For years, I was chained to the work wheel. I slept in spurts. At night in bed with Sabina, I was already up to my neck, thinking about the next day's tasks. Only my hormones reminded me that my wife was lying next to me, that I needed intimacy and closeness. Sometimes she responded, sometimes not.

The "not" times were indeed painful and lonely moments. Yet, as she made every effort to be a good and loving wife, I was on a different planet. I was in orbit on the planet known as Sabine Press and Advertising. The company's office was my home, my trophy bride. My customers were like my children. I hovered over them with deep concern. I constantly nurtured them.

I was completely immune to the effect my involvement with my new love life—the company—had on my family.

On holidays with the family, I chose where we went and when. Sabina and I never conferred. I selected the Caribbean to rest, enjoy the sun, or the mountains of Vermont so my daughters could learn to ski. Sabina dutifully waited in the lodge with a book, patiently looking forward to the day's end.

I was not in touch with reality. My personal life—the connection with my two children and the relationship I had with my wife—had been drowning, disappearing, ending. I was oblivious. Completely out of touch.

After confiding to a friend about the issues Sabina and I were having, he suggested that I take her on a holiday without the children. He advised that it would be an important break that we both needed. He assured me that intimacy will slowly return. I listened and did as he suggested.

&#8526;&#8475;

Sabina and I took a vacation alone to the Sandy Lane Hotel on the island of Barbados. She and I were distancing, so I wanted to find a romantic spot to reconnect. At the time, this resort was one of the most elegant hotels in the Caribbean. I socialized with guests, interesting individuals who were accomplished in their careers, both young and older. Sabina read. The friends I met shared stories with me, had lunch, played tennis, and swam in the afternoon. Sabina was uncomfortable, saddened and found it difficult to join the fun. I had not a single clue why she walked around with a grim face. With all that activity surrounding me, still I was compelled to search out the phone daily. I checked in on my staff and, when necessary, a customer or two. Sabina's and my communication skills were non-existent.

The hotel planned to host a gala party. It was going to be a true holiday evening. I fantasized our dancing together, drinking Champaign and just being romantic. She brought one of her beautiful Slavic folk dance dresses, just perfect for the party.

Sabina got onto a floating plastic raft the afternoon of the party, and spent a good part of the day on her back in the sun. I called out to her several times to come out of the water and the blistering sun. She may have been dozing. Perhaps she did not hear me or just ignored my warnings. When she eventually came back to our room, she was sunburned so badly, I thought we would have to take her to the hospital.

Although I remained silent, I was angry.

*She did it on purpose. She wants to spoil our vacation. She didn't want us to go to the beautiful hotel party to dance and have fun. She wants to be in a position where I cannot touch her.*

It was not the first time I felt lonely, but it was the first time I felt all by myself, isolated. Whether or not what I was feeling was untrue or unreal, nonetheless, what I felt is what I felt. I sank to the lowest level, hopeless and without the energy to fight it any longer. As I matured, from time to time I reconsidered the event. I concluded that no one in their right mind wants to get a sun burn that leads to blistering. She did not think of the consequences of the exposure she was giving to her body. It was just one of many sad sequences in our lives together. Murphy's Law, *What could go wrong, will go wrong.*

Sabina and I had been tip-toeing slowly apart. The movements were not overt or explosive. It was a silent disease, a rash that gradually covers the entire body. It was hardly noticeable to either of us until we felt a huge void—the absence of intimacy and simple conversation.

We did not attend the party at the hotel. We remained in our room by ourselves with anti-burn medicine covering her body.

A turning point came as my daughters, Lynn, Jane and I began to go skiing almost every weekend without their mother. We left Sabina at home, as was her wish. She said it was good for our daughters to have some private time with their father and I did not object. Besides my work, the girls were the only brightness I had in my life.

At Sabina's request we often returned from skiing on late Saturday afternoons, so that my wife and I could go out to dinner with her friends. It was an accommodation that I resented. She could learn to ski, as she learned to dance. She could be part of the family I envisioned. I never considered that her mind and her feelings might be elsewhere. What either of us envisioned for our lives was not the same.

There was strength in Sabina that mixed with a touch of stubbornness, which made her at times very interesting. Without a doubt, it contained a trace of anger toward me. I realize now, she needed more in her life than she was getting. She had been a wife and a mother since her teenage days. That life was an unfulfilling existence. Our desires were in a silent battle. Little did we know, there would be no winners, at least for that period in our lives.

I knew that I was part of this equation. I was the one who worked hard. I was always the one who made the commitment to shoot for the stars. I was the husband she chose. My path was to face the consequences of the risk taking. A commanding force drove me to give one hundred percent to the company in order to protect my family and give them one hundred percent of the life we wanted. We enjoyed a beautiful home, two cars, a housekeeper, and above all safety—all these for Sabina and our two daughters.

This was the story I fed myself. It was my propaganda to convince me that I was on the right track, until I found I was failing. I finally confessed the truth to myself: my hard work was for myself, not for my children, not for Sabina. I had to be better than my father and my brothers. I had to be the best. Were my efforts selfish or were they ambitious? I preferred the later adjective.

I write this not as an excuse, but to state—looking back at my life—I realize that this forty year-old man had no vision for the future. I only saw the now of what was in front of me, and I was thinking with the wrong head. I had no clue about the consequences of my actions. My ambition blinded the truth of what I created for my existence and my family. I faced the dangers and knew what the stakes were.

*Look at me, Momma, your poor son from Brooklyn with no*

*education. Look what I have accomplished. Not a single one of my friends or family member reached those stars that I now hold in my arms.*

By myself, skiing, fishing, exercising, bike riding, I celebrated my efforts and battled my loneliness. I was alone and it was her fault. I thought this myself and often blurted it out loud.

"It's your fault—it's your fault." That was the bill of sale I sold to myself. And who was a better seller than I? I convinced myself that I was not the guilty party.

She and she alone was the culpable one.

ଛୀଓଃ

Sabina wanted us to take a holiday to Yugoslavia. With great reluctance I agreed to go on a two week holiday with my wife. Her passion was folk dancing, and Yugoslavia, the birth place of many of the dances Sabina learned and performed with her new friends at a folk dance club close to our home. She was excellent, graceful and a beautiful sight to watch. That was when she was happiest—dancing.

By mistake our travel agent booked a flight to Beograd, in the south, while our trip was to begin in Zagreb, in the northern part of Yugoslavia. Once again Sabina moved to the end of the bed in a "don't touch me" position. After a miserable night at a hotel, we boarded a plane to take us to Zagreb. The plane took off. Within moments of being airborne, smoke filled the cabin, the plane lurched and began to shake in the most horrifying way. The pilot announced that everyone should put their heads on the seat in front of them and make sure we were tightly strapped into our seats.

# A Life of Risks Taken

Sabina began to scream. She crushed my hand in hers. For some strange and inexplicable reason, I was calm, unafraid. I could only think of one thing—the night before in our hotel room, she was curled up like a knot—unreachable, untouchable.

I said to Sabina as the smoke engulfed us, "The next time I say we should make love, do it. You never know when the last one is being offered."

I am not relating this story with humor. I tell it to describe the loneliness and loveless life I was experiencing. The pain of rejection was more intense than the frightening expectation of a sudden horrific death. Difficult to believe, however, true and accurate.

Soon we learned that an air conditioning unit was causing all the trouble and was quickly repaired by the crew.

The rest of the trip was pleasant and a great learning experience. In Zagreb we rented a car and drove down the Adriatic coast. There was little intimacy, but we were civil to each other.

ഇരു

Diana was a famous senior designer of a major women's apparel firm. She was talented and a well-known executive in the industry. Our rendezvous were always tricky. If we bumped into someone in a restaurant, I was introduced as the CEO of her firm's advertising agency. True, but not true. When I met someone I knew, I introduced Diana as my secret girlfriend. The answer I got on several occasions was, "You should be so lucky." I am convinced other people saw us who knew my wife but minded their own business. I was reckless and did not care if we were caught and exposed.

If a wife withholds from her husband, he will find it elsewhere. It is as simple as that. Anger has many ways of lifting its ugly head.

Diana was a very beautiful woman, taller than I, which I liked. She was raven-haired, which when undone, hung to below her waistline. As a woman in her early twenties she was a well-known model. She had five major magazine covers to her credit including several television commercials. At the age of thirty, she decided to end her lucrative modeling career and become a fashion designer. She attended Fashion Institute of Design and earned her degree in two years.

Diana and I liked each other very much. She knew I was married. I never hid that fact. She traveled often to Paris, Rome, Milan and the west coast. She told me how difficult it was for her to have a relationship because of the demands of her job. Single men she dated found her to be unavailable because of her career. Between my work and my married life, I felt similarly. Whatever limited time we had to share was acceptable to both of us. We had a few days in Beverly Hills, five days in Paris and once we took a trip to the West Coast and drove from San Francisco up though the wine country, Napa and Sonoma, into Nevada and Lake Tahoe, through Yosemite and back to San Francisco. Those were the holidays I dreamed about having with Sabina. But they were distant dreams that never happened.

On one February weekend, I asked Sabina to go skiing

with me. She declined, telling me there was a folk dance party she wanted to attend.  It took ten minutes for me to decide to invite Diana to go skiing for the weekend.

"Yes, darling. I would love to," Diana responded with delight. I was thrown off guard by her energy and desire to be with me.

I picked her up at her apartment early Friday morning. We shared the driving for almost five hours to Vermont.  We listened to music, touching, and laughing. We stopped for lunch at a cozy restaurant in Williamstown, Massachusetts, and held hands while we ate. Diana made me forget my work, Sabina and the stress of my life. I completely forgot to call my office. I was calm and relaxed.

The beautiful lodge at Stowe was our destination. A romantic four-poster bed in a beamed-ceiling suite greeted us. A fireplace was already warming the living room of our suite, and a bottle of champagne, a bowl of fruit and some cheese and crackers were waiting for us. Diana's eyes sparkled and her young face glowed. I was forty years old. I thought I was old, but did not realize how young I was. Diana was thirty-something.

We prepared for dinner. She brushed her hair and kissed me before putting on lipstick. "I don't want to get lipstick on you," she whispered. There was so much excitement in her voice. I felt the pang of how much I had been missing.

Anywhere we went, all eyes were on us.

*Everyone must know that this stunning woman is not my wife.*

I felt a quiet pang of guilt. Sabina's look and her voice

edged itself into my thoughts. Luckily, thoughts of her disappeared after my first sip of Johnny Walker Black.

Diana did not take her eyes from me for a single moment. For the first time in many years, I felt wanted. No one was angry. We were both happy. Our dinner was filled with conversation about work and life. She asked about my two daughters, the ski vacations I took with them on weekends. I told her about going to Lynn's college graduation. When her name was called, I cried out, "That's my baby."

Diana laughed. "I can just see that scene."

She told me about her younger sister and brother, both in college. Her father passed away and her mother was living with her stepfather. She talked about modeling, how she loved it, but it was a very cruel environment. As a designer, she was happier. She felt creative, appreciated, respected while earning a significant salary and bonus.

After dinner we sat in the lounge and listened to music. I sipped cognac. Diana had an espresso. Again, I thought about Sabina for a moment, and wondered if I should telephone her to tell her I arrived. I decided against it.

We left our drinks on the table to walk in the snow. Her hand in mine was warm and comforting.

*Am I awake or in a deep sleep?*

We laughed as we trudged, and I devoured the fairytale moment. The air was cold, we kissed and kissed again.

*Am I dreaming?*

In bed we were silent. Diana's body was firm and

welcoming, with skin like silk. I had forgotten what passion was about. Our intimacy continued through the night and through the weekend. It was a honeymoon.

Unfortunately, our fun increased my sense of the emptiness I felt at home.

*Why couldn't we do this together, Sabina and me? What's wrong with us?*

It occurred to me that I was living alone. I had no one in my life. And here, in this elegant spot, with this lovely young person, this was not the remedy. Diana made me forget for a brief moment how sad I was about my marriage. But her warmth and kindness were no cures. It was like taking an aspirin when you have cancer. When you have cancer, you need intervention, not pain relievers. You need surgery.

I decided to take an extra day and spend Sunday night at Diana's tiny apartment on the Upper East Side of Manhattan. I returned home Monday afternoon. Sabina was not home yet. I laid down in bed and quickly fell asleep. It was late when she returned and came into the bedroom.

I looked up at her.

"Did you have a good time skiing?" she asked, her face unusually tense.

Suddenly—without thought or preparation—a surprise answer sprang from my lips, "I think we should live apart."

*Oh my God, what did I just say? Did I mean it or was it just a bluff?*

She was silent for about twenty seconds. "I think

you're right," she answered without any look of surprise.

We were, at long last, in agreement.

෨෨෨

I met Sabina when I was twenty years old. Twenty-year-old boys do not have a clue about love and life as well as zero experience regarding anything. Testosterone guides most of their decisions.

I met my bride-to-be at summer camp. I was visiting my brother Bob. I first saw her in the recreation hall where the counselors gathered in the evening. She was dancing the polka with extraordinary energy and grace. Her ponytail swirled gently about her head. Petite as she was, she danced tall and proud, wearing short shorts. Her legs were stunning. She was quite beautiful. It was love at first sight.

Sabina became my baby bride at the age of nineteen. We married just shy of my twenty-first birthday. We were filled with excitement, hope and love, but frightened to death of life. For years, we struggled through our mutual crazies and insecurities to make a home for our new family.

She and I were bound together in an overwhelming undertaking. The Korean War was raging. Men my age were drafted. We decided to have a child. This was an excellent ploy for staying out of the war, but a silly reason to start a family. Our first child, Lynn, was born when I was twenty-two years old. Sabina was just twenty. Today when I look at a twenty-two-year-old, I wonder to myself, *Did I look that young? What a stupid kid I was. Where was my mother to advise me? Would I have listened? I think not.*

෨෨෨

# A Life of Risks Taken

It's not easy to be totally objective about a former wife. A tiny layer of anger can linger in your heart and in your memory for the rest of your life. Though I do not dwell on the past, the memory of those times occasionally perks up its ugly head.

Sabina was not and is not a bad person. We were not a good fit. I don't believe either of us was ready for a long-term relationship when we married. We were just two kids who wanted something, and neither of us knew what that something was. All we knew was that we wanted to be free, out of our parents' homes, grown up.

My first wife pushed buttons I never knew I had. Through more than twenty years of our marriage, she could say or do something and stir up the wrath of Zeus in me.

A thousand years of therapy could never explain the anger I experienced. Upon reaching my late fifties, I began to understand a little bit more. I realized that my anger had everything to do with not feeling loved, a truth I failed to acknowledge until long after my divorce. If you sense that you are not wanted in a relationship, I say get out of there. However, getting out of there is easier said than accomplished. I often think of the song Charles Aznevour sings with lyrics, *"It is time to leave the table when love is no longer being served."*

❧❦❧

A few months after Sabina and I decided to separate, we were divorced. It was after our divorce we decided to go for marriage counseling. I think for once we agreed that we wanted to be sure that we tried everything to be certain we were making the right decision.

Diana was confused and hurt when I told her I had to stop seeing her.

"Why?" she asked.

"It has nothing to do with you. You have been wonderful to me. But Sabina and I are beginning marriage counseling. It will never work if I have you in the wings," I explained. I felt miserable, but I was doing what I thought was best for my family.

"Don't do this," she cried. "I love you."

For months, we attended therapy. Finally the therapist suggested that Sabina and I move in together for six weeks to see if we could find a path of harmony. During the trial period, I did everything I could to be a better man and a better husband. I thought if I changed my ways, even just a little, that we might remarry. I was very optimistic.

On the last day of the sixth week, I came home excited. Sabina was sitting on the sofa in the apartment I had rented. Her suitcase was beside her. I was puzzled.

Sabina calmly told me she was going on a holiday with a mutual friend of ours, a man I had known for years. I was in shock. I could not believe my ears.

*Am I blind? Did I not see any signals that our test was failing? I thought it was working for me. Was I an optimist or just foolish?*

It hit me: I was not loved in this house and not wanted in her life.

৪৩৫৫

It took several weeks for me to believe the reality of my life. It took me five years to be comfortable again. I didn't know then, but in that singular, rejecting moment, I became the luckiest man in the world. I had no idea of the life that was in store for me.

We live in a "breaking up" society. Divorce is easy if you have some money. But I never thought it would be me. When Sabina left, I couldn't believe that this was my life. It was as if I was in a movie.

A few weeks slipped by and I telephoned sweet, beautiful Diana.

"Fuck you!" she said and hung up the telephone.

I shook my head and smiled. "I deserved that."

The divorce was not caused because we were both involved with people outside of our marriage. The divorce was a result of immaturity. We grew up and out. We changed. Twenty years after we married, we were adults— and strangers.

Somewhere in our lives together—I don't know the exact moment when or how it happened—she turned ever so slightly, one eighth of an inch to the right, and I moved one tiny eighth of an inch to the left. When we looked again, we were a hundred miles apart.

Looking back, I realize we were desperate for something that we could neither articulate nor offer to the other. To Sabina, my generosity was a manipulation. To me, her holding back was a power tool. Our end was not like *The War of the Roses*. It was more like, "Okay, this is it. Good bye and good luck."

Ten years raced by. I found myself at the opening of the *Queen of Mean*, a film about Leona Helmsley, produced by my daughter, Jane. We took our seats in the theater,

Marsha, my bride of a few years on my left and Jane on my right. I turned to my daughter and whispered, "Where is your mother?"

"She is sitting next to me," she responded. I leaned forward, gazed past Jane. I was thrown completely off balance. I did not recognize the woman sitting next to my daughter. She said, "Hello, Seymour." Only her voice was familiar, the rest gone from my memory.

*Sabina? Is that you?*

I was not seeing the young beautiful girl I married many years ago. I was looking at an older woman. Someone I did not know.

That entire evening I stood at a distance from her, staring at her—my partner in life for more than two decades—trying to find that memory lost somehow, somewhere in my mind. I stared from afar, observed her movements, heard her laughter, and watched her head cock back. She pushed her hair aside with the back of her hand. She held her cigarette left-handed and her drink in her right. She turned her head from one side to the other, scrutinizing the room, searching for something. I did not know what.

Within an hour, the memory of Sabina slowly returned. But in truth I wasn't looking at the fifty-year-old woman who was standing forty feet in front of me. I was seeing that pretty, petite girl I married thirty years earlier.

As of late, when there is a family celebration that Sabina and I both attend, I look at this person who says she was my wife, talks of our children, the fun vacations, the good and some of the bad times.

# A Life of Risks Taken

*How could I have married this person? I don't know her. She isn't my type. Most likely she thinks the same of me.*

Though what I've recalled here is reasonably accurate, time has inserted its warm and caring heart toward forgiveness. I have forgiven the painful rejections I experienced, and I have forgiven her by reaching out to counsel and personal help. Most important for me, I have forgiven myself. I am happy where I am and very comfortable in my own skin. I did not realize—as I say once again—how lucky I was that my overtures toward reconciliation were rejected. I would have missed the joy of my wife, Marsha, and our son, Edward. Life is strange and magical. And now for the first time, I am truly in love.

# Chapter 25

୨୦୯୫

### Illness and a Partner

A mild heart attack is a misnomer. That is the diagnosis the cardiologist gave my episode. A heart attack is exactly what it says it is. It is painful and terrifying. It happened to me when I was thirty-five years old.

I went back to work after six weeks of recuperation, but I had to take it easy for a few months. As I began to feel normal again, back to my usual strength, I learned something important that I have followed all the years after my heart incident. Caution was my new friend. Health came before everything, because illness stops everything. When one is healthy, all issues can be overcome. With illness you can do nothing productive.

The time had come to acknowledge that a one man show was not the right course of action. It was time to find a business partner.

I met Ted Tessler at a dinner party at a neighbor's home in Great Neck. He was a salesman for a printing and mailing company. We spent a considerable amount of time together, biking, playing tennis and just got to know each other better. It was a courtship. After several months of sharing ideas, philosophies, work and business ethics, I was satisfied. I sincerely believed that Ted was the right fit for me and my company. I proposed to Ted that he join Sabine Press & Advertising as a partner. Although my sales were close to $5 million and, as he told me, his were about $500,000 annually, I suggested, that we become equal partners. I wanted him to be totally committed to the business.

Our agreement included an understanding that within one year, if either of us were dissatisfied with any part of the relationship, no matter what it was, we could terminate the contract with sixty days' notice.

My competitive genes went into overdrive, and that year I produced an additional $300,000 worth of business. Ted's original $500,000 turned out to be disappointing. His performance made me unhappy. I was working too hard and was now supporting his family as well my own, when my original plan was for him to take the load off my shoulders.

My friend and lawyer, Donald, suggested that ending the relationship, which is what I wanted to do, would be doing a disservice to me and to Ted. He recommended that I consider a new division of the business. I mulled it over and finally came to a solution I thought was fair.

I explained to Ted that I was very unhappy with the way things were working out. I said it was not reasonable for him to earn equal to me when I was producing eighty percent of the business. I suggested a new distribution:

sixty-five percent for me and thirty-five percent for him. We negotiated and settled on a sixty-forty deal. I was not happy. Ted was not happy. But life went on, both of us working to the best of our ability.

An opportunity to buy another company similar to ours came across my desk. I suggested to Ted that we investigate the business and if it fit into ours, we buy it. Ted could run that business for us, and that might work out.

We bought Manchester Press, a company with sales of $300,000. We paid the seller about $25,000 up front and then five percent of all the sales for five years.

Ted held up his end of the deal and brought in a little less than $300,000 of the new business, plus his $250,000 investment. All together we had a strong company and good cash flow. Peace and quiet reigned for about four years.

Then, suddenly, Ted had a heart attack and was ill for a long time. When he returned he had decided he wanted out. About a month after we signed our separation and buyout agreement, Ted died of heart disease.

Ted was a good person. We all know when we are ill, and Ted knew how sick he was. He wanted to take care of his wife and family. He accomplished that with the buy-out contract he made with me.

Over a period of about eight years, we sent his wife a check every month, despite one or two difficult years. When the final payment was made, we received a thoughtful letter of thanks from her. In the letter, she wrote that her friends had warned her that she would never get all the money, but that she had trust and confidence in my integrity.

I ended up back where I started. The entire company and all its sales to cover were now my responsibility. I took over Ted's sales and in the first year we had significant increases. I also hired and trained a young man to work with me, but he was a disappointment. I brought my daughter into the business, but that didn't work out either, and she left.

For the next ten years, more or less, I worked alone and was very happy. In that time I started several new companies, of which one was a messenger company.

## The Messenger Company

A truck driver I barely knew, working for a company we contracted at Sabine, approached me one day with a proposition. He wanted to start a trucking and messenger service. Would my firm have any interest in that?

I thought about it for a couple of weeks and finally asked Sarah, our bookkeeper, give me our monthly costs for trucking and messenger services. Her report showed that our firm spent $1,500 a month on messenger services and about $3,500 each month on local trucking. To bring these costs in-house would be profitable. The synergy seemed excellent.

Charlie, the trucker, and I came to terms. We agreed that we would invest $5,000 each to begin this new enterprise. His job would be the management and logistics. Mine would be sales and marketing.

On the eve of our signing, I said to my new partner, "Charlie, I don't give a crap about this piece of paper. What I care about is trust. I would like you to stand before me, put your hand on your heart, and swear on your children that you will never take a single penny more than you give me as an equal partner."

"Are you serious?" he asked.

"Quite serious," I replied.

Charlie stood before me, put his hand on his heart and made the promise. When he finished, we shook hands, signed the documents, and I gave him a check for $10,000 to start the company. Charlie did not have the money to invest. I gave him a loan.

Charlie returned my investment in the first year. I convinced all of my customers to turn their messenger and light trucking needs over to our company. We soon had a team of about sixty bikers and twenty contract truckers moving important envelopes, merchandise and small packages all over the city and Tristate area.

On Friday afternoons, Charlie and I would sit down and go over the books, the sales and the expenses. When Charlie showed me he drew $360 that week, there was a check made out to me for the same amount of money. If he had taken $800, my check was exactly the same.

Charlie and I earned a great deal of money working together.

As good as the financial rewards were, it had a downside. I was unprepared for Charlie's psychological makeup. His demand for emotional support was over the top. I encouraged his organizational skills, his work ethic and complete transparency, but the requirement for emotional support was a requisite I refused to fulfill.

Charlie would call every night at about ten p.m and

talk to me for an hour or more. That was not for me, nor was it for Marsha.

After a while, I told him that his calls were unacceptable. I had to rest from my day's efforts, and his need to talk was an interruption. I asked him to end his evening phone calls. Instead we could meet weekly to discuss all our business issues. This worked for about six weeks, then the calls resumed.

After four years, I finally decided things had to change. Even though the messenger business was a cash cow, it was not worth the daily disruptions. I told Charlie that he had worked very hard to make this company strong and successful. It was time he owned it all. He did not need me around to look over his shoulder.

"Make me an offer I can't refuse," I suggested. "Whatever number you give me, I will have the choice to let you buy me out, or I will buy you out."

The abrupt end to our partnership surprised Charlie. Two weeks later at lunch, he confessed that, at first, he hadn't understood my request, but as he thought about it more, he realized I'd taught him an important lesson. If he gave me too low a price, I would buy him out. If he gave me a high price, he would have to pay me that price.

I nodded.

Then, he said, "$1 million."

"You've chosen the exact number I had in mind," I said.

We drew up the papers, and he began a ten-year buyout. I suggested a decade of monthly payments in order to assure myself of getting paid in full. The long-term payout made it easier for Charlie to write the checks. We agreed that a fair deal had been struck, and a good one for both of us.

The phone calls at night did not stop, but they did diminish. In the middle of the fourth year, I told Charlie that he'd worked very hard since the start and that he deserved to have the company all to himself. It really belonged to him. I told him to buy me out for ten dollars. He did, and the phone calls stopped.

One month after I was totally out of the company, the fax machine was invented. Messenger businesses were in big trouble. My luck was holding.

∞∞

Years later, we met at a restaurant. He said, "Seymour, you gave me a wonderful break. My family and I have a good life thanks to you. We bought a house and have two nice cars." I listened as he continued, "The best thing you did was ask me to swear on my children that we would have a fair and honest partnership. I want you to know that we certainly did."

I smiled and said, "I always thought so."

# Chapter 26

ഔ

**Marsha**

As a bachelor I had countless relationships. The '70's and early '80's were a learning period for me. There was never a week that went by that some aunt or a cousin wanted to introduce me to *"this wonderful girl that you have to meet."* I always politely took the number but seldom called. I had enough contacts of my own. I did not need any help.

Slowly, but surely, I began to pay attention. I learned how to listen, particularly to the women in my life. It was not imperative to entertain or be the clever one. I was becoming comfortably confident with the women I had around me. I discovered that I enjoyed the company of men, as well. It was easy to talk to guys who were in similar situations.

Each autumn and winter, I rented a house in the Berkshires. Every Friday I packed up my car and drove to my cottage. It was a wonderful escape, and, most of the time, I went alone. It was there in that house that I found a new friend—me. I was finally able to enjoy being alone with a good book, or the New York Times, watch the TV, or go fishing in a nearby stream and often just be with my thoughts. I stopped searching for companionship. Spending quiet time in my house in the mountains of Massachusetts was a pleasure I never expected.

හ⭕ශ

In the years after my divorce from Sabina, I dated constantly. That was my priority. I must have dated more than a hundred women in those ten years—often two or more during a given period of time. First thing in the morning at the office: *Who shall I call to have dinner with tonight?* But as the years passed that routine and lifestyle became boring. I was ready for a change. I enjoyed the luxury of a full time housekeeper. Linda was a wonderful cook who kept my apartment decent and neat. She used to call me Mayor Koch, because often I would call her and tell her at the last minute, "We will be four for dinner," sometimes even more. Our freezer was always stocked full of steaks, hamburgers and other goodies. For a fish dinner, Linda would go to the local market and buy fresh fish.

I spent nine years of being alone, but always with someone lying next to me. But no single woman I met ever met made me think of anything serious—until I found Marsha. My life changed forever.

හ⭕ශ

As a single person, I spent several weekday evenings with my friends, Donald Shack and his wife, Barbara, as well as my other very close friends, Roger Gimbel and his wife, Nora. After finishing dinner at home by myself—I was getting better at eating alone—I would telephone Roger and ask if he and Nora would like a little company. They never refused me and about a half hour later I was at their door. We shared dessert. Roger and I would sit around in his living room and talk or play a hand or two of gin rummy.

Seven or eight years had passed since my divorce. I mentioned to Roger that I felt I was ready to settle down, find a good woman and make a life with her. I was forty-eight years old, and I felt old. It takes being fifty years old to understand how very young forty-eight years is.

As a bachelor for a long time, most of the women I got involved with were people I met through business contacts. Or often doing the things I liked best: playing tennis, skiing or visiting the various museums throughout New York City, I could meet someone attractive and interesting. I had a box at the Metropolitan Opera House for the American Ballet and a series of Philharmonic concerts. The theater was another one of my interests and last, but not least, two seats in a box at the US Open Stadium. All of that never kept me from playing Gin Rummy with my closest friends, Donald and Roger, at least once a week. I was a very busy guy. Add to that schedule, dinners with my daughters and running a demanding business.

𝕾𝕺𝕽

Women were not my only interest. I had several dear buddies. Jerry Feldheim, Ron Davis and Mitch Miller were three guys with whom I spent a great deal of time.

# A Life of Risks Taken

Jerry, Mitch and another man whose name I forget and I took one the best vacations I ever had. We chartered a sail boat in the Caribbean and sailed from island to island, anchoring at each location, swimming eating, drinking, but never drunk. We laughed all the time. Jerry and Mitch were the captains and first mate. I was the chef and the other guy kept our ship clean. That trip is one of my fondest memories.

Roger mentioned that he knew a woman named Marsha at Gimbel's department store. She held a high position as merchandiser of accessories. He thought, perhaps she might be available and it could be a good thing for the two of us to meet. I agreed.

The next day Roger had lunch with this friend. He related every detail he could recall about me. He shared stories of my first marriage, my work, my children and the life I had been leading. He left nothing out. I was surprised he did not give her my balance sheet. In spite of all this information, she agreed to meet me. I knew at once this was a brave woman.

The following day, I spoke to Marsha by telephone and we arranged to meet at my apartment. Her plan, as she later told me, was to escape as quickly as possible if she didn't like me.

The evening of our meeting, the doorbell rang right on time. I quickly moved to welcome her. There, standing before me, was the most beautiful woman I had ever seen.

*Oh my, oh my, this woman is so very young and very beautiful.*

"I like what I see," I said, "I hope you like what you see."

A smile but no response.

Marsha was several years younger than I. Younger women were not my specialty. I found young girls boring and quickly lost interest after sex.

After my initial greeting, I stood there, staring and speechless. Having nothing to say is not one of my failings, and it does not happen to me very often. I invited her into my apartment.

"Like a drink?"

"Ginger ale works, if you have it," she answered

I poured two. We spoke for about an hour, sharing little things about our lives and loves. From out of the blue and without warning my daughter, Jane, came dashing into the apartment.

"I was fired from my job," she sobbed.

Marsha, of course, had no idea who this very upset person was, but I recall how she comforted my twenty-three-year-old daughter. She spoke to Jane about possibilities of other, more fulfilling opportunities in the same industry and encouraged her to see this turn of events as a stepping stone. Jane quieted down after we—mostly Marsha—spoke to her for about an hour. My daughter felt better, and she left. At the time, it did not occur to me that Marsha was only seven years older than my daughter, and eighteen years younger than I.

Marsha began her story with the death of her father two years earlier, and she missed him very much. She loved her job and cared about art and music. She told me that she was seeing a man, and they had been together for seven years.

"If you have been seeing someone for such a long time, why are you here?" I asked.

She didn't answer.

A bad question. I probably put her in an uncomfortable position, and perhaps destroyed any chance of the friendship I had in mind.

I rallied with, "If you had been with this man for a year or two, I would've thought that you weren't sure yet where it would lead, so it couldn't hurt to have a date. But," I continued, "seven years is a long time, and probably means that nothing serious is going to come of this relationship." I paused. "Or perhaps, you secretly know he is not for you, and you're just waiting for 'Mr. Rightberg.'" I smiled at her. "Whichever it is," I stated with confidence.

At first sight, I liked the woman who sat next to me. I was struck by her looks and her quiet way of assessing my observations. There was no controversy, just mutual private evaluations.

I glanced at my watch. It was ten p.m. The evening was almost over, and I was nowhere with Marsha, with the exception of a little important honesty. We both comfortably put our cards on the table.

She inferred she was taken.

*I plan to be in the game.*

I scooped up my nearby guitar and began to play and sing. Marsha knew every song, including the Yiddish songs. Much to my surprise and delight, Marsha took the guitar and began to play her repertoire.

*Is she competitive?*

We continued to talk and sing for close to four hours. It felt good. This beautiful young woman was smart, sensitive, most likely earned a good living, and she was not impressed by my obvious success when looking around my home. I liked her, and I hoped she liked me.

At two a.m., we agreed it was time for the evening to end for the second time.

I telephoned the garage in my building and requested my car to be brought out. I drove Marsha home. This was a first for me. I usually called for a cab, took my date to the doorman, paid the cabdriver and off she would go.

Before Marsha got out of the car, our lips gently touched.

"Good night," I whispered, "You will hear from me—and soon."

In the car driving home I was thinking, *Who is this girl, this person who has swept into my life? Why am I thinking of her? When will I see her again? Tomorrow? Should I send flowers to her office? Too showy . . . but that's my style. Will I scare her off?*

These questions had never come up before. My usual reaction was, *Whew, I'm glad that's over*, and I'd fall fast asleep. But not that night.

I returned the car to the garage, took the elevator to my apartment and plopped down in my bed with my clothes on. I laid there for a few minutes, my head spinning.

"This is like the theater," I said aloud.

I picked up the phone and called her.

She answered, "Hello?"

I said, "I didn't say good night."

"Yes, you did. When you kissed me," she whispered. "Good night."

"Good night."

I put the receiver down and continued to think about her. I fell fast asleep with all my clothes on and a very happy man.

၈၁၀၃

Five women were in my life when I met Marsha. I alternated with each according to their schedule and my frame of mind. Immediately, I had a feeling that Marsha was going to be important. I knew from my six-week reconciliation test with Sabina, if you want something to work, you can't have anyone in the wings. You have to be honest and clear about your goals. My goals were to have a truthful and important relationship with Ms. Marsha Maxine Tosk, merchandising manager at Gimbel's Department Store.

One by one, as gently as possible, and holding their hands, I explained to each woman, "I met someone who I think is going to be important in my life and it would be impossible to make it work if you and I continued to see each other."

Three of the women replied, "If your new fling is unsuccessful, please call me."

The fourth woman broke down and began to cry. She said, "You have deceived me. You are dishonest. You are an unkind, horrible man."

She went on using words like *asshole, prick,* and more. I listened. She sobbed. It was painful to watch. She asked, "Why were you sleeping with me?"

I could not answer. She was very distressed.

I tried to comfort her. I put my arms around her shoulders.

"Don't touch me, you son-of-a-bitch," she said, weeping.

Finally, she stopped. I asked, "Should I call a taxi?"

"I don't want anything from you!" And slamming the door behind her, she didn't even say goodbye. Six months later, I had heard she became engaged to a member of our tennis club.

One woman remained in my life for a brief time longer—a widow new to the single world. A few months after we met, I invited Mary to come with me on a weekend holiday to the Ocean Club in the Bahamas. She agreed and we had a lovely time playing tennis and swimming. The time together was pleasant, kind and lovely. On our way home on the plane, Mary was happy and felt comfortable in our relationship. She went on about it, and to thank me she offered to make me her guest on the next trip, knowing my schedule, and how every six weeks I'd fly down to Paradise Island to play tennis and rest. A month and half went by and I planned my next trip to Nassau. Mary had forgotten her offer. She asked over dinner, "What are we doing for the weekend?"

I explained, "I'm leaving for the Caribbean tomorrow morning."

"Why didn't you remind me that this was the week I was supposed to take you?"

"If I'm important to you, then you should have made the plans two weeks ago and invited me. So, I'm going on my own this time."

This happened twice with Mary. And after the second time, by coincidence I met Marsha, and Mary was finished. I did not want to hurt her, but eventually I had to tell her about Marsha.

ഇരുന്ന

I wanted to proceed slowly in my pursuit of Marsha, but before I knew it, I stepped on the pedal. We started with an evening at the ballet. How was I to know that she loved the ballet? I decided once again to face the new challenge. It was a stroke of luck. On Sunday, we went to the Metropolitan Museum of Art. How was I to know she

263

loved art? Another stroke of luck.

In time, she finally broke up with Mr. Seven Years, and we began our courtship in earnest. I sent flowers to her office. We dined together every evening, except when she had to work. We enjoyed the movies, the theater, walks in Central Park. Neither of us was making any mistakes with the other. It felt too perfect. I began to worry.

Finally, we took a weekend away to my beautiful retreat in the Berkshires. The house was picture-perfect: a converted barn with a huge living room that had a large French Bell fireplace. The converted barn had two bedrooms, a sauna, beamed ceilings, a small eat-in kitchen and a beautiful outdoor patio. It was my place for rest and quiet. I loved the solitude and wanted my new love to share it with me. She, too, had a career filled with daily stress. She, too, needed the same quiet and respite.

On her very first visit to my country house, I planned to take Marsha to the Clark Museum in Williamstown. It was in that museum on that day, Marsha told me she fell in love with me, she later confessed.

The Clark is one of the museum gems of the United States. Sterling Clark—whose grandfather was a founder of the Singer Sewing Machine Company—and his wife, Francine, had established the museum. Marsha was in awe of it. Who would believe that this tiny spot in western Massachusetts had such a special collection of paintings by Degas, Renoir, Remington, Pissarro, and many others?

ഇൻയ

We gradually began looking in jewelry store windows. We wandered into Tiffany's, and she tried on different styles of engagement rings. It was fun, but still, we did nothing. We had time. There was still much to learn about one another.

We mutually agreed to overcome our nervous anxiety and move in together. Marsha would move into my apartment for a one-week test. I remember helping her pack a small suitcase. She took enough clothes for one week only. I took some of her favorite records and a special teacup she liked and secretly put them into the satchel.

We were both very nervous when we arrived at my apartment. In preparation, I had emptied out a closet and a bureau for her things. I put on one of her records and boiled some water for tea as she unpacked. Marsha sat in an easy chair, drank her tea, and listened to the music.

Suddenly, in a very high-pitched voice, she said, "What will I tell my mother?"

"Let's not tell anyone anything yet. Let's wait a while. Both of us may panic by the end of the week and all this will end," I replied.

"How will I know when my mother calls me?"

"We'll go to your place every day and listen to your answering machine."

I loved this woman, loved her nervousness, her constant wondering if she was doing the right thing. I loved her because she cared how her mother might feel if she knew we were living together.

Marsha's mom was very smart, and I think she knew all the time. Marsha never moved out. We, of course, had to get more clothes every week—and more tea and more records.

Our life together grew comfortable. I easily gave her my side of the bed—a big move. Marsha took tennis lessons, and we played together on the weekends. In winter, we went skiing. I arranged private ski lessons for her, while I skied by myself. After the lesson we skied the easy slopes together until her skills improved.

Six months went by, or perhaps a little longer. We agreed to become engaged. I insisted that we set the wedding date. I did not want to wait seven years until she made up her mind. We were engaged in July, and our wedding date was going to be February twenty-seventh, 1982.

My good friends, Donald and Barbara Shack, generously offered us their home in The Beresford, a historic Manhattan apartment building, to have our wedding ceremony and celebration. It was an elegant and intimate party, just family and a few friends.

ℰℭ

Marsha's career and my business schedule kept us so busy that we had to postpone our honeymoon. After much persuasion on my part, and a great deal of soul-searching on hers, we agreed to take a three-week honeymoon. That was a long time to be away from our work, but we did what we wanted to do.

I said, "No one in your office or in mine will ever complain about the length of time we take for a honeymoon."

Our holiday began in Paris at a beautiful four-star guest-house, Le Residence Dubois. The suite we booked was exquisite. A European-style king-size bed with a canopy stood prominently in the center of the room to welcome our exhausted bodies. Huge Louis XIV dressers and a giant mirrored armoire adorned the room. Twin sinks in the bathroom stood comfortably next to a four-legged tub large enough for two. The innkeeper, knowing we were on our honeymoon, gifted us with a bottle of Moët & Chandon, which when we arrived was standing in ice next to a large bowl of fruit and a platter of assorted cheeses.

We hungrily reached for the fruit and cheese, ate quickly, gulped the Champaign and left the unpacking for the next day. We showered, got into bed and switched off the lights.

Marsha tapped me on the shoulder. I turned to her. We looked into each other's eyes and simultaneously said, "What the fuck did we do?"

We burst out laughing. We were both scared to death. We never imagined getting married would be such a frightening experience. Still we made the commitment. We were in love, we were young, much smarter than before, and we had a little money—a perfect combination for the beginning of a life together.

Secretly I thought, if this did not work out, everyone would think that I was the culprit— like in my first marriage to Sabina. Clearly, Sabina was not alone with issues of communication and compromise. I also had problems with many important marital rules for respect and understanding.  I refused to let that happen again. I planned to seriously focus on not making the same mistakes.

Paris was wonderful. We shopped in very expensive stores, ate in four and five-star restaurants, and visited the great museums of the city. We just walked and talked everywhere. We were by ourselves together and in love, exhausted, but never allowing that to interfere with the good time we were experiencing.

From Paris we boarded The Orient Express to Florence, Italy. We checked our luggage and went to our compartment. The train ride overnight into Italy was very romantic. Dinner in the dining car included wonderful wine, pasta and a delicious veal Milanese that we shared. We tripped our way back to our compartment shushing each other's laughter. When reached our compartment, we found the beds made. One upper and one lower. We looked at each other, shrugged our shoulders and undressed, cuddling together tightly in the lower birth. It was a charmed experience, except we didn't realize that travelers are supposed to take their luggage on the train with them. Ours bags arrived in Florence two days later.

In Firenze, the art center of Europe, we stayed at the remarkable Villa Cora. Again our suite was incredible, overlooking the outdoor pool. Marsha dove into the beauty and art that Firenze had to offer. I listened and learned as she explained. Each museum, each shop, each street, my bride knew everything. I was excited. I married a beautiful woman who was an Encyclopedia Britannica.

A week sped by and it was time to say goodbye to Italy. We hired a car and a driver who chauffeured us through the Alps. Our final destination was the Alex Inn in Zermatt. Along the way, we stopped at a lovely gem of a restaurant the driver knew. It stood on plateau overlooking the magnificent mountains. The food was excellent. The owners of the restaurant could not do enough for us. We looked at each other. We smiled and wondered what the chef was saying in Italian.

No cars were allowed in the ski village of Zermatt. It nestled at the base of the beautiful Matterhorn. A horse-drawn sled took us from the entrance of the village to our warm and comfortable hotel. We skied, slept, ate, drank and enjoyed the guests from all parts of the world. These were the last days of our three week, never to be forgotten, honeymoon.

℘℘

At the end of the first week of our marriage, Marsha gave me a check. I asked what it was for. She told me it was her paycheck, and we should put the money into our account. I looked at her and understood this act of trust and confidence demonstrated her total commitment. It was how her parents lived and how my parents lived. One pocket book, one bank account.

From that day forward, all accounts had both our names on them and either of us could sign checks. We made a deal that each of us could spend a certain agreed amount any time we wanted without consulting the other.

Every weekend we drove up to a house we bought in Great Barrington, Massachusetts. It became our place of rest from the very hectic lives we were living—no entertaining, no customers, just the two of us, quietly alone in the serenity of our lake front cottage. We read, listened to music and occasionally watched the small black-and-white TV that stood next to the fireplace. Once in a while we went into town or drove to the village of Egremont to have dinner and see a movie.

Four years quickly flew by. I never thought I could be as happy as I was. At long last understood what being married was about because of Marsha.

A secret something special had been on my mind for quite a while. I never discussed it with anyone or with my bride. I wanted to have a child with Marsha. It was a private fantasy, not shared with anyone. The courage to tell her came to me one Sunday afternoon as we were driving home from the house on the lake.

I turned to my wife and said, "There's something very special in life that I don't want you to miss."

Marsha looked at me quizzically.

"What are you talking about?" she asked.

"I think we should have a child."

There it was, my wish exposed.

Marsha did not respond for a minute. "You already have two children. Why would you want any more?" She never considered that I would want another family. I never thought of it myself during our courtship. It was not on my agenda when I first met her or in my thoughts when we married. However, when my friend and neighbor, Ron Davis, advised me one day, "You are in love with a very young woman. Yes? You, my friend, are going to have a baby." I smiled and said, "If it is meant to be, it will happen." I found myself open to anything good that could happen in life.

After four years of total bliss, I had fallen in love with Marsha for a second time. I wanted her to have everything I could give her. I wanted her to know what I have known. The deepest love anyone can experience is the love of your own child.

Each weekend after that day, driving home on Sunday afternoons, I asked her the same question. Each time she said she was still thinking it over. I told her that I was not worried about her biological clock. I was worried about mine. I was past fifty-four years old. Who knew when sperms got lazy?

Sunday rolled around, and once again we got into our car to drive home.

We were both quiet, listening to music. I can't remember what I was thinking of. Marsha turned to me and said, "You are fifty-four years old. I'm thirty-seven. Don't you think we're a little too old to have a child?"

"When you are thirty you think you are old, at forty you realize how young thirty is. Now at my age, I think you are very young. We are not too old at this moment in time, but we will be too old soon."

More quiet, more music, more countryside flying by.

Marsha took my hand. "All right, let's try to have a baby."

I must confess I was a little surprised. I had to pull over to the side and park the car.

"You drive, please," I said.

"Make sure you know what you want, because you are liable to get it," my father advised me. I knew what I wanted, and that was a baby with my child bride.

Wow! She had agreed to try. We had taken the first step to parenthood.

*Was I just attempting to be that super loving, super giving husband? Did I really mean it? Do I want to have a child?*

I thought so. Now my mind raced.

Marsha drove for a few minutes. Finally, I spoke up, "Having a child is a great thing, and I don't want you to miss this experience. If we're lucky, it will happen. Look at me. Don't you think I enjoy having two terrific daughters?"

We both laughed. Lynn and Jane were not easy children. They were smart, demanding, and sometimes they were pests, but I loved them and it was because of my experience with them, that I wanted Marsha to know the experience of parenthood. You discover how much love you can have in yourself for another human being. There is no other experience in life that is better.

And so, we placed trying to conceive on the calendar and made all the fertility calculations. We took more time off to rest and be together. We laughed a lot. We both enjoyed sex, but this was work!

One day my bride whispered, "I think today is the day."

On the way to work a few weeks later, my car phone rang. I answered, and it was Marsha. She spoke into the phone in her delighted voice. "We won!"

Then she told me the pregnancy tester had turned that color—she was pregnant.

*That woman knows her body!*

I suggested she call Dr. Reckler, my urologist, to ask him to recommend an obstetrician for her. Reckler said it would be his pleasure to do a pregnancy test that very day.

Two days later it was confirmed: Marsha was pregnant, and the baby was due at the end of July.

At first, we both intelligently decided to wait a while before we told anyone.

We tried to contain our excitement.

Marsha asked me, "Do you think it's all right to tell my mother and my sister? And can I tell my brother?"

"Okay. But no one else, okay?"

She agreed. And then she said, "We have to tell Joe and Diane." Joe and Diane were friends we had up in the Berkshires who also had an apartment around the corner from us. I played tennis with Joe very often at the club. Joe and Diane were similar in age to us, and they had a little boy, Jeffery. He was a wonderful child. Marsha and I loved him very much.

"Okay, okay," I gave in.

Within seconds, the mother-to-be was on the telephone with her mother, "Mommy, I am pregnant," she announced with joy. My mother-in-law was not one for delirious delight when it came to children. She knew the truth. It would be a very hard job for two "old" people like Marsha and me. But she congratulated her daughter and wished her the best. Then Marsha called her sister, her brother and Joe and Diane.

It had been done. Now the world knew. It was not bad news. It was happy news. In the back of my head, I thought about our ages and the possibility of complications. Then I pushed the thought as far from me as possible. I did not want to think about bad stuff. We were going to have a healthy boy or girl, and that would be it!

When I told my friends that Marsha was going to have a child, they rolled their eyes in surprise and astonishment. They thought I was insane to have a baby at my age, but they were all happy for us.

&#8359;&#8906;

Our son, Edward Harris Tosk Ubell, was born nine months later on July twenty-eighth, the same day as Roger Gimbel's birthday, the friend who had introduced Marsha to me. We found that coincidence amazing fate.

In the delivery room, dressed in a surgical gown, I tried to comfort Marsha's brave efforts to push out this reluctant child. From the start, he had plans of his own.

With a burst of energy and a final push, this little guy came flying from his mother's womb into the hands of a nurse, who swiftly turned to me and placed him in my arms. He was yucky. In milliseconds, my eyes scanned his tiny body to see two arms, two legs, eyes, ears and a nose— all together and nothing missing. I was a happy father. I returned the little boy to the nurse to be cleaned up, ready for Mommy's arms. But that didn't happen. They laid him right on top of Marsha, who started laughing and crying simultaneously. Having a child is a man-and-woman-made miracle.

I removed my dressing gown, and washed up. I put on my double-breasted, navy blue, pinstriped suit, fixed my tie and my shirt, and made myself ready to welcome my son into the world.

All dressed, I approached the nurse and asked her, "What time are visiting hours?"

She looked at me and scowled. She said, "Grandparents are not allowed in this room. Please go to the waiting room."

I was stunned, "Don't you recognize me?"

"No, I do not." She eyed me for a moment. "Who are you?"

"I'm the father, not the grandfather. You just put that beautiful little boy into my arms."

The poor woman did not know what to do.

"Are you Mr. Tosk? I'm so sorry. Please forgive me." If there were a hole in the floor, she would have thrown herself into it.

"No, I am not Mr. Tosk. Mr. Tosk is my wife's father. My name is Mr. Ubell. I am the Edward's father."

She placed her face into her hands, almost crying.

I put my arms around her and said, "This is not a crying moment for me. This is a happy one. Your mistake was a natural one. Please forget it. And thanks for doing a great job in there."

She continued her apologies anyway.

"Forget it. Someday I'll tell this as a funny story."

From that moment on, I knew what the future would be. Everyone would call me Grandpa. But I realized that having that title was not a frustrating experience. Now that I *am* a grandfather, I enjoy the comfort of being around to be called, "Grandpa."

It was a warm sunny spring day. I was pushing his stroller in Central Park. Ed was a handsome blond child. He always attracted people no matter where we were.

A couple came over to us. They looked at Ed and said, "What a lovely looking boy. You must be the grandfather."

274

Ed challenged her, "He is my father. He only looks like a grandfather because he has a big business and worries a lot." The couple smiled and ran to a place they could hide.

⁊⊙�҃

Eddie has been a fortunate child. He has had both father and grandfather in one man—the somewhat tough, strict, disciplining dad, and the loving, generous grandfather. He hadn't known, nor had I, what was in store for both of us during the next quarter of a century. It was, and still is, a special experience. Our lives have included skiing, tennis, fishing in the North Pole and many vacations. I cheered him at fencing meets and lacrosse games. We sent him off to college and watched him mature in his first job. Finally, we are working together in the family business.

As I write these words, Marsha and I have passed our thirty-second wedding anniversary. Our son is about to celebrate his twenty-seventh birthday. How swiftly the years pass—especially when you're having the time of your life!

# Chapter 27

ഇൻൽ

## Retirement

Sixty-two years old sounds ancient, especially when you are thirty or forty. I was not old. I was tired. I found myself emotionally and physically spent. That condition is not the ideal time to make important decisions. In hind sight, I am smarter now, but then and there I was not thinking about my tomorrow, only about today. Today I was fatigued. And so I ended my career. My wife and I made the decision to sell our beautiful home in the Berkshires and our apartment on the Upper Eastside of Manhattan. In exchange for total financial security, or so we thought and planned. We rented a lovely triplex on East Sixty-Seventh Street in Manhattan.

We were safe and comfortable with hardly a worry.

My existence was simple. It was the first time in my adult life I experienced a stress-free period of time. What a pleasure, not thinking of anything with the exception of how to fill the day. I would wake each morning at six-thirty a.m and be off to the tennis club in Long Island City.

# A Life of Risks Taken

Twenty-five men and several women became my close tennis friends over a period of ten years. We arranged tennis dates and we all met to compete six—and at times—seven days each week. We arrived at seven a.m and played a set of singles, followed by a set of doubles.

Friday morning each week was set aside for a special get-together after our tennis matches. Each Friday one of the players volunteered to bring bagels, cream cheese, lox, sturgeon and other tempting things to eat. Our competitiveness extended itself into who brought the best breakfast. We sat around, exchanged stories, kidded each other, relaxed and had a good time. Some of my strongest friendships developed at the tennis club. Marsha and I still enjoy the company of Lynn Syms, the wife of my good friend Sy, who passed away, as well as Pepe Jelenik and wife, Vera. Tennis also strengthened an already-strong relationship with my brother Earl, and my brother-in-law Marvin—both sadly now gone as result of Parkinson's disease.

If it wasn't Friday, when the singles and doubles matches were over, the group dispersed. Most showered, dressed and were off to their jobs. I remained by myself. I ordered a light breakfast, and in total relaxation I read *The New York Times* from first page to last. I never knew what a luxury this would be.

From the tennis facility I went to the gym. After exercising, I showered and left for a hard-to-get lunch date. I discovered quite quickly that former business colleagues, including friends, had little interest in me or my post-career life. They were the working majority, and

# A Life of Risks Taken

I was a sixty-two-year-old retiree, a minority with nothing to add to the success of their day.

*This is the life I've chosen, and this is the life it would have to be—for now.*

Those two years of my life held a very special meaning for me. I had worked hard my entire career, and I finally gave myself the time to experience the rewards of that effort. My final years would be filled with comfort and financial safety and the privilege of being able to do anything I wanted. I enjoyed the feeling of no responsibility to anyone or anything, except to my wife and my three children.

It didn't take long for me to realize that I was not a happy retiree. I was lonely. I missed my coworkers. I hungered for the ring of the telephone. I felt deserted and abandoned. I noticed, too, that my memory was not as sharp as it had been when I was on the job.

Ultimately, I discovered that what I worked for all my life—the goal of retiring financially solid, healthy and interested—was not what I really wanted.

*Did I truly want to give up my work style, my leadership needs and the excitement of making the deal and earning the rewards?*

I felt young. Two years had quickly past, at sixty-four years old, I began to think I was not at the final curtain of my life. I wanted to work, I needed to work.

*What if I lived until eighty-five or ninety? For sure, I would not have enough resources to live that long.*

A friend said to me that I was lucky to have earned the treasure of safety for the rest of my life. I responded,

# A Life of Risks Taken

"I have enough money to live all the years I have left, if I died at seventy or I only ate four days a week." We both laughed, but it was true.

I believed retiring from business was what I wanted. The truth was that I was running away from the pressure of my job. In retrospect, I should have taken a long vacation, and then decided what path to take. I had been impetuous and was shooting from the hip, when I should have thought about this path more carefully.

I *wanted* to work every day. I *hungered* to work. I *was born* to work. Oh, yes, another important fact I had learned—I needed *the money* to live in the style to which we had become accustomed. Work is the only thing one gets paid for. Rent, car, vacations, food, education—you pay for everything. Only working changes the cash flow from out to in.

As time passed, it became clear: I needed an office, a staff of people, the "good mornings" and the phone calls to customers and suppliers. I had to return to a job as soon as possible. Just thinking about what my next steps would be was a new beginning that was both exciting and frightening. Two years had zipped by and I was now sixty-four years old. Who wants a man that old in business?

As I write these chapters at the age of eighty-two, I think back and can tell you how young I was at sixty-four years old. Planning to return to the labor force invigorated me. Here I was in my life planning to go back to work, when most people at the age of sixty-four are looking forward to ending their careers. I was going in as they were going out.

# A Life of Risks Taken

I scoured *The New York Times* and *The Wall Street Journal* for work opportunities or a business to buy. I answered ads, went on interviews and spoke to as many people as would listen to me about possible openings in firms that needed an experienced entrepreneur.

At last I saw an ad that interested me in the *Wall Street Journal*, it read:

SUCCESSFUL FULL COLOR PRINT
ORGANIZATION SEEKING EXPERIENCED C.E.O.
STAFF OF FORTY PEOPLE. A TAKE OVER OPPORTUNITY.

YOU ARE THE BOSS.

That sounded like something I would be interested in. I prepared a simple résumé and mailed it. Three weeks later, I received a response requesting a meeting with the representatives of the printing firm in the lobby of the Sheraton Hotel on the Avenue of the Americas in Manhattan.

The day of the meeting was dreary, misty with an occasional drizzle. I was feeling comfortable and a touch anxious. The last interview I had was forty-five years ago, with Mr. Handwerger at Rose Brothers.

*Ah, there is that old, slightly edgy, going-to-work-in-the-morning feeling. Welcome back! That's the Seymour I remember.*

I arrived at 8:50 a.m., ten minutes early. I gazed around the lobby. I saw three people looking quite lost—two men and one woman. The woman was tall and attractive. She was dressed in a black, fitted skirt suit. She had a beautiful, gold, frog pin on the lapel of her jacket. The two men were in sports jackets and open-collar shirts, no ties. I always had a tie on.

I walked over to the trio.

"Hello, everyone. I may be guessing, but I'm Seymour. Are you looking for me?" A big smile on my face. No answer.

"Are you Mr. Ubell?" The women asked.

"Yes, I am."

The woman introduced herself and her colleagues. "I'm Emily Jacobsen. This is Sandy Freestone, production supervisor, and Bob Handes, our general manager." We all shook hands and they gave me their business cards.

I had none, I told them, "Sorry."

Emily suggested we go to the conference room reserved for our meeting. Coffee, sweet rolls and some fruit had been ordered earlier. A waiter greeted us and served the coffee.

They started the conversation by telling me that my résumé was too brief for them to get a thorough understanding of who I was and what skills I had. They admitted that my letter was intriguing, and they were curious to know more about me.

I asked, "Why didn't you call me?"

Again, no answer.

I turned to Emily. "May I ask who are you in this company?"

She told me her family, the Jacobsens, owned this business for two generations, and she and her husband were the third generation.

I asked, "Where is Mr. Jacobsen?"

"If you are referring to my husband, Thomas was killed in a car accident about three months ago. He was the C.E.O and his name was Tom Brookman."

"I am so sorry," I replied.

"We're meeting with candidates to replace him and continue to run the firm with our present staff," she said.

"Please tell us about yourself. Our job is to find out about you. If we're satisfied, we'll tell you all about our company."

*Smart woman. Wastes no one's time. Cuts to the chase.*

I liked her at once. I poured a cup of coffee, reached for a danish on the table, munched and sipped, and then I began.

Speaking directly to Emily, I explained, "This is the first interview I have had in more than forty years."

I related the entire story of my business life. When I finished, they looked at each other in surprise. They did not expect such an in-depth, transparent description of my career.

The trio detailed the structure of their company, each taking a turn to describe the part that they managed. They had prepared slides of their factory, the equipment, and their staff—all very interesting. Their sales were close to twelve million dollars. Their company headquartered in Harrisburg, Pennsylvania.

My instincts signaled—after an hour and half of talk—Emily, the owner, wanted to hire me. The exchange continued until lunch, at which time we broke and enjoyed a pre-ordered meal served in the meeting room. Our banter turned to family, children, vacation sites. I experienced good chemistry between Emily, Bob, and me. Sandy, the Vice President of Production, gave me zero signals. He was a little suspect of me, I thought. I was confident he was not my competitor for this job. I vowed I would win him over. Those are the challenges I have a passion for.

After lunch, we continued the discussion of work.

"How many candidates have you met with?" I asked.

Once again, no response.

"Wow! What a way to kill an interview. Looks like I blew it. Am I fired already?" I asked.

They all laughed.

Emily said, "Well, we must confess, you're our first interview." She went on, "We received about fifteen responses to our advertisement, and although yours was brief, we found it direct, to the point and honest. We were curious to meet you."

"Are you disappointed?"

"No, we're not. At least—I speak for myself—*I* am not."

The general manager nodded in agreement. Sandy said nothing.

I realized I was the only candidate.

"Let me tell you what I'm about to do," I said. "In the sales world, we use the word 'closing' to mean the end of the sale. Let me make my closing speech. As long as two out of three of you are not disappointed in this meeting, and one is non-committal, may I suggest that we have another meeting next week, in Harrisburg at your plant?"

"Good idea," said Bob. Emily nodded in agreement.

"A very appropriate second step," Sandy added.

"How about next Wednesday?" I asked.

They all looked at their calendars and agreed to the date.

# A Life of Risks Taken

"Here is my suggestion: I'll arrive on Tuesday afternoon, check into a hotel that you recommend, and rest. We can all have dinner Tuesday evening. Please invite anyone you think would be relevant to the decision-making process. I'll spend most of Wednesday visiting your offices, your plant and your warehouse. I'll meet with anyone on your staff that you believe is relevant. Does that sound like a plan?"

All were in agreement. First, I took Sandy's hand, the silent one, smiled into his face, and told him that I was looking forward to his showing me his entire production facility. I shook hands with Emily and the general manager, and said goodbye. I was certain that I had the C.E.O. position, if I wanted it.

The following Tuesday afternoon, I arrived at the *Marriott Hotel*. The phone rang at 3 p.m. It was Emily, asking if I would like to meet for cocktails and dinner afterward? She would pick me up at 5 p.m.

Cocktails and dinner were at a very elegant private club. Wood paneled walls, plush leather seats, a full stocked bar with an abundance of snacks. Present were Emily, her father Selwyn Jacobsen, the chairman of the company, his wife Tricia, Bob Handes, general manager, Ralph Soglow, the chief financial officer, and Sandy Freestone, production supervisor and vice president. Also attending was Jed Jacobsen, Emily's brother.

Selwyn did not waste a moment. He blurted out, even before I had a drink in my hand, "What kind of name is Seymour Ubell?"

That was a punch right to the midsection. Here we go again. I've heard this question throughout my career, and

I immediately thought he wanted to know if I was Jewish.

I replied, "Jacobsen sounds like a Scandinavian or Scottish name," remembering several men I knew whose names ended in -s-e-n.

"It's neither," he replied.

A waiter walked over to me. I looked up.

"I'll have a Bombay Gin martini, olives."

I excused myself. I walked to a buffet table, where I took two pigs in blankets. I had to calm down from my introduction with this sarcastic son-of-a-bitch.

When I came back to him, I proudly began, "Shimon is my given name, and Ubell is the name they gave my father when he arrived at Ellis Island. Dad told the immigration officials that his name was Yubouroffsky, and they said that it was no name for an American. They renamed him Ubell."

I looked Selwyn straight in the eye. "In our religion, a newborn is usually named after a recently deceased member of the family. Since no one in our family had died, my parents turned to the Old Testament. I was such a strong little boy at birth that Mom named me after Samson, the biblical hero of the Jews."

*You asked that question to find out if I am Jewish. I am and very proud of it!*

Selwyn looked right into my face and said, "We belong to the Reform Synagogue here in Harrisburg."

I can't remember if I was surprised by my presumption, but my jumping to conclusions certainly embarrassed me. It was not the first time my ties to my Jewish culture caught me off guard and swept me away.

# A Life of Risks Taken

I always promised myself that I would be more careful about my back ground and give my opposite a chance. He shook my hand and smiled as our momentary duel ended. He asked if I needed my drink freshened up. I told him that one drink was enough. The first martini had done too much talking already.

During dinner I repeated much of the same dialogue I had with Emily and her colleagues. We spoke about a very important printing job that was on the presses that very evening. It would be running all night and finish tomorrow around noon. It had to go into their bindery no later than Thursday morning and be ready for delivery by the next Monday afternoon. They suggested that tomorrow we should go to that printing press and look at the job and get my comments.

I countered, that we finish our coffee, go over to the plant now and see the job as it was running. Everyone looked at each other warily.

Sandy said, "We have Eric there. He's our second-shift foreman. It would look like we were checking up on him."

"How big is this job that's on the press?"

"Fifty thousand copies of a thirty-two page book, four colors, special blue plus U.V."

"$100,000?" I asked.

"More," said Ralph, the general manager.

"So, let me tell you all right from the start. Should I become part of your team, and we have a $100,000-plus job on the press during my watch, I will be there, and so will one of you two guys along with our art director,"

I continued. "And by the way, have you invited your customer's art director or ad agency to be on press to okay the running sheets?"

Once more, no answer…and finally….

"There wasn't time for the art director to come to the shop for an okay. She okayed the color proof," Sandy finally said.

"Sandy," I answered calmly, controlling my contempt for their amateurish style. "My experience always, one hundred percent of the time, tells me, that when you have no time to make certain there are no errors, errors mysteriously jump off the printed sheet when the job is finished. Suddenly there is plenty of time to reprint—an action that brings the profits to zero or worse, a loss.

I heard myself speaking as if this was my company, as if I already had the job.

I saw a glimmer of a smile on Selwyn's lips and watched Emily look around the table.

Selwyn said, "Let's do it."

It looked to me as if I just saw the *real* boss give an order.

The plant was immaculate. I heard the constant hum of the six-color Kimori. Four men were at the press watching the sheets piled up as the run kept going. The foreman walked over to Selwyn, shook his hand and said, "How ya doin', Selly?"

I was introduced, and Eric, the foreman, began to talk about the press run. He told me that this was the second side of a thirty-two-page run. The first sixteen pages were finished, and they were backing it up.

"May I go up on press with you?" I asked.

"No problem. What did you say your name was, Sir?"

"Seymour."

"Well Mr. Seymour, welcome aboard."

I walked to the receiver side of the press, where the printed sheet was floating out onto the catcher. I asked for a loop and checked the registration. It was right on. Excellent. I looked at the blueprints and flipped through the pages. Then I looked through the folded dummy of the two-sided printed sheets. I saw something that I honestly thought would never happen—one in a hundred thousand chances—I saw a mistake. It was a mistake that no one would ever catch while on press. It would only be caught in the bindery. This had happened to me once before. But we did not catch it and had to rerun the entire job.

"Eric," I whispered. "There's an error here. Get the blueprint and get the folded dummy."

When Eric brought the two documents to me, I said, "Compare them."

"I don't see anything," he said.

"Look at page twelve and page sixteen and the backup. They're mismatched."

In a split second, Eric pressed the emergency stop button, and the presses came to a halt. The four pressmen jumped from their positions to the floor and came running to Eric. They looked around at one another, all somewhat pale. They turned their sights to me and then to Selwyn, who was standing nearby.

Eric told the group, "How lucky it is that Mr. Seymour came by to see the plant. He caught an error in time to save the day—not only the day but also the week."

I added, "It was just a lucky catch. One in a thousand. We are all fortunate. No big deal."

But it *was* a big deal. I had saved the company two full days on the press, plus perhaps $20,000 worth of paper. I knew this win gained me serious points with the Jacobsens.

At the plant the next day, I met all the managers, pre-press people, the art department, plate makers, film strippers and the head of the bindery. I talked with the chief financial officer, whom I'd met the night before. I also met the senior vice president and sales manager, Jed Jacobsen, Selwyn's son. He was thirty years old, attractive, polite, and well dressed.

I looked like an expert at every job on the floor. The word had spread about my very lucky error catch. I was a secret genius with super vision.

Emily and Jed took me to lunch. No one else was invited. This was the money meeting, about the role I would play and to whom I would report.

"Who brought in the Hess Oil account?" I asked.

"I met a senior officer of the company at a conference in L.A., and we hit it off. However, it took about four months before we met the people who decided to give us our first shot at some business," Jed said.

"That is the exciting thing about our business— getting the order."

Jed nodded.

"The tough part is getting it done right and delivered."

Again he nodded.

I went on, "Here is a suggestion. By now the press

must have the job finished. Take twenty sheets, have them folded and stitched and trimmed. You and your sales team and the art director should look these twenty books over carefully. Select as many as are perfect. Get in your car or plane or train. Run to your customer with these samples today and show it to him in person. They will be very impressed with the job and with you."

"Great idea!" Jed exclaimed.

He reached for the phone and gave instructions. He wanted the twenty books finished by the day's end.

Emily turned to me and smiled. She told me confidentially that coworkers approved of me, which was beyond her expectations.

"Here in our company, we seldom have one hundred percent approval about anything— including the color of the tiles in the men's room. We all feel that you can be a huge asset to our firm in sales and management. You seem to be a take-charge guy and a true leader. We also believe that you can give Jed a lot of help and support him."

Emily went on to say that I had even won Sandy over, who was always a very difficult case. She wanted to know what my priorities were. What was my salary range, and were there any perks that were a must?

As I sat there listening, I wondered if I was interested in living away from Marsha and Ed three nights a week.

"Emily," I began, "your company is a very good family business. There are at least three family owners who earn an excellent living here. I am confident that I could continue that easily and perhaps increase sales and profitability with Jed working close by."

Emily nodded sternly.

"My job would be to keep those presses running twenty-four hours a day, seven days a week. When that comes to pass, everyone will earn huge amounts of money, including the staff. When a shop is running two full shifts, and we start to fill the swing shift, that's where we can get more money for our work. That's the spot in this business where the overhead is free," I explained. "So let me tell you what's on my mind. I want a $200,000 signing bonus."

Emily blinked. I took a chance that did not work out.

"I would insist on a two-year contract, after which, it would be renewable each year upon negotiation. I would require an opening salary of $450,000, plus six percent of the gross over twelve million of your current sales. I want a profit-sharing plan to begin on the anniversary of my second year. I want healthcare insurance for my wife and son. I will soon have Medicare, but I would need a policy on costs after Medicare. Last, I will require a car and driver."

I took a breath. Emily was writing furiously.

"I run the company without any interference. I report only to your father or the board of directors if there is one. I hire and I fire. I have veto on bonuses and salaries to anyone on the staff. I arrive Monday morning and leave for home Thursday night. When there is an emergency, I would, of course, remain at the plant or with a customer.

"Should you decide to terminate our agreement, I get a six-month paycheck up front on departure or the total payout of the balance of our agreement, should that be larger."

I saw little reaction from Jed, perhaps a bit of a smile. Emily was shaking her head as if to say, *This will never happen.*

"You have certainly been thinking about this, haven't you?" Emily said. "No one in our company has ever earned a $450,000 salary."

"I have never earned a $450,000 salary either. I've always earned more."

Emily smiled, maybe in disbelief. I didn't care. "My immediate response is that I think your needs are a little too rich for our blood," she said. "But I will submit this to the board, and we will see. I know my dad likes you very much. What do you think, Jed?"

"Emily, Mr. Ubell is without a doubt out of his class here in Harrisburg and at our company. We're too small, and our town is too small. But we need him. I like him, and he can teach me a lot," he said.

I offered my hand to Jed, and he grasped it and shook strongly.

"Jed, my salary request is not too expensive for this company. My sales were less than half of Jacobsen's, and I know what I earned. At sales of twelve million a year, you can afford two people like me. With a little luck and our efforts teamed up, we can all profit."

"This guy is good, very good," Jed responded, looking at his sister.

"Why do you need a car and a driver?" Emily asked.

"If your husband had had a driver, I would not be here talking to you," I said.

She nodded with understanding.

# A Life of Risks Taken

❧❦

A full week went by before a FedEx envelope arrived. I opened the envelope, and in it was a single-sheet letter. It read:

*Dear Mr. Ubell,*

*We regret to inform you that we have made other plans for the position we had open. We thank you for your time and appreciate your input. It was indeed a personal pleasure for me to have met you.*

*Sincerely yours,*

*Selwyn Jacobsen*

*Chairman*

That was some blow to my ego! I was crushed. I replayed the entire visit in my mind. Had I been too cocky and too aggressive in my demands? Or maybe I wanted to run the show more than they had wanted me to—but their ad had said, *"You are the boss."* Maybe I asked for too much. Perhaps, I really didn't want the job and had made it impossible for them to accept my conditions.

I felt lonely and disappointed. It was a feeling I was not familiar with in my business negotiations. I had no additional plans.

*Did the future just slip away from me?*

❧❦

Two months later, I received a call at home from Emily. She wanted to come to New York and meet with me that same day. I had a feeling of I-told-you-so glee. I could only imagine that the person they had hired had not worked out, and now they were desperate.

# A Life of Risks Taken

We met at the Russian Tea Room on West Fifty-Seventh Street. When Emily walked in, I hardly recognized her. She looked terrible. I assumed she had driven from Harrisburg to New York and hadn't stopped to rest. She was a tired, unhappy looking woman.

I was already at a table, sipping a Diet Coke. I stood up as Emily sat down opposite me.

"You look exhausted," I began. "There must be a problem back home. How can I help?"

"Seymour, I want to thank you for agreeing to see me," Emily exhaled. "I wrote that awful note to you, and I want to apologize. The board of directors at our firm includes my dad, my mom, my sister, my brother Jed and me, plus our banker and our lawyer. My dad, Bob Handes and I went with our gut feelings and voted to offer you the job. We had some reservations about your demands, but we thought you might accept our counter-offer. The other members of the board, however, couldn't accept most of your requirements."

I nodded. "How about a drink?" I asked. "And calm down."

"I'll have a vodka martini, very dry, onions," she responded.

She let out a sigh after her first two sips. She looked at me as if she was about to cry.

"We checked your references. Each one gave you a glowing and extraordinary recommendation. But three out of the four gave us a friendly concern of theirs—perhaps we misunderstood their gentle warning. They told us, 'If you hire Seymour, he has to be the boss or it won't work.'"

"I believe when we spoke, I had made that perfectly clear. My references only confirmed it. Isn't that accurate? And didn't your ad say, 'You are the boss'?" I responded.

"Yes, the ad did say that, and you made yourself quite clear, but we were focusing more on the financial side of your proposal and not the emotional side. One of the people on the board, said, 'Who is this fancy New Yorker who needs a car and a driver?' My father went berserk and blasted him for saying that. I told them what you had said: if Tom had had a driver, we would not be going through this shit now."

I smiled. She had heard me.

"So what has happened since then? Who did you hire?"

"Before I begin, Jed went with the samples to the Hess advertising agency as you suggested. It was a magical move and a great suggestion. The agency has hired us for three other projects including the next Hess catalogue. Now Jed has incorporated that with many of our accounts and it is doing wonders for our firm. We are going to hire someone just to take care of  getting samples to our customers hot off the press."

"That is great. I am so pleased that I was able to help. Now tell me about the person you hired."

"Oh my God! We hired a very nice young man, married with one little girl. He seemed well-suited for small town life and a small town business. We got him for a third of your salary, with no perks, no contract, just a handshake deal. It turned out he had no people skills. He could not talk to customers and alienated one of our most important clients. I had to step in and take over. And his wife was a pain, always calling the office, four or five times a day."

"You should be the CEO, Emily. You would do a great job. Why don't you take over and run the company?"

"I have thought of that, but I cannot do battle with my father every day and go home happy. I'm lonely and miserable as it is."

"So are you here to offer me the job?"

"We can't afford you. You're the perfect candidate, but you're too expensive…"

"Emily, the firm *can* afford me. I know your sales and your margins. But I must add—even if I wanted the job, which I'm not certain I do—do you know what it would be like to begin to pull the power from your father? He's no pussycat. He's a tiger, and he's tough. And I'm tough. I'm spoiled and I insist on my way or the highway when it comes to running a company. We would be at each other's throats every day. And if your dad ever countermanded any of my instructions, it would be a disaster. I'm not the problem. Selwyn is the problem."

Emily appeared frustrated and confused. It confounded her that I had allowed her to drive all the way to New York and then told her I wasn't certain I wanted the job any longer.

"Let me tell you a story," I said. "Many years ago, my daughter came into my company. She worked hard every day. She was single, also lonely. Time went by, she made decisions. Some I liked, others not. I tried not to butt in, but one time I had to. I countermanded her decision, and she lost it! She was right. I was wrong. I should have let her do what she wanted to do, and learn from it. But that's who I am. I couldn't stop myself. The same thing will happen with your father."

"You may not believe this, but Dad was the one who convinced me to come to New York and see you. He said to ask you if I were able to assure you complete management of the company, would you reconsider an alternative offer from our firm?"

"I would have to think about that. Tell me, what's the offer?"

Emily took out a piece of paper from her purse and read: *"A $50,000 signing bonus. A $375,000 annual salary. Four percent of all sales over $12 million. A car and driver for working days only. A profit-sharing plan from day one. Health insurance as specified in original request. You are responsible for the success of the company. You come and go as you please. You have complete management responsibility. You report only to Selwyn on a consulting basis. Your decisions are final."*

She took a breath. She said, "If you can live with these things, we can have a deal today."

"Who wrote this proposal?" I asked.

"Selwyn and the board wrote it. I recused myself."

"Why?" I asked.

"I thought you would be best for the firm regardless of the cost. And to be honest with you, what you wanted is very similar to what my Tom wanted for himself and could not get—only he liked to drive." She smiled. "Any comments on our offer?"

"I won't accept it as it is. There's no such thing as a

handshake agreement. Would your firm take an order for a thousand letterheads without a purchase order? But I'll take your proposal and think about it. As soon as I decide, I'll contact you."

"We would like to have your decision by the end of the week."

"You mean by Friday?"

"Yes."

"Impossible."

"What is the earliest?"

"Today is Wednesday. How about next Monday? I'll either call you or write to you," I said.

"Please call me. Here is my home number as well as my office." She handed me her card.

"Okay, I'll do that."

We finished our drinks. I asked if she was returning home tomorrow. She said no, she was leaving from the restaurant. I warned her that it was not fair to her children to have her to drive home that night. She had a drink and had been exhausted when she arrived. She should stay over. She nodded and agreed that was the right thing to do. She thanked me. We shook hands and said goodbye. I saw in her eyes that she knew what my answer would be.

On the following Monday, I telephoned Emily and told her I could not take the position. I did not want to spend so much time away from Marsha and Ed. We never spoke to each other again.

# Chapter 28

ഇരുക

### Another Opportunity

A former employee of mine, who decided to go into his own printing and packaging business, contacted me. Joe and his partner, Paul, had a plan to produce shoe boxes for the footwear industry here in the States, ship them to China where the shoes were manufactured and packaged, and thus save their customers millions of dollars in duties, because the boxes were made in the United States.

Neither were skilled sales executives. One was a smart businessman, the other a good production person. Their thought was that I would be the perfect addition to make an unbeatable combination.

The plan was great, but they didn't have any customers. It was the start of an entirely new concept in international footwear packaging.

I thought about it for a month or two and turned it down.

Sometime later, I received another call from Paul. He asked for a meeting to further discuss the possibility of my joining his firm.

# A Life of Risks Taken

After a month of negotiation, I decided to give Joe and Paul a shot.

For one thing, I was impressed by the numbers that existed in the shoe business. The opportunity combined with the deal we structured was very inviting. The shoe companies we were planning to pursue were huge. I felt I could sell about ten million boxes a year in no time. My role would be as an independent contractor solely responsible for sales and customer follow up.

The three of us worked together well. We all worked hard together and had good rapport.

I joined Joe and Paul on a trip to Taiwan. I remember being a little anxious on my very first trip to Asia. I found the Far East a little intimidating. It is a massive continent. Looking at a map, cities that appeared close to each other were actually thousands of miles apart.

Joe, Paul and I shared many trips together that first year. I opened up four or five new accounts through connections that recommended me as a new box supplier in the industry. As time went by, I was disappointed that their business tactics were not my style. They hadn't gotten any of their own new business. They switched paper quality to increase profits. They never paid their suppliers on time, and held up their payments to me as well.

Joe and Paul quietly thought that I was too old to carry the burden of sales. I was sixty-five years old at the time. They decided to hire another salesman, Frank. The two of us went on a business trip to Florida, where *Footwear News*, the shoe industry's newspaper, held a meeting for major shoe retailers and wholesalers. At that meeting, my new co-worker watched me in action, moving in on every major wholesale executive and making strong contacts. I was having the time of my life. This is just the kind of business meeting that fits my skills.

"Why are you working for Joe and Paul?" Frank asked during the flight home. "You should be in your own business."

"Why don't we do it together?" I countered. "I'll be the outside seller, and you'll be in charge of production in the United States and China."

We agreed. I should have known that if he could double cross his friends so soon after being hired, he would do the same to me.

His son's name was Jason Carl, my son's name was Edward, and so we decided we would call the company JC Edward Corporation. We agreed to invest $10,000 each. A contract was drawn, letterheads and business cards produced and a bank account opened. I deposited my $10,000. Frank did not. After a few weeks of no response from him, I was determined to go it alone.

I was shocked to find out that Frank had betrayed me to Joe and Paul, telling them our entire plan. He, like Joe and Paul, was manipulative and not to be trusted.

Joe and Paul sued me for breach of contract as our agreement had a non-compete clause.

In court the judge said to them, "If a sixty-five-year-old man is a threat to your company, you should not be in business. He has the right to earn a living. Case dismissed."

So, I left the firm to be on my own. I also left over $60,000 in commissions on the table, plus a $25,000 option

# A Life of Risks Taken

I had paid for in a ten percent interest in their company.

Now, once again, I was in business by myself, ready to succeed or fail based on my own talents. At sixty-five, I had begun a new chapter in my life. This was a serious challenge and quite a risk to be taken.

My good friend, Roger, gave me a tiny office on the twentieth floor of the Empire State Building. I had a phone and a memo book and an IBM electric typewriter.

I traveled throughout the United States visiting every major footwear company that would let me talk about my business model. I was at least earning my business and household expenses. I had no overhead and a very small outlay of cash. I hired a young woman as an assistant. She answered the phone and did whatever bookkeeping there was. I also hired a middle-aged man with knowledge of freight forwarding and some production skills. Other than that, it was just me and my two colleagues.

JC Edward Corporation had a slow start, but I was not deterred. Soon growth accelerated. My very first customers were two major shoe companies, Fila and Wolverine. With those two clients, we could earn over one million dollars each year. It was exciting and a great deal of work.

The first order from Wolverine was a five-year contract for one hundred million boxes. We would manufacture boxes for their U.S. factories, expanding to China the following year.

Unfortunately, the box company I initially partnered with was so clogged with bureaucracy that it was difficult to communicate. Every issue required a meeting. I spent hours on planes going to and from the box plant and the Wolverine Company. My frustration mounted.

# A Life of Risks Taken

I found out the manager of the box plant bribed my production man to disclose all our operations. They canceled our contract and began taking over the business and relationships I had already acquired.

On a Friday night just before the contract was to be finalized between my supplier and Wolverine, the manager of the box plant telephoned me and canceled our agreement. I was dumbfounded.

This giant Fortune Five Hundred Company did not know who they were dealing with. I was furious. I would not let them get away with this. I hired Arthur Handler, a young, aggressive litigation lawyer, and we sued for twenty million dollars. It was a huge risk, but I put my horns down, reared back and charged them.

The defending company was in shock. Who is this old guy from New York starting a fight with us? I did not start the fight, they did. They could not believe what was happening. When a bully pushes you around, you just kick him in the balls. All the bully bullshit disappears. We went into depositions.

During the depositions, one of the defendant's managers that I worked closely with was being questioned. He made up stories and twisted the facts. I whispered to Arthur about each lie. Arthur destroyed him in cross-examination. Arthur challenged each and every fable. The defendant had changed his story repeatedly and suddenly couldn't remember what he had said five minutes earlier. The witness developed shortness of breath and almost fainted on the stand. Arthur made a knock out.

The arbitrator suggested a ten minute break. He

called both parties into a conference room and ordered the defendant to settle the case. The settlement was a seven-figure check.

The chairman, the president of this huge paper mill and the team that had worked with me were all fired because of their tactics. Two years later, they lost the entire Wolverine and Fila business for failing to produce a quality box on time.

ဆၢ

In the beginning, my business was based on the commission I had created. By the end of the first year, the business grew to be very profitable and it was growing swiftly.

Time passed rapidly. I now had over ten major companies as my customers. I expanded our business into commercial design. The freebee from Roger was over. He had additional space in an unoccupied area of his office that covered two entire floors of the Empire State Building. I rented two-thousand-square-feet, which gave us the room to grow.

The combination of my trips to China, the travel throughout the U.S.A. and the work of my team on the ground in New York, was beginning to show fruition. Each month we cultivated a new client. Currently in the 2014, JC Edwards produces boxes for more than one hundred and fifty brands world-wide.

# Chapter 29

৯০৫৪

### Big, Great, Wonderful Hong Kong

Hong Kong is that magnificent Asian island situated just a stone's throw from its formidable neighbor, the People's Republic of China. Hong Kong galloped into my heart in October 1994. Upon entry, my fatigue from a twenty-two hour flight suddenly disappeared.

My Cathay Pacific flight set down at the old Hong Kong airport at the tip of Kowloon that October evening at seven p.m. I passed through customs. The lines felt endless. Travelers from every corner of the world queued up to present their passports. They carried babies, luggage, and shopping bags filled with gifts for friends or relatives. I fantasized that everyone had come here to find their fortune, as I had. I told myself that the purpose of my visit was to see a new customer, but it was not true. I made the trip because I was curious.

Moving quickly down the arrivals ramp, with luggage in tow, I exited toward the taxi line. Suddenly, I caught my breath. An army of people confronted me, more humanity than I had ever seen in my life! Hundreds, perhaps thousands, of Chinese family members and friends were greeting the arriving passengers with signs that read "Welcome home" in Chinese, English, and Arabic. The excitement they showed for seeing their loved ones was contagious. The sea of human joy that flooded the space moved me. I felt that I, too, was being welcomed home.

At the exit gate, thirty or more taxi drivers approached, hawking a fare in their car or rickshaw. A cabdriver came right into my face, "Hotel?" he asked.

I nodded and said, "Royal Pacific."

He moved his head up and down signaling his understanding and politely took my luggage to a waiting taxi. Putting everything in the trunk, he returned to the front of the cab, opened the door and said something to the actual driver in Chinese. I heard the words, "Royal Pacific Hotel."

Inside the cab I shouted, "Royal Pacific Hotel," in a staccato tone, trying to mimic the first man. The driver nodded and smiled. Perhaps I spoke too loudly or he may have been amused by my effort to sound Chinese. I was, of course, trying to make myself understood, while simultaneously trying to conceal the fear inside me.

The taxi zigzagged through the maze of traffic as the driver maneuvered his way in the mish mash of crowded streets.

The city of Hong Kong was aglow with lights, lanterns and Chinese symbols. Hundreds of signs hung down the center of each street, attached to wires suspended between the buildings. Advertisements were in Chinese and

English, and sold everything from a watch to a custom tailor or a massage parlor.

Battalions of men, women and children were everywhere, walking, laughing, and taking photos. Vendors crowded the streets. Shops were filled with customers. Traffic jammed every intersection.

Bicycles whizzed by like lightning flashes across the avenues, as well as rickshaws. I saw a motorcycle with a man driving at full speed, a woman behind him, holding two children in her arms and an infant in a papoose. I involuntarily put my hands to my eyes as I could not bear to see a collision. Crowded buses were crammed with passengers and a human line, ant-like, spilled down to the subways.

It was a city whose heartbeat you could hear wherever you stood, a city filled with pulsating, thumping life. The excitement electrified everything, especially me.

In the Nineties, business was booming from the overflow of Chinese coming to this great city with money to burn. Hong Kong was awake, alive, and brightly lit. I fell instantly in love with the great metropolis.

৪৩৫

Deep in the heart of Hong Kong, the Royal Pacific Hotel exuded a majestic quality. Bellmen stepped rapidly to greet me, taking everything from my hands as they emptied the cab. They did not permit me to carry anything. The manager knew my name, what my room number was, and he personally escorted me to the eighty-eight-dollar-a-night mini-suite on the executive nineteenth floor. Eighty-eight U.S. dollars, a great price, including breakfast!

# A Life of Risks Taken

I was escorted into the executive lounge to register. Everyone behind the desk stood to greet me, politely bowing as I entered. I, with some reservation, returned their greetings with a bow. A uniformed attendant brought a damp towel to clean my hands and blot the perspiration from my face. A fresh bottle of water was pressed into my hand. I sat down at the desk, registered and presented my passport and my credit card. I handed the well-tailored clerk a US$100 bill, and he returned HK 780 to me.

My room was comfortable and clean. I flopped down on the bed with my clothes on, staring at the ceiling fan going round and round. I had just traveled half way around the world. Just a day ago, I was sleeping in my bed in New York, today I'm at rest on Canton Road in the center of Hong Kong. My life was amazing, I thought. I did not, nor could not foresee how much more amazing it was going to be.

A knock at the door announced the bellman with my luggage. I gave him five Hong Kong dollars, which was about forty-five cents in U.S. dollars. A look of surprise crossed the bellman's face. No tipping in Asia. A lesson learned.

This tired and hungry traveler called for room service. In ten minute,s I had Swiss cheese and ham on a roll. As I ate, I noticed a sign on the table by the phone. It read, "CALL EXTENSION 88 FOR MASSAGE SERVICE." It went on to say, "90 MINUTES, HK$310." That came to about thirty-five U.S. dollars for ninety minutes. Who could resist such a bargain?

I dialed the extension. A woman told me she would bring the masseuse to my room in twenty minutes.

# A Life of Risks Taken

The high-powered water stung my tired body as I quickly showered. I stood under the pressure for about ten minutes. I hadn't realized how fatigued I was. I put on my bathrobe and laid down on the bed. The knock on the door startled me, as I had quietly dozed off. Through the door, a woman's voice, in perfect English, said, "Massage."

Two women, not one, came into my room. I was curious. One of them took a large, fresh towel from the bathroom and covered the sheets on the bed. She instructed me to remove my robe. She told the second woman in Cantonese, as she touched her arm, to follow her. She led her to where I was stretched out on the bed. The second woman put oil in her hand and began rubbing my back. Then the first woman left, saying she would order more towels for my bathroom. "I shall return when you are finished in about ninety minutes.

The massage was firm, strong and steady.

*I needed this more than I realized.*

I heard a noise and turned my head to see what had happened. The bottle of oil had tipped to the floor. I saw my masseuse on all fours, feeling around the floor for the bottle. I suddenly realized, she was blind—absolutely and totally blind! I leaned over from the bed, reached down for the bottle and placed it in her hand.

"*Um goy,*" she muttered, "Thank you," in Cantonese.

"You're welcome."

The phone rang. Ninety minutes had disappeared in a flash. The woman went to the phone with the precision of a sighted person and had a conversation in Chinese. She then gave the phone to me.

# A Life of Risks Taken

A young woman on the phone informed me that my time was up and she was coming to get the masseuse.

When the woman arrived, I asked, "May I give her a tip?"

The first lady said, "We do not accept tips. Tips are a degrading Western custom."

Lesson number one again.

In a few moments, both women left, wishing me a pleasant evening. I fell asleep before the door clicked shut.

The following day, I awoke at five a.m. and I took my time getting ready for the day. I showered, except the hot steamy water I had the evening before was now ice cold. I leisurely dressed and prepared for the day. At seven a.m. the executive lounge opened, and I arrived for breakfast. A huge buffet of Asian and European foods was offered.

At the time, breakfast looked like a men's club, not one woman was in the dining room. Today more than half the traveling people are female. Women fill the planes and hotels and they're self-assured. This new generation of female entrepreneurs, travel with a keen knowledge of Asia, its customs and its challenges.

A man sitting alone in the breakfast room turned to me.

"You are an American, aren't you?" he asked.

I nodded. "I am from New York."

He invited me to come to his table. I took my coffee and joined him.

"How did you guess I was from the States?" I asked.

"It was no guess," he said. "You dress like an American. Very few men in Asia wear ties." He continued,

"You had the *International Herald Tribune* at the table. Typically American."

I peered into my coffee. *How about that.*

We spoke at length as he described many aspects of doing business in China. "Don't be an American," he told me. I felt a little offended. This guy was really aggressive.

"In Asia, relationships are the key to a successful and complete business deal. Let your customer or your supplier get to know you. Talk about your family, your friends, school, anything, but not about business. Your opposite has to trust you. And when trust arrives, so will the business," he said.

I listened eagerly. I felt that the philosophy was the same in America, but moved quicker.

Before we parted, we shook hands and exchanged business cards the Asian way.

"You hold your card in both hands on the long side, almost half bowing as you present it," he explained. "The other person takes your card and you accept his. Look down at the card, actually read it. Doing otherwise would be considered rude."

I had one appointment with the agent for my first and only customer in Hong Kong, Kenneth Cole Productions. It was the reason I gave myself to come to Hong Kong and then move on to China. To this date I had only been in Taiwan.

The agent's offices opened early. Upon arrival, I met Mary Tai, a woman of about thirty-five and general manager of the office. Mary had dark hair and was tall for an Asian woman. When she smiled, she raised her hand to cover her mouth. All I could see were her shining eyes and her nose peeking over the back of her hand.

Mary appeared pleased to meet me. I was the very first shoebox supplier who had ever come to visit her. She told me she had been saving an order of Kenneth Cole boxes for my arrival, a total of thirty-five thousand Reaction brand boxes. I expressed my gratitude, explained how pleased I was to be doing business with her firm.

"I am looking forward to working with you for a long time," I said.

She smiled and bowed. I did the same.

I confessed to Mary that I was totally unfamiliar with the customs in Asia. I asked her not to be insulted by my Western behavior. In the United States, I explained, it was traditional to invite a customer to dinner in the evening after a business meeting. Would she honor me with her company for dinner? Mary was quiet for a moment before she covered her mouth with a smile and accepted. I suggested we meet at seven p.m. She said she preferred eight-thirty. We agreed to meet in the lobby of the Royal Pacific. I asked the concierge to arrange a reservation.

Mary arrived exactly on time. She wore a Mandarin dress, with high heel shoes, hair pinned back in a bun, collected and held with a beautiful bone hair comb. She was elegant and stunning.

When Mary saw the restaurant, a famous Western/ Asian restaurant, she said, "Oh no, Mr. Seymour, that one too expensive. I take you to restaurant where food is very good. Half the price."

I gazed into her stunning face, now at least three

inches taller than I. What could I do but capitulate to this beauty? She led the way and I dutifully followed.

The restaurant was noisy and packed with people young, old and very old and children as well. Mary and I sat quietly at a corner table. I felt many eyes upon me. I appeared to be the center of attention, the only Western face in the restaurant. Children walked up to our table to view me close up. They stood at our table and stared. Mary explained and apologized that I was probably the first Western person they had ever seen. She spoke to them gently and politely. She assured them I was not from outer space. They laughed and ran away.

Mary ordered everything. Dish after dish was placed on a lazy Susan at the center of the table, all different types of fish, chicken, snake, and pork and rice, dumplings and noodles.

I struggled with my chopsticks. Most of the food that I tried to maneuver onto the chopsticks and into my mouth either landed back on my plate, on my lap, or on the floor.

Mary looked at me and smiled sympathetically. She took my sticks into her hand. Slowly and precisely and with trained delicacy, she placed tiny chunks of chicken and noodles onto the chopsticks, raised the sticks to my lips.

A flush of affection, warmth and flavor flowed onto my lips, my tongue. What a wonderful sensation it was to have someone feed me such delicious-tasting food! The feeling was a direct route back to my childhood, when my mother had fed me, a button that had not been pushed in over sixty-five years. I savored the memory.

# A Life of Risks Taken

Mary taught me how to improve my use of chopsticks and with a little practice I became more adept. My expertise arrived after a year or two of traveling in Asia.

During our meal, she apologized for arranging such a late dinner, aware that I may have jet lag. She explained that she lived about an hour from Hong Kong in the New Territory, and she wanted to return home to bathe and put on fresh clothing befitting dinner. I was surprised that she had traveled two hours back and forth just for our dinner appointment. For a moment, I recalled how, as a teenager, I dressed for the occasion of going to dinner. Asians began to impress me more and more.

As the evening came to an end, I insisted that we call a taxi so she could return home safely. She argued it was too expensive, but here I won the battle. We shook hands, bowed and said goodnight. She left quietly, unaware of what she had given me: a life-long memory of my first evening out in Hong Kong.

ॐ

Early the next morning, I arrived at the Hong Kong ferry terminal, whose entrance was right below the Royal Pacific hotel. A bellman helped me buy my ticket to Fu Yong, the port where I would take my first steps in Mainland China.

The China Sea was choppy and the ferry moved slowly. The journey took about an hour and a half. I peered out of the foggy window. The gray, cool morning light made it difficult to see the sea.

One hundred people or more slowly shuffled off the ferry. Two soldiers with machine guns were mounted on an overhanging bridge, while others eyed the exiting travelers. Needless to say, I was a little frightened going through the customs process. China customs x-rayed every piece of luggage, shopping bag and carton carried by the passengers. No chances were taken.

Once cleared, I looked for a taxi. No one spoke a single word of English. There were probably six Westerners on the ferry. I approached one passenger and explained that I was going to Dongguan, to the Silverland Hotel. He took out a pen and his business card and wrote in Mandarin the name of the hotel. He walked me to a taxi and told the driver in Chinese where I was going. I was surprised and pleased that this Westerner with an English accent was so fluent in Chinese

This amazing stranger suggested, in the future, wherever I traveled in China, I should hire my own car and take directions written in Chinese, which are available on every hotel business card, including addresses and phone numbers of the endpoint and the departing hotel. I realized at that moment that learning to speak in Mandarin was an essential part of my education if I was to succeed in this country.

The taxi ride to Dongguan was on a two-lane highway. The road was crammed with cars and trucks from the ferry pier in Fu Yong to my destination.

I arrived at the *Silverland Hotel*, which, although clean, needed a total refurbishing. My room was very small, with a stall shower and a small television. It cost about forty-five U.S. dollars each night.

By the third evening at the hotel, I noticed something

very strange. At the rear of the hotel was another small building. Hotel guests floated in and out while I watched with intense curiosity.

In the restaurant, most of the wait staff were women who spoke no English. We communicated in awkward but reasonable sign language. I finished my dinner and strolled into the front lounge where other travelers were sitting in oversized leather chairs, reading newspapers in English and Chinese. I purposely sat down next to a man who appeared to be an American. I said good evening to him. He didn't lift his head but nodded. I took a magazine from the table in front of me, a *Forbes* dated four months earlier.

"Are you an investor?" the man sitting next to me asked in what I thought was an English accent.

I replied that I was a businessman on my inaugural trip to China, and I was making every effort to adjust and learn.

He put down his newspaper and began a nonstop lecture about the country, its business customs, lifestyle, and character. To my surprise, he wasn't from the United Kingdom. He was from Australia.

I asked him questions about money exchange. Who should I trust about car service? What restaurants did he recommend, and what is that building behind the hotel?

His answers were to the point and truthful.

"The yuan to the dollar s at 9.5 exchange rate," he said. He gave me the card of a car service he used. "You are better off eating only at the hotel, unless you are with a local person that you know well." He put down his newspaper, leaned over to me and whispered, "And the building behind the hotel is a spa and a brothel. For eight dollars, you can have a two-hour massage and a hand job, sex for another three dollars. Don't over-tip or you'll spoil them."

I sat there not surprised, not stunned. It was just different. He stood up, we shook hands, and he said, "Nice to meet you. Travel safely." I never saw him again.

The food at the hotel was limited in variety, although it looked fresh and appeared well cooked. I ate carefully, stayed close to home, and prepared for my next-day's trip to a shoebox factory.

෪෨

The People's Republic of China welcomed me. The businessmen I met were friendly, hardworking and very interesting. Mostly they came from Taiwan and Hong Kong. They made investments in China and were planning to make their fortune in the next ten years.

I visited twelve box plants and four shoe factories in one week's time. Each box plant had several hundred people working. The managing staff was all Taiwanese. Their efficiency was excellent, and the laborers were all focused on their tasks. There was no conversation as they worked the printing presses or the die-cutting machinery. Everyone was busy at his or her job, and everyone took the responsibility seriously. I was impressed.

Each day that passed, China reminded me more and more of the United States in the 1920s, when workers put in twelve-hour days. There were no unions, no safety rules, and very little training opportunities. You learned as you worked. All the Taiwanese lived near the factory.

The Chinese workers lived in small but clean dormitories adjacent to the plant. Each worker was given three meals a day and several uniforms, which had to be clean. At the end of the month, the salary was equivalent to sixty U.S. dollars at that time. Now the wage is about 1800 yuan a month, equal to about $300 US a month, which is still quite low compared to Western countries.

The shoe factories I visited were different from the box plants: Each shoe facility had several thousand employees. Every plant in itself was like a small city. The campus had a school, a hospital, a recreation facility, a mess hall, a dining room and huge, brand-new housing. Everyone lived at the manufacturing works. The first year, women were not permitted to leave the premises without permission or accompanied by another seasoned worker. Those rules were for the girls' protection and strictly adhered to. Most of the young women working in the shoe factory were country girls and unaccustomed to city life. In the past, girls had been taken advantage of, some seriously injured. One or two had been found dead.

Things were regimented. At seven a.m. each day, several thousand employees lined up outside their housing for exercise. Everyone followed instructions and began exercising. This continued for close to thirty minutes. At the end of this ritual, each person marched into the dining hall for breakfast. This took about forty-five minutes, after which a whistle blew and all marched to their work-stations.

# A Life of Risks Taken

The work area I saw consisted of seven lines of tables that were as long as a football field, with workers on either side of each table. Every employee had his or her specialized task. One by one, they performed their jobs as a carrier belt moved the developing shoes slowly along to the next operation. By the time the shoe reached the end of the line, it was finished, examined, approved, and placed into a box wrapped in tissue paper.

These factories manufacture around one hundred thousand pairs a day. A shoe company, called Pou Chen, and their facility, called Shoe City, had more than one hundred thousand employees producing one million pairs a day.

It was mind-boggling. Numbers flashed across my mind. If the company earned only five dollars a pair, the math is easy. The shoe giant earned 5 million dollars a day. Quite extraordinary, I thought.

The cleanliness of the facilities was also impressive. There were no scraps or garbage or any superfluous material lying around. The employees were all attired in clean uniforms. A cleaning staff constantly swept, wiped and polished.

In an environment where thousands of workers are on the job daily at huge facilities, health is paramount. Disease is likely to spread quickly, and an epidemic could shut down production.

As each day went by, I became more fascinated by the Chinese way. There were no coffee klatches or conversations while working. Once in the morning and once in the afternoon, there was a fifteen-minute break for bathroom and rest. Everyone focused on his job. My sense was that each employee had a feeling of loyalty and pride for the company he worked in.

Walking to my car one day, I saw hundreds of young men and women lined up and waiting outside the shoe factory, hoping to be selected for a position in a new plant. The enormous wealth of willing and available labor was beyond imagination. Most were unskilled, just-out-of-school youngsters, ready to roll up their sleeves, work hard and learn, participating in the industrial explosion of the century. It began to occur to me that I was in a Communist country, experiencing a global change as it turned its gargantuan infrastructure into one of the world's great capitalist nations. Yes, this third-world country was becoming wealthy right before my eyes. This phenomenon was something that had never occurred to me. What a moment in history I was experiencing!

The United States of America became one of the richest countries in the world by producing, buying, and selling with less than fifteen percent of China's population. I thought at that time, very soon this population was going to have the money and the desire to buy everything they see. Can you imagine how strong and wealthy this country can become just producing and selling to their own population. The USA did it with only one hundred and fifty million people. Here in China they have one billion, three hundred million people.

ൠ

Since that first visit, I have returned to China perhaps fifty times. During each stay, the country has embraced me and welcomed me into her heritage and heart. I love being in China. I could live there for long periods of time if I had to.

The heart of China beats rapidly and with great energy, as a cloud of its soft-coal-produced power hovers over each huge city.

The United States is my home, where the people I love reside, but China, ah, China! Ask any C.E.O. of any major U.S. company and they will tell you exactly what I discovered: China is where the action is. I was in the right place at the right time.

Since that first trip to Hong Kong and China, almost eighteen years have gone by. Our firm weathered the storm of America's most serious down turn since the Great Depression, through honesty, loyalty, cooperation and thinking outside-the-box. We stayed the course through the difficult years of 2008 and 2009. My company, my business child, JC Edward Corporation maintains all the customers we have mustered·for many years.

Years of experience taught us it pays to be loyal, truthful and fair, and our reputation has opened the doors to countless new clients. We have become the premier packaging organization in the footwear industry. We have a sense of pride in our customers and we distinguish ourselves with total commitment to our product and our ability to solve problems no matter what the cost. The best part is that our clients have, over the years, become our friends.

And finally, I have learned that preparing for the future is essential. I have established a successor. My son

Edward joining the firm, with his enthusiasm, hard work and commitment, has resulted in JC Edward experiencing its very best year in close to two decades.

As Mom used to say, "Every child brings its own luck to the family."

# Chapter 30

ༀ

## My Last Venture...Marsha Tosk, Inc.

Marsha was a born artist. She decided to study sculpture in her mid-forties. Beginning as a hobby, her art blossomed into a satisfying fulfillment of her creative needs. Each year, she grows to be a more accomplished artist. She attended classes at the National Academy of Arts almost every day for ten years, never missing a lesson.

Her art explores women's issues, war, battered children, beauty, and love. Her creative instincts and their creations surround us in our home. For me, to live with her art is to live in splendor and serenity.

*Bravery* is the word to describe what it took for her to submit her sculpture into competitive shows. It takes courage to offer one's work for critique by other artists and professional judges. When someone views your work, the results could be the joy of winning or the pain of criticism and rejection, or even worse, silence. But like me, my bride is a major risk taker. She married me, didn't she?

# A Life of Risks Taken

Slowly but surely, Marsha began to win awards. At first, runner-up, followed by second-place, and then on to first-place prizes. Ultimately, she won the grand prize for several of her creations.

I returned home from work one day to see a new sculpture standing on a pedestal. It was a little pig with a blanket wrapped around its torso. It was funny and beautiful—its face, sweet and warm, creating a sense of love and laughter for the observer.

"Marsha!" I called out. "I can sell a thousand of these sculptures."

She laughed and asked how I was going to do it. I told her we were going to start a new company, Marsha Tosk Corporation. She would produce works of art that had double meanings, like *Pig in a Blanket, Hot Dog, Peeking Duck, A Horse of a Different Color.*

At first she was reluctant, but my enthusiasm was contagious. She agreed to my gambling instincts and we were on a new adventure. We were partners in a business together.

We hired a PR person and an art director who developed a website. We made many mistakes at the beginning. One right thing we did was putting an ad in *The New York Times Magazine*—Marsha sold thirteen pigs the first day. Our goal wasn't to make money. Our purpose was to create a Marsha Tosk brand—and international name recognition

Three years flew by and it is slowly happening. Orders came in from all over the United States, Europe and Canada—each buyer amused by and enjoying the piece of art Marsha sold to them. Letters came from college kids, friends and relatives with suggestions of figures of speech to sculpt: *Cereal Killer, Kangaroo Court, Holy Cow, Bare Hug.*

Orders popped up in my BlackBerry e-mail. No matter where I was in the world, whether China, Indonesia, Thailand, Canada, or somewhere in the United States, I telephoned Marsha, night or day, and whispered, "You have an order."

We could not have imagined the fun it turned out to be.

By 2012, Marsha sold more than two hundred and fifty sculptures. The staff of CNBC saw her *Pig in a Blanket* ad in the *Times* and invited her on their show.

As we arrived at the studio in midtown Manhattan, we were both nervous.

During the interview, the anchorman asked, "Do your sales and the high price of your sculpture mean that the economy is improving because people are buying such expensive art like *A Pig in a Blanket?*"

Marsha held her own, explaining her art, its purpose, and its success. There was a moment when one of the commentators tried to push her around. Marsha would have none of it and stood toe-to-toe with him, explaining the insight she had with people who love art and humor, and see beauty in the creative results.

At my seventy-ninth birthday celebration, I made a toast to my wife. It went something like this:

"To Marsha, my soul mate,

"We have been married more than twenty-eight years, which equals 10,220 days. During that time, we must have said 'I love you' to each other four times each day. That equals more than 40,000 'I love yous.' We've kissed hello, good-bye, good morning, and good night each day no less than five times, which equals over 51,000 kisses. We have asked each other, 'How are you, darling?' at least twice a day, and that equals 20,400 moments of concern. Add to that, holding hands as we walk, hugs, smiles, kindnesses and quiet dinners together, gift-giving on occasions and non-occasions, as well as concerned words when one of us is worried or ill. Tie all of those experiences together and you have a million or more expressions of love, respect, admiration and happiness."

That is our life together.

# Chapter 31

૭૦૮૩

**The Next Generation**

I missed my son Edward when he was away at college. Fortunately—for both of us—he has joined our firm. Edward and I working together everyday has been a nourishing new adventure in my career.

What better reward can a man ask for? Going to the job and the company he owns and loves each day and getting the cream on top—seeing and being with his son every day, watching his son enjoy and love the same company and business as he does.

Edward is smart, hardworking, and hungry—not hungry for food or power, but for success—the perfect combination for the highest level of achievement in one's career. All these come from talent and very hard work. If one examines the lives of the most successful and talented people, he will observe their unflinching commitment to a tireless work ethic.

That being said, taking my son into the company with me did not happen easily or quickly.

# A Life of Risks Taken

Ed's passion was and remains the art world. Just out of college, he took a job with a major art gallery. The Pace Gallery hired him as an intern, and within months promoted him to assistant to its president. His boss was tough and challenged him relentlessly. Edward was still living with us at the time. In the evening he would return home after a long and difficult day, sharing with me the battles he had to fight. I listened with a sympathetic ear, secretly delighted that he was getting the perfect training for his future.

Before we offered him the opportunity to work at the company, I spoke to at least ten fathers who had sons or daughters in their companies. Nine out of ten cautioned me about how difficult the relationship can become, and several warned of the danger of a complete breakup between parent and child.

I already knew the dangers. Years ago, I had an unsuccessful experience with my daughter, Lynn, who worked with me at Sabine Press & Advertising. I was a much younger and more aggressive at that time. I put my business before everything: before my children, my wife—everything was second to the company. The success of the company overshadowed our relationship. That was one of my biggest missteps, one I often regret.

Evan Janovic, a neighbor and a new friend—a very successful entrepreneur in his own right with two sons working his business—gave me the best advice while I was considering bringing Edward into the firm. Evan counseled me to give my son the opportunity to earn as much money as possible. The word "earn" is the crucial word. He cautioned me with tongue in cheek that the only time I should quarrel with Eddie is if he makes such a major mistake that he puts the firm into bankruptcy.

"Do not rush to anger over minutiae," he advised me.

I never offered Ed a job, but simply requested his help.

"Edward, I need you to join our firm and help me run and manage our business," I offered. That was the challenge I presented to him. Because Ed had the guts, he accepted immediately.

The turning point between Edward and me came by not offering him a job, but simply requesting his help.

Two days later, we were both on a plane to Hong Kong.

Hong Kong was a stopover spot before continuing on to Macau, where we had been invited to speak at the vendor meeting of V.F. Corporation. Our firm was the only packaging company to be so honored at that time.

As the pilot took us over the North Pole, I turned to Ed and announced that he would be making the presentation to all the attendees. He responded with a rolling eye and a slight gulp, asking me what the topic was. I advised him that he would have to talk about our firm. He would have to explain how we operate, what our philosophy was, and how we work with customers, suppliers, colleagues and people in the footwear industry.

"How will I know all that, Dad?" he gasped.

"Just go on the internet and look. Study our website and prepare. Ask me any questions that cross your mind."

Two days later at the hotel in Macau, we walked into the meeting hall and took our seats with more than two hundred other employees and vendors.

# A Life of Risks Taken

The senior vice president of the firm introduced each speaker, finally reaching my name. I was invited to the podium.

I began by introducing myself and saying, "This morning, ladies and gentlemen, I am announcing a sudden change in the program. I will not be speaking as scheduled."

A whispered hum ran through the audience.

"Instead, it is my pleasure to introduce my son, Edward Ubell, who has joined our firm as a director. He is the future of JC Edward Corporation. Ladies and gentlemen, please welcome to the center stage, and to our industry, my son and business colleague, Ed Ubell."

A mild round of applause followed. I stepped down from the platform. As Ed approached the podium we passed each other. He stopped and we both kissed each other on the cheek. You could hear the entire assembly give a warm sigh, along with the sound of few clapping hands.

Ed had already won over the entire audience. When he completed his presentation, he enjoyed a standing ovation. Though a little nervous at the beginning, he finished with a flurry of excitement and bravos. Two senior executives jumped from their seats and gave him strong handshakes.

I enjoyed with pleasure the feeling of fatherly pride. Ed's first moment representing our firm had been a triumph.

That evening at the dinner for all the attendees, I was no longer the star of JC Edward Corporation, a role I had enjoyed for almost two decades. Ed's performance had catapulted him into the new role. His youth, good looks, and enthusiasm were contagious. It was a unique experience in my career, a new beginning for our firm and our father-son relationship.

# Chapter 32

ဆာ

### Nepotism

It never occurred to me that having my son join our family business would be the most exciting adventure of my long career. Here I am in the Autumn of my career having more fun and enjoyment than I ever dreamed about.

It is a fact that most family companies encounter difficult domestic issues interfering with the day-to-day fundamental transactions that good business sense demands. It is rare that family constituents are able to put aside growing up intrigues and hurtful memories that linger from past family experiences. These experiences could be painful recollections of missed graduations, recitals, hockey games, or simply forgetting to say good night, or missing the parental gesture of saying "I love you," and possibly not reading enough to the child, or the parent saying something in front of the child's friends that the parent feels is cute. At the same time the "cute comment" totally wipes out and causes embarrassment to the offspring. Those incidents long forgotten by the parent-employer are never forgotten by the employee-child.

My eldest child, Lynn, joined the family business in the early days of my career. Her presence in the company was a total failure, resulting in a painful estrangement from her. But it was not because she was incompetent. On the contrary, she was skilled, conscientious and as ambitious as anyone could be.

My bad habit was the constant need for total control. I exercised this style in the running of the company. This and this alone made the father and daughter partnership turn into a malfunctioning association, and its eventual conclusion, resulting in her desire not to work for the company. The structure of our relationship, sadly came tumbling down.

My failure alone caused a long separation and we lost the beauty of just being daughter and dad. Here we both paid the devil's price for my lack of experience, as I placed business priorities above the need for a stronger and loving bond with my daughter.

How does one explain the botching of one father/child collaboration, while a second business alliance with a child from  another marriage, rose to an almost 98% success. Still, nothing is perfect.

I discovered that both my son and my daughter in our family firm, strange as this may sound, neither child ever viewed me as the head of the firm. To my employee-children, I was not seen as the final word in business choices made regarding every issue of the ongoing day-to-day work matters that constantly arise. My children-employees were able only to see one vision of their father and one vision only.

To them I was not the CEO, the President, or the managing director of the firm as other employees saw me. My children viewed me 100% of time as the Dad—the man they grew up with—upon whom their personal welfare and financial support depended.

If I, as the CEO Poppa, criticized my son or daughter, no matter how gentle or how strong, the child thinks, "How can Dad speak to me that way....and in front of all those people?" Yet, I, as father, think, "What did I say that was so bad that my darling child ran into the lady's room to cry her eyes out?" All I did was order her to take the "Goddam samples to the customer NOW!!!"

I grew up in that kind of business atmosphere, which I believed was good training. My hurt child could not accept the tone of my voice, which is the boss' privilege. All I was trying to do was toughen her up for the true difficult things in business life yet to come.

As I perceived it, there was no difference in the tenor of my voice to my daughter as to my other employees. How difficult it has to be for both parent and child to be at each other daily. I was excusing my behavior, believing I was teaching. I did not have the experience and perhaps the sensitivity to understand that you cannot teach by command, only by example.

My children did not know my private and silent joy was seeing them every single day of my business life. That was my reward.

Children understand that the child always, whether

in business or not, has the upper hand. The parent always loves the child more than the child loves the parent or more difficult, the parent-employer.

A customer once asked my son how he was getting along with his dad in the office. Eddie answered, "My dad is just happy when I eat. Can you imagine how ecstatic he is when I also earn money for him? He is the most amazing man in the world. And he rewards me not only with money, but with a reaffirmation of my talent. Though I am successful and applauded for it, I continue to have my doubts about my own ability. But Dad never stops. That is what helps our relationship. My dad does not need all the credit. He shares it with me. He gets the money and I get the adoration. In a sense we both get what we need—for now."

It was unfortunate that I did not have those skills as Ed described, during the days when my daughter was in the family business. I was in my mid-fifties. Though not young by today's standards, I was at the top of my game. Every business transaction, every order, every meeting, every customer was more important than anything else. That attitude may benefit the family business, but it does harm to the family.

When my daughter was a child, about twelve years old, we were driving in our car. She asked, "Daddy, if I were to get married in Paris, would you come to my wedding?"

"Of course I would," I laughingly replied.

"If I were to marry a man that you did not like, would you still come to my wedding in Paris?"

"Absolutely," I answered.

"Would you still come to my wedding in Paris, if I married a man you did not like and he was not the same religion or the same race?"

"Sweetheart, there is no doubt in my mind that I would come to your wedding in Paris if all those situations existed," I responded, thinking, *Where is this going?*

"Daddy, would you come to my wedding in Paris, knowing all the things I just told you—and a customer called you for an important meeting."

My hands were on the wheel of the car. I thought for a moment and in all humor I responded.

*"Don't push me!"* This response was made as a joke and with a sense of humor. I do not think my daughter enjoyed my so-called joke. Unfortunately, I made a serious mistake.

Though the entire conversation was about a child testing its parent's loyalty, my daughter instinctively knew and understood how important my customers were in my life. She tested me to the max. I responded as she may or may not have expected. Somewhere in her life she felt that she was not my number one priority. She knew, but did not understand why her competition was my customers. This of course, in my mind, was untrue. But my behavior and my work ethic and the responsibility to my job and my company gave my daughter the insecure feeling that she was not number one in my life. One of my major regrets.

My response should been the opposite. "Of course darling, your wedding is more important than any customer."

# A Life of Risks Taken

As time went by, and I was in my second marriage with a new family that included a ten-year-old son. I promised him I would show up at a fencing match he was competing in at school. One of my most important customers telephoned me a few minutes before I was to leave for the match. He asked me, in fact, he ordered me to be at his office for an important meeting by four o'clock.

"John, I promised my son I would be at his school to see him in a fencing match. Can we do this in the morning, early if you wish?" hoping he would cooperate.

"That works for me. See you tomorrow." John complied, much to my surprise.

In the morning when I arrived at the breakfast meeting, John's wife, Laura and his senior VP were waiting for me. The very first thing John (my customer) said to me was, "I learned something yesterday. You chose your son over an important business meeting. I should do that more often. How did the fencing match go?"

"It was great, Ed won."

John also had children and his wife in a huge firm. The family business was difficult for all of them. And John himself had a difficult life in the family business when his dad was the boss of bosses in a huge industry.

My decision to ask for a meeting postponement was difficult for me. But I did what was best for me and my son and the family. I was in my sixties and much smarter than during my daughter's days of growing up. Another one of my major regrets.

As a sixty-six year old man at the time, with much more experience, my sense of priorities had changed.

My son needed to see me at that match. That was more important to me than the profit I would garner from the business meeting. In my thirties, I had no way of knowing that both my daughters needed the same attention and commitment that I gave to Ed. I was stupidly busy earning money and trying to support my family. I have since gotten to understand that moderation for every commitment you make is the right road.

## Showing the Way

It was a week before the Christmas Holiday, employee evaluation time. Eddie sat with me in my office as we discussed each employee's contribution. He watched and absorbed every word as I spoke clearly and honestly to each member of our staff.

I demonstrated to Eddie that every employee knows who they are as I offered each my opinion of their annual performance from the very best employee to the one who performed their duties only as instructed. My criticism of the last young woman was firm, honest and direct. It was more like guidance than a threat.

She clearly understood my position as she tried to defend herself and then retired to her office, where her tempo quickened while her participation with her colleagues became more apparent. I advised Ed that most people do not change their work styles. I never met an employee who improved their work habits because he or she received an increase in salary. Nor does a lower pay check deter a hard worker from his or her total commitment to their work responsibilities.

# A Life of Risks Taken

We sat in my office alone as I presented my opinion of Edward's contribution for the past year. I examined in detail the difference in his performance from the beginning of the year including this very day. He heard my sense of pride in the strides he had made and in his improvement of follow up and sales success. I complemented him on his relationship skills with customers and employees. All that being said, I presented him with a bonus equal to his contribution to the company. It was apparent that he was satisfied.

I proceeded to discuss the future. He was delighted to hear that I offered him a small partnership. He would lose his commission-based compensation, and would now participate in the total success of the firm, similar to the financial arrangement I gave to our China CEO. I am an employer who shares the business success and profits with key people.

Eddie's response to this spectacular development was impressive. He was calm and accepting. I did not know at the time that, inside, he was screaming with delight and excitement. He was proud of his accomplishment and that I, his Dad, recognized his efforts.

I was satisfied that I rewarded him in a way that was a total business decision. Simultaneously, I ensured a future heir to the responsibility of running our successful family business skillfully and honestly. Still there was much for him to learn. As an older father, we both understood that the window of learning was swiftly approaching an end. He is constantly aware, as I am, that no one lives forever.

My decision was an opportunity to strengthen the

company, the  bond between us and for the future of our family.

Our firm is a China-based company.  We produce shoe boxes for the footwear industry.

More than 90% of our business takes place in China. All our employees there are bi-lingual Chinese, college-educated people. They are steeped in Chinese tradition of respect to employers and a commitment to giving all to the job. There are always some who do not fit that mold. Though this statement is a generality, it is reasonably accurate.

When Ed was in college, our firm's Chinese CEO at the time, Mary Tang, questioned me as to whether Ed was going to join the firm after graduation. I was quite candid in my reply. I honestly did not know what he was going to do. Nor was I going to force or insist that he consider coming into the family business. Mary's immediate comment was: "He has no choice. It is his responsibility to follow in his father's footsteps. He has to carry on the family tradition."  Her answer did not surprise me. It was another cultural custom I learned about China. Mary was not afraid that my son would take her place. Mary knew a son coming into the company was insuring the future of the company and her place in the business for the next generation.

The more I thought about that exchange, the more I realized that most firms we did business with in China were strong family businesses. Not only sons and daughters, but wives and cousins, brothers and uncles all were in the business working together. The entire clan worked as a team with the singular understanding that the company was primary and was best for the family. They understood and accepted that the father was the final word in any decision. They also accepted the eldest son was to be the heir apparent. Nothing else existed.

Nepotism was not a condition of employee envy or discomfort in China, it was a given. It was the Chinese way. There was nothing else to be said. The fact that the eldest son was in line to take the father's place when father's life or his work days were over was, in fact, a guarantee that employees would continue to have a job, a place to go to earn a living for their families. Nepotism was a guarantee for the employees that their working life will continue into the future safely and securely.

In the United States the concept in most cases is totally different. An aggressive and ambitious employee sees nepotism as a hindrance to his or her future. The family heir apparent is a sign that the future is limited and can only go so far. No matter how hard the employee works, he is held back by the son or daughter in front of him.

There are many American firms where partners agree early when the company was formed, that no offspring will be allowed to join the firm. This usually ends in partnership disputes, as the son or daughter of one of the partners asks why they are not permitted to come to work for the parent in the family business.

I know of one company where the partners are in court over that agreement. One partner wants a son in the company. The other exercised the agreement that may have been signed twenty-five years earlier when the children were very young and the future was far away. It does not take long for the future to become today.

Before my son joined the firm, I interviewed a dozen businessmen in my industry about the pit falls and disappointments when inviting an offspring to join the family business. Most of the father-bosses advised me against it. They cautioned me about the relationship issues. Three of the businessmen I interviewed, sadly advised me that they have been estranged from their sons because of the controversies that were encountered in the business. All this frightened me. I certainly did not want to lose the relationship I had with my only son.

I knew a neighbor of mine who had not one son, but two of his sons in his company. I met him one day in the elevator and invited him to lunch to ask how he succeeded with two sons in business.

At our get together about two weeks later, he painted a picture of all the possible issues that could come up as road blocks to a successful working relationship. In his itemization he mentioned an unknown future daughter-in-law who may not be in sync with family tradition, who may envy the difference in the rewards between boss-father and husband-son-employee.

As sons and daughters quickly reach working age, so do grandchildren whose presence adds an additional complication to the family business. Summer jobs are simple. Life long careers offer another glitch in the road to harmony.

I took my neighbor's advice seriously and one day Eddie and I did have a dispute.

# A Life of Risks Taken

I raised my voice to Edward. "I never said it would be easy working together. You are my son and I love you, but I will not compromise this firm's reputation or its financial stability for the sake of keeping the peace."

He looked at me with a straight and determined expression on his face. He backed out of my office in silence and walked into his. I knew this conversation was not over. He would return with a clever twist to his point of view. He wanted us to take on a customer with a much lower profit and greater risk than I was willing to agree to.

One hour passed. Ed returned to me as I finished an e-mail to a good friend and customer.

"Want lunch?' Ed asked.

"Okay. Where?" I answered.

"Kosher place?"

"Ten minutes."

Six months later, Ed's customer filed for a $9 million bankruptcy.

# Chapter 33

༄༅

## A Few Comments

I have had more than a normal share of adventure, gambles, love affairs, laughter, friends, sex, profits and losses. Money losses are simple defeats. True bereavements are the very painful losses of loved ones. Gone are my parents, my brother, Earl, my brother-in-law, Marvin, and my niece, Amy. My school friend Bernie, as well as aunts and uncles and other people in my life, whom I valued, are also no longer with us. Experiencing the death of a relative or friend is the most powerless feeling one can have. It is sudden, even when expected, and it is final. No return, no fixing. Nevertheless, we must move on. Being here and alive remains an exciting voyage.

༄༅

Laughter is important to me. I value it as much as music or a good book. My brother, Earl, and I shared a funny story almost every day by telephone or e-mail. If one of us knew the other's joke, we fired the punch line, ending the conversation, both of us laughing at our constant one-ups-man-ship.

My very dear friend, Roger, who sadly has lost his vision in the later years of his life, laughs at every one of my stories. His personality is wonderfully upbeat. Blindness is a horrible disease, yet in spite of the cruel handicap, his sense of humor and his kind spirit keep him from sliding downhill. Roger and I speak to each other almost every day, no matter where we are in the world. We are like family, but our roles change daily—sometimes he is the father and I am the son, or I am the mentor and he is the child. Always, we are brothers.

At the very beginning of my shoebox business, Roger offered me space in his offices at the Empire State Building. During the first two years we paid no rent, no phone bill. We had zero expenses. That indeed was a very serious assist. Many years later when Roger retired, I returned the favor with the same perks.

Roger is the consummate businessman. We are involved in many joint ventures, where both of us have been successful. Whenever I share with him a new concept for my own firm, his response almost one hundred percent of the time is, "I wouldn't do it that way." That's Roger. His point of view always makes me laugh. I listen to his suggestion and I do what I want to do.

On the other hand, my equally close friend, Donald, is a more critical recipient of my humor. He's a serious man. His world view is enmeshed with politics, the U.S. Constitution, civil rights, women's rights and much more. But when I reach his funny bone, his handsome face lights up with a burst of reluctant laughter. It's always a special moment for both of us.

Donald is an extraordinary person and a special friend, who has also become a brother and has had an enormous impact on my life. I love him very much. However, as brothers tend to be, our competitiveness or criticism often get in the way of our relationship. Sometimes, we just need time and space away from each other. His point of view about my business style, my financial decisions and my family relationships often sound imperious to me, as my ideas probably sound to him. At the same time, I know that his comments are meant to be helpful. He wants only the best for me.

Lunch at the Harvard Club is a favorite of Donald's. It's a place where Roger, Donald and I have conversations about politics, friends and business. I was particularly silent at one of these meetings, listening to Donald and Roger argue about economics and politics. Roger is a diehard Republican, Donald, a liberal. I sat and listened, preoccupied with my own thoughts. Our lunch finished and coffee arrived, Donald turned to me and asked, "How is that box business of yours going?"

I paused for a moment and answered quite bluntly, "I'm short about $300,000 to make it a big success."

Both men were silent. They looked at me, looked at each other. I cannot remember who said this, but one of my two best friends turned to the other and said, "Let's lend it to him."

Within five minutes, I was given two checks from these two men, who in one swift and impulsive moment of friendship and brotherhood that changed my life.

# A Life of Risks Taken

That act of kindness and trust is the height of loyalty and comradeship. It was an extraordinary act of generosity. The box company became my most successful venture, and within two years, I was able to repay the debt. I am forever grateful to these two generous human beings—and to Barbara and Nora, their wives.

80C3

"Pull the plug" are my instructions, should I become ill, a burden to my family, unable to take care of the normal functions of life. I have already donated my body to science. Whatever part of me is usable to another human being at the time of my departure, I hope that person enjoys it as much as I have.

A religious ceremony at the time of my death would be the antithesis of my beliefs. Cremation and a simple farewell will do the job, followed by the family getting together in our home. Perhaps some people with whom I was closest will want to remember some funny episodes in our lives together by telling those stories—that will be my farewell. For now, I am still here and want to get on with my writing.

# Chapter 34

ಐಎಲ

### My Fantasy of Family

I wish my daughter, Lynn, had the ability to forgive and forget. She has a very short fuse. She is quick to internalize anger about an incident that the other party may not have a clue about. I often am that blameworthy person. Her reaction to my infractions leaves us in silence for long stretches of time, sometimes years. What a waste of time and bad feelings. I often wish it were different. My yearning is to see my daughter more often. We have yet to make it all right, and it is equally unfortunate for us both. She is blinded by the hurts she experiences, real or imaginary, leading only to the distant steps between.

Still, I am very proud of Lynn for raising two wonderful boys, my grandsons, Javier and Ben. She is to be congratulated for managing a successful printing brokerage business, for changing careers and becoming a public school teacher, and for receiving two master's degrees. My hope is that as she grows older, she will learn that even the people you love, and those who love you, are not perfect. I certainly admit I haven't been the ideal man.

# A Life of Risks Taken

I was not a great husband to my first wife or the best father to our daughters. But now I work hard at it and I believe I am getting better each day.

I've discovered that one cannot keep friends or family under a microscope, watching every movement, scrutinizing each word said, and translate those actions into misdeeds or insults. Forgive and forget. That is the path to take. It is a twisting, difficult path to being comfortable and loved.

Families at best are a different union. Yet, I continue to have the fantasy of family—a family that gathers together to commemorate the birth of a new member, a bar mitzvah or a graduation. I would welcome a dinner in our home with everyone around the table, eating, drinking and talking to one another. I would love to see my children being kind to each other by sharing a vacation story or a career promotion. That is my hope—to be part of that dream scene.

I can only imagine Lynn's pain of choosing to be excluded from family events. She must believe that exclusion gives her power. At this moment everyone is immunized to her choice of retaliation. Nothing is accomplished by anger, only more of the same. I try to respect that and hope our situation will improve. She is the prodigal daughter whom everyone will welcome back into the family when she feels it is right.

ᏚᎧᏟᏒ

Jane Ubell Meyer, my youngest daughter, telephones me almost every evening. She and I have a connection that is valued and nurtured by both of us. Jane is a unique and dynamic woman. Her drive and desire for success is endless and combined with tenderness and sensitivity.

Jane has forged a diverse business career and she is successful in her ventures. She adopted the motto of "no risk, no reward." Her effort, her energy and her dedication make me very proud of her. Jane sees the good in everyone. She forgives indiscretions of words or behavior. It is better to live in peace than in anger. She has taught us all that.

She and Ed and I have recently invested in a new business. Jane has a plan to sell eyeglasses on the Internet. As I write at this very moment, at 11p.m. on April 23, 2014, Jane is China-bound putting together a collection of special sunglasses for sale on the Internet. It is a new adventure for the three of us. We speak to each other every day from New York to China. Jane gives me daily reports on her activities. I voice my opinion on business directions. Most times we agree. Sometimes we do not. But there is no anger or criticism. My business inner voice tells me that we may have winner. Who would have thought that I would be blessed a second time with another of my children in business with me?

෫)ଓ

Once a week or at times more frequently, I hear from my grandsons Javier and Ben. Javier, now twenty-four years old, was a soloist ballet dancer with the Oregon Ballet Company. He now dances with the Munich Ballet Company in Germany. Javier is maturing into a very thoughtful man. He knows who he is and what he wants. Still he is concerned about his future. He is aware that the window on a ballet dancer's life shrinks every year. The ageing process pays a price to a body in movement. As he thinks of the future to teach ballet or be a choreographer, I think and begin to plan the concept of a new ballet company for our grandson's future. I have shared this with Javier, and he is very excited about it.

ཨུཕ

Ben, twenty-two is a senior in college. This summer he worked in our firm's China office. He lived with an Anglo-Sino family learning the culture and the ways of those who live in The People's Republic of China. My office arranged that a Chinese language teacher come twice to our office and give him lessons twicee a week in Mandarin. On his return to college, he took the Mandarin language as one of his electives. When he returned from China, I saw a significant change in him. Maturity was showing its head. Ben is not sure of what he wants to do with his life. But whatever he chooses, I am confident he will give it 150% of his effort. He is a gifted writer and a talented storyteller. He came in at the top of his class with poetry he wrote during his last two semesters. Each poem reached into the depths of feeling and indelibly touched the reader's heart. Ben's sense of humor often makes my heart smile.

ཨུཕ

Matt and Alex, our step grandsons—Jane's stepsons—are less communicative with us. We will hear from them on special occasions, sometimes on birthdays or holidays but not on a regular basis. I am hopeful that the connection will strengthen. The two boys are still only kids. Someday they will understand the value of the relationship we offer. That offer will stand for their lifetimes.

# Chapter 35

ಬಂಡ

## How I See Myself

Most of my life, I have felt that I was swimming upstream. I've had to use all of my wits and energy to survive the force of life's battles. Being at the top of the game constantly is not easy. It takes a great deal of perseverance and commitment and a never-give-up attitude.

I've always refused to accept the world as it is. I raised the bar for myself and worked hard to reach my goals. I've never lacked self-esteem, but I believe my courage comes from the lack of fear I have to take risks and challenges in business and with the people I meet and engage with. I do not fear challenges or face-to-face confrontations. If I have made an error, that to me is a learning experience. If an apology is needed, I do not hide.

My most successful battle has been overcoming the bad genes I was born with. And though I've often been negligent in self-care, I'm fortunate to be married to a woman who has never been intimidated by me. She guides me on the path to a healthy diet, minus alcohol, and a regime of exercise. At eighty-two years old, I feel young and energized. At a session one day with my cardiologist, Dr. Holly Andersen, I confessed that I have given up smoking, coffee, alcohol and ice cream. Holly responded, "Not ice cream!"

As I dash up the steps at our Gym or the steep staircase of the box factory I am working with, I am amazed by my energy. I cannot believe my age. I tease myself by whispering, *I think my mom made a mistake on my birth certificate. I was not born in 1931, it must have been 1951.*

ഇ

My lack of formal education has pained me. My knowledge comes from experience, from my educated friends, and from as much reading as I can squeeze into my very busy schedule.

I regret that I did not attend university and earn a degree. Would I be more content? I don't know. But I believe I would have been a happier man being exposed to literature, the arts and music. Education would have enabled me to enjoy more of the cultural events that my wife, my son, my daughters, and I seek out.

As I write these pages, I am frustrated by my lack of extensive vocabulary, by my difficulty with grammar and the strain I experience in developing a complete and clear thought. I must write and rewrite time and time again, until I get it.

I am someone who loves his family and his friends. I am passionate about that part of my history. I forgive, I support and I care about those close to me.

These pages, which have occupied about three and a half years of my life, remind me that I have had an interesting and exciting existence. It has been filled with love and success, as well as my share of pain and disappointment. I have enjoyed my time and the life I have led. My only regrets are the risks I did not take.

No guts, no glory. No risk, no reward.

I have been careful what I have wished for in life, and I've been lucky enough to get much of it.

*Not the End.*

## ABOUT THE AUTHOR

Seymour Ubell is an entrepreneurial spirit whose life-long pursuit of success has taken him from the mean–streets of Brooklyn to the heights of international business. He has created six businesses in his lifetime, and now shares his story in this engaging memoir called A LIFE OF RISKS TAKEN. Mr. Ubell resides in New York with his wife, Marsha, where he continues to write, to work, to travel and to enjoy life.

CPSIA information can be obtained at www.ICGtesting.com
Printed in the USA
BVOW11s1747080914

365755BV00005B/16/P